Born in Somerset in 1947 and educated at Clifton College and Trinity Hall, Cambridge, Will Fowler has since 1972 concentrated on military history, current affairs and defence technology. He was a researcher at the Royal United Services Institute, Whitehall during the Falklands War in 1982 and from 1983 to 1990 Land Forces editor of *Defence* magazine. He has filed for international defence magazines and covered conflicts in Europe, the Middle East and Asia. In 1998 Will Fowler set up and edited the first edition of *Jane's Amphibious Warfare Capabilities*, the reference work that covers the world's amphibious forces, including some in South America with no seaboard that operate exclusively on lakes and rivers. In August 2002 HarperCollins published his book *The Commandos at Dieppe*, the first full account of the successful action by No. 4 Commando at Dieppe in August 1942. A long-time territorial soldier in the Royal Green Jackets, he served with British forces in the Gulf War of 1990–91 and graduated from the French Army Reserve Staff Officers course at the Ecole Militaire in Paris in 1993. Though he retired in 1997 as a historian he has led TA and regular Army battlefield tours. Will Fowler has broadcast on British international radio and television. He is married and lives in Hampshire.

OPERATION BARRAS

The SAS Rescue Mission, Sierra Leone 2000

···

William Fowler

CASSELL

Cassell Military Paperbacks

Cassell
Wellington House, 125 Strand
London WC2R 0BB

Copyright © William Fowler 2004

First published in 2004
by Weidenfeld & Nicolson
This Cassell Military Paperbacks edition 2005

British Library Cataloguing-in-Publication Data.
A catalogue record for this book is available
from the British Library.

ISBN 0 304 36699 4

Printed and bound in Great Britain by
Cox & Wyman Ltd

www.orionbooks.co.uk

To the memory of my father

Wilfred Fowler
1907 – 1971

'A Good Man in Africa'

Contents

List of maps   viii

Introduction   1

Chapter 1   **Kidnap**   9

Chapter 2   **Lion Mountains**   19

Chapter 3   **Independence**   31

Chapter 4   **'No Living Thing'**   47

Chapter 5   **UNAMSIL: The International Dimension**   66

Chapter 6   **Operation Palliser: Intervention by Air and Sea**   78

Chapter 7   **Negotiations**   106

Chapter 8   **Operation Barras**   139

Chapter 9   **Aftermath**   159

Notes to the Chapters   185

Appendix   **Ministry of Defence Press Release: Operation Barras**   205

Glossary   209

Bibliography and websites   213

Maps

Sierra Leone and West Africa   20
Sierra Leone   67
The Western Region   83
Forodugu and Magbeni   120
Gberi Bana   140
Magbeni   143

Introduction

'I learned that the only two species who wage war
against their own kind are ants and men.'

AMINATTA FORNA
The Devil that Danced on the Water

The library and the librarian were unlike anything we had ever encountered before.

The librarian, a warrant officer (WO) in the British Army Intelligence Corps, checked that the alarm was off, inserted keys into two Chubb five-lever locks and swung open the steel-clad solid timber door.

Inside was a modest room with books and pamphlets ranged around the shelves and, in the centre, a table flanked by a couple of chairs. The room also housed security containers fitted with combination locks and several locked four-drawer filing cabinets. The entire building was alarmed and visited regularly at night by sentries from the guard. He explained that we would be required to sign in order to take out books or pamphlets, and that some of the more highly classified material could only be consulted if the reader remained in the room.

This was definitely no ordinary library.

The 'we' who were ushered into the Secure Library of the School of Service Intelligence, Templer Barracks, Ashford, Kent, were students on the intense two-week Regimental Intelligence Officers' and NCOs' course run for British Army Reservists.

It was the late 1970s; the Cold War was a chilly reality and the immediate enemy for NATO and the British Army was the well-trained and superbly equipped 'Group of Soviet Forces in Germany' or GSFG.

Within the borders of the German Democratic Republic, the DDR – to us, East Germany – were the depots and barracks of the Soviet 2nd Guards Army, 3rd Shock Army and 8th Guards Army, with the 20th Guards Army in reserve close to the Polish border.

In addition, East Germany had its III and V Armies in place to support a Soviet attack on the West and to the south were two Czech armies with huge Polish forces, in position to reinforce the offensive with fresh troops and equipment.

At that time, NATO lived and planned for a terrifying world in which the international situation would unravel, and as tension escalated between the West and the USSR and the threat of war increased, reserves would be mobilised and other military forces deployed to positions facing the Iron Curtain. The wives and children of regular British forces in Germany would be transported back to the UK as married quarters were emptied and the domestic pets that could not be brought home were destroyed.

The West German police could be relied on to be completely ruthless with fellow Germans who might be tempted to flee west with their families and valuables piled into Mercedes, Volkswagens and BMWs. These cars with their terrified passengers would be directed off the roads into improvised parking lots in fields to allow military vehicles to move forward to the border.

As regular and reserve soldiers dug in, engineers would prepare bridges for demolition. Some would be blown in advance and in other areas minefields would be laid to canalise Soviet armoured vehicles into anti-tank killing grounds.

The mobility corridors had been identified – gaps in hills, woodland and cities through which Soviet tanks and armoured personnel carriers were expected to drive. Villages would become focal points for defence – from within their cover, anti-tank guided weapons would be fired to streak low across the farmland, trailing their guidance wires, before exploding against the T-54/55 and T-62 tanks and BTR-60 PB and BMP armoured personnel carriers.

This was World War III, and for many years it had been fought in theory and in practice on maps and in exercises that had ploughed their way across fields and clogged roads in autumnal West Germany.

One evening, talking to a German World War II veteran, I commented that as a British platoon commander it would be difficult to prepare a house for defence if the German owner was still in residence. Even before any fighting began, windows would have to be smashed, furniture used as barricades and staircases ripped out. The hard-working homeowner would have strong feelings about these operations since they would almost certainly ensure the complete destruction of his home if fighting developed in the area.

There was a pause in the conversation that summer evening. Then the veteran turned to me and said quietly, 'If a man came between you and your plan for defence – you should shoot him.'

That evening I heard the true voice of the last desperate months of Nazi Germany in 1945 when old men and boys faced overwhelming Soviet artillery barrages and tanks driving remorselessly westwards towards Berlin.

Hanging over the apocalyptic vision of the new war for which NATO was planning was the terrifying prospect of 'nuclear release'. As fire from NATO troops slowed down the encroaching Warsaw Pact tanks and vehicles, huge traffic jams would develop, and such a target would become big enough to merit attack with battlefield or tactical nuclear weapons. To many NATO theorists, 'tactical nukes' seemed like nothing more than larger versions of conventional weapons. It would take the accident at Chernobyl in the Ukraine on 26 April 1986 to show how lasting and damaging nuclear radiation can be, and to hasten serious disarmament discussions by both sides.

This was the war for which we, as intelligence officers, were training and the library held the raw material of our calling. The librarian explained that the classified books and references ranged from 'Secret' through 'Confidential' to the lowest level of 'Restricted'.

In front of us he had laid out four classified manuals open at the same map – the positions in East Germany of our old friends the GSFG. Pointing to each map in turn, he said, 'This map is Secret, this is Confidential, this is Restricted and this one is in the public domain – now, if you ever draft a report or write a classified paper, make sure that you know where you have sourced your information and do not mix it up.'

This principle of knowing the source or attribution of all material has informed everything I have written about modern military operations.

I have been privileged to meet and talk to men and women who have trained and served in several armies in various theatres. Their experiences and anecdotes have been shared with me in friendship and in turn I have always respected their confidence.

As we looked at the manuals ranged on the table at Ashford, a version of World War III was actually being fought – but not on the North German

Plain. There were several proxy wars that had begun with Korea in 1950. In Vietnam, the USSR defeated the USA, but in Afghanistan the USA achieved a final victory against its ideological adversary.

In Africa, the 'Wars of Liberation' in Angola, Mozambique, Namibia and Rhodesia (now Zimbabwe) were fostered and supported by the USSR and Communist China. To sustain these conflicts, the continent was flooded with robust, easy-to-use, well-designed Soviet small arms. One of the suppliers was the erratically led state of Libya, which also provided training facilities for the fighters. Their weapon of choice was the *Avtomat Kalashnikova Obrazets* 1947, an assault rifle universally known as the AK-47 or the Kalashnikov, after its designer's name. Since their introduction in 1947, around fifty-five million AK-47s have been sold at almost 'knock-down' prices. In one African country, for example, they cost no more than £3.38 each. Once seen as the weapon of revolution and liberation in Africa, the AK-47 has now become a tool of repression in the hands of undisciplined gangs and militias.

An automatic weapon like the AK-47 fires 600 rounds per minute. This allows the user to kill quickly at a distance from his or her victim. In Africa, the machete or *panga*, a half-metre-long agricultural knife intended for clearing scrub or cutting sugar cane, has become the other weapon of choice. It has been used to kill or to maim by lopping off hands and arms. This is hands-on killing – close enough to feel the heated breath of the victim's desperate screams.

This book is about a post-Cold War African conflict.

It is about what is now known rather grandly as a 'resource war' – in reality, a war driven by greed for a country's natural wealth rather than the impulses that drove earlier wars – a desire to impose a new religion or ideology on a reluctant population or to liberate a colony from its colonial masters.

In writing this book, I have followed the guidance of the Intelligence Corps WO at Ashford and have used exclusively material in the public domain. This includes books like Will Scully's *Once A Pilgrim*, which has become a sort of 'set text' for many British soldiers posted to Sierra Leone since 1997. Aminatta Forna's brilliant and haunting *The Devil that Danced on the Water* also gives a unique insight into life in Sierra Leone.

Reports from Irish, African, US and British newspapers, notably *The Daily Telegraph* and *Guardian* in Britain and the *Expo Times* in Sierra Leone, and BBC radio and television have conveyed the drama of the hostage crisis as it developed in August and September 2000. Inevitably, some of those interviewed by Freetown-based journalists may not have been reliable witnesses but rather individuals motivated by greed, a desire to deflect criticism or simply a wish to tell a good story and be the centre of attention. Emphatically this cannot be said of the interviews with victims of Revolutionary United Front (RUF) and militia brutality conducted by the international charity Human Rights Watch. They give a tragic human face to the statistics of cruelty. Other material has come from the United Nations (UN) and non-governmental organisations (NGOs) operating in Sierra Leone.

From these diverse sources, I have drawn my own conclusions about Sierra Leone and the nature of the operations conducted by the UN and British forces that culminated in Operation Barras. I have cross-referenced and checked the reports where possible and have included material from background features, since they give an excellent feel for the personalities and the country.

Military history, however, can be an imprecise art. An attempt to bring structure and order to what is actually often violent and unstructured can sometimes distort the reality of war. A veteran of the British Army's discreet low-intensity campaign in Oman in the 1970s recalled reading a report of an action in which he had participated. 'I did not recognise any of it – it was only by checking the date, time, group and grid references that I realised that this was a description of the fire fight in which I had been involved.'

If the official record can be imprecise, the historian and the journalist should also be warned that many soldiers of all ranks and ages have a mischievous sense of humour and a highly developed instinct for 'spotting one coming'. It can be irresistible for some soldiers to see how tall a story can be spun to the gullible and impressionable before eventually they realise that they are the butt of an insider's joke – but some victims of such wind-ups never do come to this realisation.

Some 'insiders' may find minor factual errors in this book, but hopefully these will not detract from the overall story. It is essentially one of confusion and courage, out of which has emerged a more secure, if battered, Sierra Leone.

As I worked on this book, it brought back long-forgotten memories of a happy childhood spent in West Africa where my father gave the best years of his life working as a colonial officer. During World War II, Freetown had become a familiar port for my mother when the ship on which she was travelling joined the convoys forming up there for the hazardous run to Britain. With the war over, my parents decided that the debilitating climate and tropical diseases of West Africa would not suit their children and so we made only occasional visits. To a five-year-old in the 1950s, it was a world of strange and sometimes wonderful sights, smells and tastes and of universal and generous affection. There was also local curiosity and amusement, such as when on one occasion, unknown to my mother, as a blond fair-skinned European child, I squatted by the side of a dusty laterite road contentedly making mud pies.

Explaining their decision to limit our visits to West Africa, my mother would sometimes quote the grim doggerel rhyme about the climate and incidence of malaria and yellow fever that gave the area the name 'the White Man's Grave':

> *The Bight of Benin,*
> *The Bight of Benin.*
> *Where few come out,*
> *Though many go in.*

Sierra Leone, along the African coast to the west of the Bight of Benin, is a brave young country that shares a similar climate. The spirit of optimism and laughter through tears that has sustained the country through some grim and terrifying times is typified in the Krio proverbs collected by Peter Anderson that appear on the Sierra Leone website and which head each chapter of this book.

In the preparation of this book I have been helped by numerous friends who have been generous with their guidance and advice. I owe thanks to Tom Reah, Guy Nash, Andrew and Tom for their help and to Simon and Anne Chapman for medical insights. Lisa Rogers most ably copy-edited my manuscript. I am grateful to the Fleet Photographic Unit, Portsmouth, Defence Media Operations, LAND Command for photographs and the Defence Geographic Centre (DGC), Feltham, for their guidance in the production of sketch maps. The staff at Romsey Public Library, a branch of Hampshire County Library Service, have as always been invaluable in locating unusual titles.

Finally, my thanks to Carol, who has brought the shrewd eye of an editor to this book and the love and support of a wife to my life.

Will Fowler
Romsey, Hampshire, 2004.

Chapter 1
Kidnap

Howehva tin trangga tete, I de dohn.
However bad things are, they won't last.

The West Side Boys were stoned.

They had been smoking ganja since the late morning. In the humid afternoon sunshine of 25 August 2000, twenty-five of them – grinning men and women – crowded around the vehicles of the 1 Royal Irish Regiment[1] that had arrived unexpectedly in the dilapidated village of Magbeni. They chatted and cadged cigarettes off the 1 Royal Irish soldiers and their Sierra Leone Army (SLA) liaison officer.

The patrol had driven down the dusty red laterite track into the village close to the muddy waters of Rokel Creek in the Occra Hills of Sierra Leone, West Africa. Oil palms had grown close to the verges for most of their route, but as they emerged from the jungle there was open ground on their right, sloping down to a ferry point from which boats would cross the 275 m-wide Rokel Creek to the village of Gberi Bana. Magbeni village itself stretched for about 200 m down either side of the track in front of them. It was from this village that the crowd of armed West Side Boys had unexpectedly appeared.

The patrol of three Land Rovers included one with a weapons-mount installation kit (WMIK) including a Browning .50 inch (12.7 mm) heavy machine gun (HMG) and one with a radio – probably a PRC352 with a range of over 16 km. The eleven soldiers in the vehicles were armed with SA80 5.56 mm rifles.

Among the West Side Boys, twenty-two-year-old Ibrahim Koroma recalled the first moments of the encounter with the British patrol: 'They got down from their vehicles and talked with the Boys. We didn't know they were coming, but everything seemed calm.'

The West Side Boys asked patrol commander Major Alan Marshall to wait for the return of their leader, twenty-four-year-old 'Brigadier' Foday Kallay, a former sergeant in the Sierra Leone Army.

Thirty-three-year-old Marshall, one of the youngest majors in the British Army, was an exceptional officer marked for fast-track promotion. Under his command, the patrol had driven out from their base at Benguema Training Camp (BTC) on a liaison visit to Colonel Jehad al-Widyan, commander of JordBat 2, the 2nd Jordanian Battalion in the UN Mission in Sierra Leone (UNAMSIL) based at Masiaka. The visit, it would later be explained, had been approved by Brigadier Gordon Hughes, Commander British Forces in Sierra Leone, and was part of routine liaison with adjacent friendly units to obtain increased advance warning of any imminent attack or threat.

Over lunch in Masiaka, Marshall and the other officers learned from the Jordanians that the West Side Boys were beginning to surrender to the UN as part of the disarmament programme. Marshall subsequently diverted his patrol, which included the regimental signals officer (RSO), a captain, the company sergeant major (CSM) and other non-commissioned officers (NCOs), into Magbeni to check this information out and to help build up the wider intelligence picture.

Significantly, Marshall's was not the first British patrol to visit the area. In the past, British forces had enjoyed a reasonable working relationship with the loosely structured group that gave itself the rather pretentious name of the West Side Soldiers. The group was, however, more commonly known in Sierra Leone as the West Side Boys (WSB)[2].

When Kallay arrived, the atmosphere changed.

When the Royal Irish patrol arrived, he had been summoned from his hut in the nearby village of Gberi Bana by a West Side Boy and had crossed the Rokel in a motorised canoe. He was belligerent and suspicious. He regarded the area as his territory and was angered because there had been no request for clearance for the British troops to visit Magbeni. He was probably also feeling aggrieved that his group was beginning to disintegrate, with men slipping away to the UN disarmament, demobilisation and reintegration (DDR) centres.

As the youthful, slightly built leader stamped angrily into the area he snapped out orders and the group suddenly became agitated and aggressive. A captured SLA Bedford MK 4-tonne truck mounting a twin ZPU-2 14.5 mm heavy machine gun swung out from behind the huts and blocked the road south of the village.[3]

Hemmed in by an armed and now hostile crowd, the Royal Irish soldiers were soon surrounded. The soldier manning the Browning HMG up in the WMIK knew that he could not open fire without killing or wounding his comrades and almost certainly triggering a massacre; however, the radio operator was able to report back to their HQ at BTC that the patrol had been detained.

When Major Marshall attempted to reason with the WSB and then resisted their attempts to grab his rifle, fists and rifle butts thumped into him and he was badly beaten. Worse would follow for Lieutenant Musa Bangura, the Sierra Leone Army liaison officer (LO) attached to the patrol. The attack on Marshall was a piece of brutal psychology: it sent the message to the rest of the patrol that the WSB did not respect rank and if the CO could be brutally assaulted – so could they.

West Side Boy Koroma witnessed the brief struggle. 'They had no chance to resist,' he said later.

Within five minutes the Royal Irish soldiers were overwhelmed and disarmed. They were stripped to their olive-green T-shirts and underwear, wedding rings and watches were removed and, it was later reported, collected by Kallay. In the first of many humiliations, he put the rings on his fingers and, turning his hands, admired the glitter of the gold in the afternoon sunshine.

The men were goaded down to the walled ferry point, bundled into two motorised canoes and taken north upstream across Rokel Creek to Gberi Bana, Kallay's headquarters and the militia's main base near a deserted palm oil plantation. It was a shrewd move by the former SLA sergeant to put the creek between the hostages and any friendly forces that might approach overland. In addition, areas of marshland to the east and west of Gberi Bana restricted access to the village from the right bank of Rokel Creek.

Whether at this time or later, it appears that the radio in one of the Land Rovers may have been unbolted and shipped across the creek, or the RSO may have been transported back across the creek to the vehicle at some point. Whatever actually happened, the radio would allow the British soldiers to communicate with BTC, albeit under the eyes of their captors. They initially sent a brief radio report saying that they had been surrounded and held against their will. Later the radio would play a vital part in the rescue operation.

In London and Freetown, Foreign Office and Ministry of Defence (MoD) staff tried to assess what had happened. Initially, the Whitehall ministries were optimistic. They reported that the men had gone missing on 25 August in the Masiaka–Forodugu area about 100 km east of Freetown. They confirmed that the soldiers were safe and well, but not free to leave.

Both London and Freetown asserted that the Royal Irish patrol had been on an authorised liaison visit to the Jordanians. Brigadier Gordon Hughes said they had been co-ordinating security arrangements with Jordanian peacekeepers at Masiaka. 'The British troops completed their mission . . . and on their way back to Benguema they were stopped and detained.'

However, this statement was rejected by the deputy commander of UNAMSIL, Nigerian Brigadier-General Mohammed A. Garba: 'That is one thing I want to categorically deny, because the rate at which things are going, the British may have a tendency to shift blame on the UN troops deployed in that place.'

Garba denied the British claim that the soldiers were travelling back toward Freetown when they were captured. Instead, he said, they were travelling east from the capital when they made a left turn into an area known to be controlled by the West Side Boys. 'They went in over six miles,' he claimed. He denied that the British soldiers had met the Jordanian troops, and said that UN peacekeepers did not know what the British troops were doing when they were captured. 'The British did not say to UN peacekeepers in Masiaka that they were going into West Side Boys' rebel positions, which I would describe as very dangerous.'

There would continue to be an undercurrent of tension between UNAMSIL and the British HQ in Sierra Leone during the days following the kidnap of the Royal Irish patrol. The UN command would be keen to distance themselves from the incident. There was also a suspicion that within UNAMSIL there was a degree of *schadenfreude* that the British, who had been so confident, were now suffering the same humiliating experiences that some UN units had already endured.

A day later, Brigadier Hughes played down the dispute, saying that it would not help to secure the men's release. 'It is really far too early to speculate on the circumstances surrounding the detention of our soldiers. Whenever they have been safely released there will be a full and accurate report released; that is normal procedure. My focus is very much making sure that our soldiers are released safely and quickly.'

The MoD said that negotiations had begun to secure the release of the soldiers from the renegade faction, which had a reputation for kidnapping and robbery. To UNAMSIL HQ it looked like a repeat of one of the numerous incidents of 'hostage and ransom' that had almost become routine in Sierra Leone.

Kidnapping had become a worldwide problem, notably in Central and South America, and security firms working in the risk-management and hostage-negotiation business know it simply and rather bleakly as 'H and R' – hostage and ransom.

Writing a year after these events in the academic journal *Small Wars and Insurgencies*, Richard Connaughton – formerly Head of Defence Studies for the British Army – remarked, 'Immediately, the British media roundly condemned the British government's Sierra Leone policy. The "H" word, "hostage", will always pressurise liberal Western democratic governments because of the implication of political and military failure.'

Though many of the kidnappings in Sierra Leone went unreported, they were utilised often as a show of strength by a militia or faction. The victims would be held and then released after negotiations that might produce a ransom but often served simply to reinforce the status of the faction. Kidnappings did not normally end in executions. However, many African men who were kidnapped were used as porters and labourers and women were coerced into sexual slavery.

The pattern could be seen as far back as 14 February 1998 when three missionaries from Spain, Italy and Austria were kidnapped from Lunsar's hospital in an area 80 km to the north of Freetown occupied by the aggressive and violent Revolutionary United Front (RUF).

Three days later, two aid workers – one Canadian, one French – from the medical charity *Médecins Sans Frontières* were kidnapped in the interior of the country.

On 27 February, the missionaries who had been kidnapped at Lunsar by the RUF were released at Mashaka and taken to Gboko by Bishop Giorgio Biguzzi of the Roman Catholic diocese of Makeni.

On 14 November, at least sixteen people were killed and a further fifty or more kidnapped when over 100 guerrillas attacked the northern border town of Kamaporoto.

Ten days later, guerrillas loyal to Solomon 'Saj' Musa, the Armed Forces Revolutionary Council (AFRC)[4] chief secretary of state, were reported to be holding an Italian Roman Catholic priest, Mario Guerra.

Throughout 1999, missionaries, aid workers and UN personnel continued to fall victim to kidnapping. On 12 January, five monks – four Italians and a Spaniard – together with six nuns – four Indians, a Kenyan and a Bangladeshi – were kidnapped by anti-government guerrillas in Freetown.

Eight days later, Japan's honorary consul and ten other local businessmen were kidnapped by anti-government guerrillas in the city.

On 22 January, Archbishop Joseph Ganda of Sierra Leone and five European priests were rescued from their RUF kidnappers by troops from the Economic Community of West African States (ECOWAS) Military Observer Group (ECOMOG).

Javier Espinosa, a Spanish journalist, was kidnapped by anti-government guerrillas on 25 January but freed two days later.

However, not all kidnappings ended as quickly or happily.

On 27 January, three of the kidnapped nuns were reported to have died during fighting between their captors and ECOMOG forces.

The reality was somewhat different from this report. The death of the nuns was witnessed by twenty-year-old Beatrice who had been abducted with her sister a week earlier and force-marched into the hills by the rebels along with thousands of other people. She described the actual events to Human Rights Watch:

There was this rebel, and he had it out for the nuns. He said his name was Colonel Foday Bah and for the last day we'd heard him threatening to kill the nuns. Another rebel named Tina Musa, she was Saj Musa's wife, kept insisting that they be left alone and they argued about it. So that morning she had to go on a mission and no sooner had she climbed the hill behind Allen Town, than Foday Bah started in again on the nuns.

At around 10.00 a.m. he got out his pistol and started threatening, but seriously now. The nuns started crying and praying and we did as well, so he announced, 'I am Colonel Foday Bah. I'm an SLA man. We came for peace but you people don't want it. You're the ones selling out our country.' In the process he was hitting the nuns and others with a stick. Another rebel told him to leave them, but Foday threatened to kill him as well.

When it became clear he was serious, the nuns started praying. And then he walked over to the black nun, and shot her with his pistol in the head. Then he shot a white man. And then, even as the others were begging and begging, he shot a yellow [Asian] nun and then another yellow [Asian] one, and then the others. When he was finished he went over, removed their slippers and gave them to a few of the abductees.

When Tina came back down the hill and saw the nuns had been killed she was furious and upset. She even cried for them.

On 12 February 1999, RUF guerrillas kidnapped Father Vittorio Mosele, an Italian Roman Catholic missionary, and looted his mission in Kambia, 100 km north of Freetown. He was eventually released on 9 April.

On 4 August, the AFRC, a guerrilla group loyal to rebellious SLA officer Lieutenant-Colonel Johnny Paul Koroma, kidnapped thirty-seven people, including British soldiers, in the Occra Hills, 40 km east of Freetown. Five of the hostages were released almost immediately and two more were released the following day. Another nineteen hostages, including two Britons and a Canadian, were released on 8 August.

On 15 October, a group of humanitarian workers, two priests and Bishop Giorgio Biguzzi of Makeni were kidnapped by armed men at Masongbo, 50 km from Freetown. Koroma denied that his supporters had been responsible but claimed that they had secured the hostages' release three days later.

On 14 May 2000, eighteen UN peacekeeping troops and military observers who had been kidnapped by the RUF were handed over to UNAMSIL.

A week later, the RUF freed a further fifty-four kidnapped UN peace-keepers – including thirty-two Zambians, ten Kenyans, a Norwegian and a Malaysian – at Lungi International Airport.

At the end of May, the RUF released the last of more than 500 UN peace-keepers they had kidnapped in the first week of May.

With this pattern of capture and release in mind, the MoD was initially reasonably sanguine. The Royal Irish patrol had lost contact with their base at 15.45 hours on Friday 25 August 2000 as they drove through the bush near the gang's jungle stronghold. In London, MoD spokesman Major Tom Thorneycroft explained: 'They are in the hands of the West Side Boys, although we have not received any ransom demands.'

British diplomatic staff in Freetown urged Koroma to intervene to secure the soldiers' release, since the WSB asserted that they were loyal to him.

In Freetown, the crew of a Lynx HAS 3 helicopter on board the Duke class frigate HMS *Argyll* (F231) were alerted and flew over the area in which the patrol was last reported. Initially, *Argyll*'s aircraft was the only British aircraft in the country and would be critical in early reconnaissance. Lieutenant Commander Al Jones, the flight commander, and Lieutenant Nigel Cunningham had flown many missions over the jungle and their knowledge of the area would prove invaluable.

Within hours, the WSB admitted that they had taken the patrol hostage and demanded that Lynx flights should cease. At this point, fears began to grow for the safety of the missing men.

The militia group holding the Royal Irish soldiers was made up partly from former SLA soldiers who had staged a coup against the elected government of Tejan Kabbah in 1997, former members of the RUF, kidnapped civilians and common criminals released from Pademba Road Prison in Freetown during the coup. They now operated as bandits. People who had encountered the group said that it was usually possible to pay them off with alcohol or other bribes – though they were most likely to use their weapons in the afternoon and evenings, when they were most inebriated.

The gang was organised into five groups that they called 'battalions' which were based in the villages in the Occra Hills. The Royal Irish patrol had encountered the HQ and a sub-group of the gang that called itself the 'Gulf Battalion'. Though they saw themselves as soldiers, the WSB were regarded in Freetown as armed criminals with an eccentric taste in clothing and accoutrements who robbed travellers on the roads around their bases.

Travelling with a UN convoy one morning in 2000, Aminatta Forna[5] encountered a lightly manned West Side Boy road block near Masiaka. 'It became evident we were in rebel territory when we passed through the first checkpoint: a wooden pole, lowered and raised by means of a length of rope. To the side of the road stood the operator: a boy of ten or eleven, bandy legged and barefoot, wearing a pair of ragged shorts and nothing else, save a large sub-machine-gun strapped to his back.'

In addition to military uniforms, designer T-shirts, women's wigs and flip-flops were also sometimes sported by the West Side Boys. Their behaviour was unpredictable, fuelled by drugs like cocaine[6], acquired through contacts in Central America or the Caribbean, locally grown cannabis[7] and, to a lesser extent, alcohol.

According to both Liberian and Sierra Leonean rebels, this taste for cross-dressing was a military mind game, a tactic to intimidate their enemies: an armed and aggressive man wearing a summer frock or a pastel-coloured housecoat is a grotesque and disturbing sight. The clothing also made the soldiers feel invincible because of a regional superstition which holds that soldiers can 'confuse the enemy's bullets' by assuming two identities simultaneously. Though the accoutrements and female garb looked bizarre to Western eyes, they were, in a sense, variations on the camouflage uniforms and face paint used by Western soldiers for concealment and, hopefully, invulnerability during combat.

The WSB had not been seen as a threat by the British forces in-country and had indeed assisted in operations by the SLA against the RUF in May 2000, but there was a darker side to their character that would only become evident later.

A four-months-pregnant, twenty-year-old Sierra Leonean woman known to her Human Rights Watch interviewers as M. K. calmly described her traumatic experience of abduction, rape and forced abortion by the WSB in July 2000:

I was abducted with two other civilians, including my brother-in-law, by the West Side Boys. They were all wearing uniforms; some uniforms were new, and others wore old ones. We were taken to their base in Magbele Junction where there were many other abductees. At night time one of the rebels called Umaro Kamara came to me and said he wanted to have sex with me. He spoke nicely with me and said that he wanted to take me to Makeni and make me his wife. He raped me that day. The rebels saw that I was pregnant and said to Umaro, 'We are not going to work along with any pregnant woman, we should kill her.' Umaro said that he wanted to take me as his wife and that I should be given an injection instead. Umaro called me and tried to convince me to get rid of the baby. He said, 'They will kill you if you do not agree so you better have the injection.' I was taken to the doctor who gave me an injection and some pills. Two days later I started bleeding. I felt weak and had pain all over my body. Then I lost the baby.

When Umaro was on patrol, three other rebels raped me. When we moved out to go to another base, I saw the body of my brother-in-law. After one day I started bleeding again so Umaro took me to the doctor who gave me another injection. When we reached Lunsar, Umaro wanted to make me his wife. Even while I was bleeding, Umaro used me. He told me to wash myself before raping me.

The WSB were also involved in scams selling stolen goods. In March 2000, Human Rights Watch released an interview with Vandi, one of fourteen men abducted from a coal pit in Lalsoso by the WSB on 20 February. He was used as slave labour for six days and forced to work long hours removing zinc panels from the roofs of houses in abandoned villages. He described how the panels were then sold to individual soldiers from both ECOMOG and the loyal Sierra Leonean Army. He had whip marks in at least five places on his neck, arms and face where he said he'd been beaten by the rebels.

'We went village to village unroofing the houses,' he recounted. 'The rebels would sit down and watch us as we worked and then force us to walk long hours, sometimes throughout the night, with twenty-five zinc panels on our heads. Sometimes I could barely move and they would beat me with a whip or the blunt end of the machete. Their base was Gberi Bana. An hour before reaching the main road, where they sold the panels for 1,000 leones [£0.45] per sheet, the rebels stashed their guns and took off their uniform.'

Even with ready access to women, drink, money and drugs, Kallay was concerned about the flagging morale of the gang. In the month before the capture of the Royal Irish soldiers, a total of 212 of his men had come in from the jungle to surrender their weapons to the Jordanian DDR. Kallay suspected that twenty-seven more of his men were also possible waverers.

If these young men were not on side they were potential enemies for the WSB. So, days before the Royal Irish patrol was captured, he ordered that his 'soldiers' be taken to the bullet-scarred dip near the camp that some knew as the 'Dead Zone'.

There, a squad of West Side Boys formed up, depressed the safety catches on their AK-47s and raked their comrades with bursts of fire.

Chapter 2
Lion Mountains

Dat ship we bringg Baibul, na-in bringg rohm.
The same ship that brought the Bible also brought rum.

In 1460, rain was lashing the tiny craft of the Portuguese explorer Pedro da Cintra when the lookout in the crow's nest perched at the top of the main-mast shouted down that he could see land.

It is said that to the sailors the outline of the mountainous peninsula on the western coast of Africa resembled a crouching lion. Hence it became known as *Serra Lyoa* and later *Sierra Leone* – Lion Mountains. Another version of the origin of the name asserts that the rumble of thunder and the drumming of the heavy rain, which is at its most intense between April and November, sounded to the sailors like the roaring of a lion. This may not seem so fanciful in light of the fact that the average annual coastal rain-fall in the area is 3,810 mm.

The circumstances that led to the encounter at Magbeni between the West Side Boys and the Royal Irish patrol on 25 August 2000 had been determined over the course of almost 400 years by a chain of interlocking historical events that brought Europeans to West Africa. Sierra Leone had initially attracted sailors in the 16th century because its huge natural harbour offered protection against the Atlantic and it was on the trade routes to India and the East.

It was here that Sir Francis Drake anchored on his circumnavigation of the globe 120 years after the Portuguese had discovered the area. The country inland was at that time ruled by a small number of independent tribal groups including the Temne, Sherbro and Limba and, except for visits by Mandingo traders from the area that is now modern Mali, Senegal and northern Guinea, it remained almost unexplored.

By the 16th century, the Portuguese were using Sierra Leone as one of their African slaving bases. Nearly 500 years later, children would still be

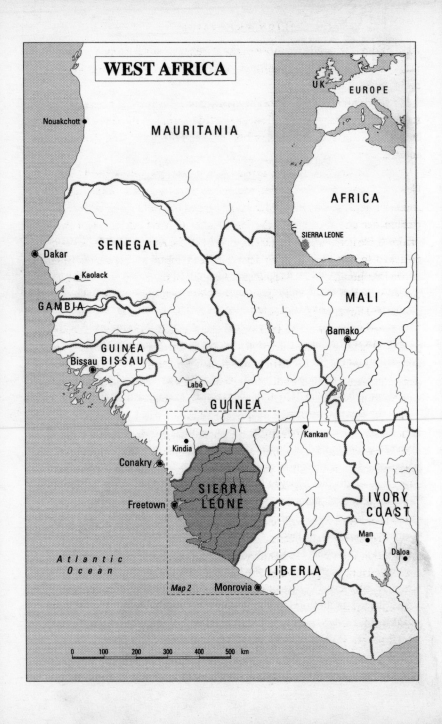

WEST AFRICA

MAURITANIA

Nouakchott •

UK EUROPE

AFRICA

SIERRA LEONE

SENEGAL

Dakar

Kaolack

GAMBIA

MALI

Bamako

GUINEA BISSAU

Bissau

Labé

GUINEA

Kankan

Kindia

Conakry

SIERRA LEONE

IVORY COAST

Freetown

Man

Daloa

Atlantic Ocean

LIBERIA

Map 2 Monrovia

0   100   200   300   400   500 km

drawing on a grim folk memory of the Portuguese slavers: when meeting fair-skinned strangers travelling in rural Sierra Leone they would still shout 'Oporto, Oporto!'

The harbour at the mouth of the Sierra Leone River would play a significant part in the 'Triangular Trade', so called because of the shape formed by the three trade routes worked by British, Portuguese and American colonial merchants.

Along the first route, ships carried fish, lumber and other goods from New England to the West Indies, where they were traded for the sugar and molasses used to make rum. Merchants carried the rum, along with guns, gunpowder and tools, from the West Indies to West Africa. Here they traded these items for slaves, taken prisoner in the African tribal wars and marched to the coast by their fellow African captors. The slavers then carried the human cargo, packed into the holds of their ships like cattle, to the West Indies where they were sold. Here the traders would take the profits and buy more molasses.

A reverse version of the trade route saw finished goods from Britain, produced in the new factories of the Industrial Revolution, exported from Liverpool and Bristol to Africa and traded for slaves. The slaves were shipped to America and traded for raw materials like tobacco, cotton and sugar – which would, in turn, be supplied to the British factories.

Untold numbers of slaves died in the ghastly conditions of the slave ships or were worked to death in the plantations of the Americas. They were doomed men and women from the moment of their capture; in former times, their African captors would have killed them, but now slaving allowed them to make a profit from the spoils of tribal war.

Between 1750 and 1800, the fort on Bunce Island in the mouth of the Sierra Leone River was a collecting point for slaves. It had been built in 1663 by the British as a trading centre. It was destroyed by the French in 1702 but rebuilt soon afterwards. The Dutch and Portuguese held the fort at various times until it finally returned to British control in 1750.

In 1787, the British stopped their slaving operations and established a settlement on the Sierra Leone peninsula as a home for slaves repatriated from England and North America and for slaves liberated from ships intercepted by the Royal Navy's anti-slavery patrols. Abolitionist groups in Britain headed by Member of Parliament William Wilberforce, cleric Thomas Clarkson and the enlightened pottery manufacturer Josiah Wedgwood were instrumental in the purchase of the peninsula and the establishment of the settlement as 'the Province of Freedom' and a refuge for 'the London black poor'. The town and community became known as Freetown. The Freetown Peninsula is approximately 40 km long and 16 km wide and rises to 100 m above sea level. At the western end of the peninsula, the Aberdeen Creek divides the Aberdeen Peninsula from greater Freetown

Within three years, however, 90 per cent of the former slaves and white settlers, many of the latter prostitutes deported from London and Liverpool, had died of tropical diseases or fled from the new province. Of the 15,000 slaves who had fought for King George III against the American Revolutionaries during the War of Independence, thereby winning their freedom and having subsequently made their way to London, some 1,200 were brought to Freetown in 1792. In two years only 800 were still alive. To the chagrin of the British philanthropists, some of the settlers, both white and black, joined in the slave trade.

Between 1807, when the slave trade was abolished, and 1864, some 50,000 freed slaves were landed at Freetown by the British. The area, like others along the West African coast, later earned itself the name 'the White Man's Grave'. In the late 20th century, HIV/AIDS would join malaria as a regional killer in Africa. In 2001, out of a population of about 5,732,681, an estimated 170,000 Sierra Leoneans were suffering from HIV/AIDS and there had been 11,000 deaths from the disease.

In addition to malaria, the heat stroke and dehydration caused by the climate killed both black and white settlers. Sierra Leone has a marked wet season with high humidity followed by a dry season.

'In Sierra Leone the rains begin on 1 May every year,' writes Aminatta Forna. 'From then on it rains at eleven o'clock every night, gradually moving forward in the day until the rain falls almost continuously. As the season advances, so the rain recedes at exactly the same pace. Next the sun shines for seven months until the clouds come back again. On 2 May, if for some reason it did not rain the night before, people in the marketplace might remark, "The rains are late this year, not so?" This in Sierra Leone is what passes for a conversation about the weather.'

Like so much of the early British Empire, this West African enclave was run as a business. The Sierra Leone Company, formed in 1791, administered the settlement until 1808, when it became a Crown Colony. By 1850, over

100 ethnic groups were living in harmony in different areas of Freetown under the firm but paternalistic British rule.

The liberated slaves who settled in Freetown became known as Krios (Creoles). They benefited from missionary education and the British appointed many of them to positions within the civil administration. The Krios have remained in Freetown, some still living in distinctive wooden-framed houses, and although they now make up less than 2 per cent of the population, they are still the country's intellectuals and professionals and are further distinguished by being Christian. The Krios' influence on the political and social life of the country is sometimes described disparagingly as 'Creocracy'.

The Krios have a strongly defined identity and speak a distinctive patois. Canadian journalist Ian Stewart recalled his first experience of Krio when meeting a customs officer at Lungi Airport, who was speaking 'a complex and charming language based on English, but peppered with expressions from other languages'.

'"How dee bodee now?" the officer blurted out in a rapid-fire staccato. Loosely translated, this means "How are you?"

'I had been taught a bit of Krio . . . so I answered, "Tank-ee Gah, dee bodee in dee clothes." ("I'm fine").'

The two major tribal groups within Sierra Leone are the Temnes of the north and the Mendes of the south. These tribal distinctions would play a significant part in the political future of the country.

The British imperial infrastructure became fully established when the hinterland of Sierra Leone was declared a Protectorate in 1896, and the port and town of Freetown prospered. Its grid pattern of roads even today retains many of the original street names, such as Waterloo, Wellington, Liverpool Street and, close to the harbour, the appropriately named Wilberforce Street. Some names have changed – hence East Street has, since independence, become ECOWAS Street after the Economic Community of West African States. In the middle of Freetown, like a version of a provincial British town, is Victoria Park. Within the peninsula were communities with typically English-sounding names such as York, Hastings, Gloucester and Bathurst, while Dublin was established on the offshore Banana Islands. Further inland, many of the country towns retained their indigenous names. An unusual exception was the community that sprang up around the road construction camp that had been set up about 150 km from Freetown during the late 19th- and early 20th-century road and rail expansion. It was known as Mile 91.

In 1898, the Colonial Authority imposed a 'Hut Tax' and, under the leadership of Bai Bureh, the indigenous population rose in rebellion against the British and the Krios.[1] It was a significant moment in the history of Sierra Leone.

A railway network was built from the peninsula to link the port with the towns in the hinterland. At the junction at Bauya the lines divided, running to Makeni in the north and Bo and Pendembu in the south and east. Though the railways were phased out in the 1970s, the station names and buildings remain, and so Sierra Leone still boasts a Waterloo Station. Surfaced roads ran inland to Kambia on the Guinea border and to the Liberian border. In 2002, the country had 11,700 km of roads, of which 936 km were paved – but in poor condition.

By 1900, Freetown, positioned at the divide between the North and South Atlantic, was an important coaling station and Royal Navy base. In addition to the capital there were ports at Bonthe to the south and Pepel on the Sierra Leone River. An enduring memory for the crews of warships and commercial vessels visiting Freetown was the lively business conducted with the waterborne traders in their 'bullum boats'. These long, narrow, wooden workboats named after the Bullom Peninsula were inevitably known to British sailors as 'bum boats'.

The Sierra Leone Police Corps was formed in 1829, from which a succession of police and paramilitary formations would emerge, culminating in the formation in 1971 of the Sierra Leone Regiment, Republic of Sierra Leone Military Forces. In 1890, the Sierra Leone Frontier Police was established and, eleven years later, the Sierra Leone Battalion. Sierra Leone contributed troops to the West African Frontier Force established in 1928. The Sierra Leone Battalion, Royal West African Frontier Force, was formed around 1940.

Even after independence the formations retained the title 'Royal', as in the Sierra Leone Regiment, Royal West African Frontier Force 1959, and the Royal Sierra Leone Regiment, Royal Sierra Leone Military Forces, until the Republic was formed in 1971.

In World War I, soldiers from the Royal Sierra Leone Regiment fought alongside British troops as they attacked the Imperial German colony of Cameroon, for which the regiment received the battle honours Duala, Cameroons 1914–16.

In the aftermath of World War I, Lebanese emigrants from the former Turkish province in the Levant began arriving in Sierra Leone. Known at the time to the British as 'Syrians', they would play a significant part in the economy of the colony and gain control of much of the diamond trade, with contacts throughout the Middle East and Europe.

One of Sierra Leone's notorious Lebanese would be the lawyer turned militia leader Nabih Berri. Educated in Lebanon in the mid 1970s, he went on to head *Amal* (Arab acronym for 'Movement of the Disinherited'). This Shiite militia fought with the Maronite Christians and Sunnis for a more equitable share of power in Lebanon. It funded its operations with diamonds smuggled from Sierra Leone.

In World War II, Freetown became the base for Force K, a Royal Navy task force composed of the battle cruiser HMS *Renown* and aircraft carrier *Ark Royal*, which were among the ships on call to sink the German 'pocket battleship' – the heavy cruiser KMS *Admiral Graf Spee* – in 1939. As the U-boat war bore down on Britain, Freetown and Halifax in Nova Scotia, Canada, were the two assembly points for convoys making the hazardous journey to Britain. In 1941, a flight of Supermarine Walrus flying boats was based in Freetown harbour. These aircraft were the first seaplanes to be based in Sierra Leone and would be deployed to attack U-boats or recover downed RAF aircrew in the Atlantic.

From 1941, the waters outside Freetown were a graveyard for merchant ships caught by lurking U-boats, with a few even being sunk in the last year of the war. By the end of 1942, coastal defence artillery had been installed and manned in all the principal West African ports. Soldiers from the Royal Sierra Leone Regiment fought alongside the 14th Army in Burma against the Japanese. The regiment was awarded the battle honours North Arakan, Kaladan, Myohaung, Burma 1943–45. When British forces returned to Sierra Leone in 2000 they found that there was still a proud and vigorous Burma Star Association composed of tough old veterans of the campaign in the Far East.

Evidence of the two World Wars and of the social attitudes of previous generations still remains in Freetown today in the two Commonwealth War Graves Commission cemeteries. One appears to be for British and white Commonwealth dead and the other for men from Sierra Leone.

The King Tom Cemetery on the headland between White Man's Bay and Kroo Bay, close to the oil tanks by the docks, contains 248 Commonwealth burials from World War II, two of which are unidentified, and 129 World War I burials. Many of the men who died in World War I were victims of the worldwide pneumonia epidemic of September–October 1918. Some were Australian and South African soldiers on troop ships returning from France. The cemetery also contains 135 non-war burials and twenty-one war graves of other nationalities from the European community in Freetown that are in the Commonwealth War Commission's care. Among the civilians are merchant marines from ships like the *Trinity Star*, which was sunk by the *Admiral Graf Spee*. A memorial in the cemetery commemorates thirty-five casualties from both World Wars whose graves elsewhere in Sierra Leone cannot be maintained.

Freetown's Lumley Cemetery contains seventy-four Commonwealth burials from World War II, seven of which are unidentified. The names on the headstones suggest that Lumley is the African cemetery. Many of the soldiers, like Regimental Sergeant Major (RSM) Foindu Kaily, served in the Sierra Leone Regiment, or in the Sierra Leone Naval Volunteer Force like Leading Seaman Charlie Brown, a Krio. In Sierra Leone, the rural population has little concept of dates and measures the passage of time simply as 'Yesterday – Today –Tomorrow'. Consequently, few of the men buried at Lumley have an age recorded on their gravestones.

Many of the British servicemen who died in Freetown in World War II were in the garrison or working in the docks and were probably victims of malaria and waterborne diseases rather than enemy action. During World War II, the country was continuing to live up to its reputation as 'the White Man's Grave'.

In 2000, the return to Freetown of British servicemen and women allowed the war dead at King Tom and Lumley cemeteries to be honoured with ceremonies in November on Remembrance Sunday.

Following World War II, the airbase at Hastings was replaced by a new airfield at Lungi, which developed into the international airport. It has a ferry link from the Queen Elizabeth II Quay at Kissy, east of Freetown, across the harbour to Tagrin. Inland, nine airstrips would eventually be constructed, seven between 914 m and 1,523 m long and two under 914 m long. The strip at Hastings would play a significant part in operations in September 2000.

In her haunting book about her father and her childhood in Sierra Leone, *The Devil that Danced on the Water*, Aminatta Forna conjures up a picture of Freetown, the same city described by Graham Greene in his grim novel *The Heart of the Matter*. Though separated by nearly fifty-five years, they both describe a lively city, but one at peace.

In the centre of the town, at the junction of five roads not far from Victoria Park, stands the 500-year-old Cotton Tree. It towers above the streets, a symbolic landmark. Greene writes, 'Round the corner, in front of the old cotton tree, where the earliest settlers had gathered their first day on the unfriendly shore, stood the law courts and police station.'

Aminatta Forna describes the minibuses – or *poda podas,* Krio for 'hither and thither' – manoeuvring around Freetown: 'Other *poda podas* inch their way around the massive trunk and soaring branches of the Cotton Tree, which appears on postcards and in calendars as the symbol of Freetown, home of the freed slaves, once but no more the Athens of Africa. The words are always written with capitals: the Cotton Tree. In between the massive roots the lepers sleep on, undisturbed under their makeshift awnings.'

The white residents in Freetown met at the exclusive Hill Station Club on the heights overlooking Freetown. This was the world described by Graham Greene. Though some of the expatriate population developed a real affection for Freetown, after a few drinks in the evening some of the Colonial Office staff would sing lugubrious words set to the lilting tune of 'The Mountains of Mourne':

> Oh Sierra Leone, Sierra Leone,
> Thousands of miles from Sierra Leone,
> I shall be happy wherever I roam
> If I'm thousands of miles from Sierra Leone.

Writing about Freetown in World War II, Greene would concur with this pessimistic view of the port: 'In the evening the port became beautiful for perhaps five minutes. The laterite roads that were so ugly and clay-heavy by day became a delicate flower-like pink. It was the hour of content. Men who had left the port for ever would sometimes remember on a grey wet London evening the bloom and glow that faded as soon as it was seen: they would wonder why they had hated the coast and for a space of a drink would long to return.'

In his book *Once a Pilgrim*, former SAS soldier Will Scully recalled his first impressions of Freetown in 1997 when he arrived to take on a military training post: 'Freetown is the pits. The air was tropical-warm and smelled thick and sweet of decay. The roads were narrow and in a terrible state of repair, congested with people wandering along the beaten red earth at the side or milling about by stalls set up between mounds of rotting vegetables and rubbish, selling bananas, yams, cassava, beer, whiskey, brandy, varieties of cigarettes, shirts, pots, pans, shovels – in fact anything.'

Political development came early to Sierra Leone. The first elections for a legislative council were held under the constitution drafted in 1924. The ministerial system was introduced in 1953; Sir Milton Margai, a former doctor and leader of the Sierra Leone Peoples' Party (SLPP), was appointed chief minister in 1954 and prime minister in 1960. The SLPP represented the interests of the Mendes and was supported by the Krios. In parliament, the All Peoples' Party (APP) or All Peoples' Congress (APC), who were the opposition, was headed by former trade unionist and popularist politician Siaka Stevens and consisted largely of Temnes. This mix of tribal and political loyalties would be volatile and ultimately destroy the democratic process in Sierra Leone.

The country that Margai headed is 71,740 square km – about the size of Scotland or South Carolina – and shares a 306 km land border with Liberia in the east and south-east and a 652 km border with Guinea to the north and north-east.

Freetown, the capital city and main political and commercial centre, has the highest population density. In the years that followed independence, this would grow as internal refugees flooded in from the rest of the country, trying to escape the civil war.

The country consists of a coastal belt of mangrove swamps and low-lying land, forested hill country, upland plateaux and mountains. The extensive network of rivers includes the Great and Little Scarcies Rivers in the north, the Moa River in the east, the Mano River in the south-west and the Rokel River in the west. They provide the country with a network of 800 km of waterways, of which 600 km are navigable throughout the year. The Great Scarcies and the Mano flood between May and October. The only other natural hazard is the *harmattan*, the dry and sandy Saharan wind that blows from November to May and coats the façades of buildings with red dust. In Freetown, when the *harmattan* is blowing hard, the dust can erase the horizon, the hills and even the shape of houses.

Sierra Leone has an agricultural economy with export cash crops that include coffee, cacao, ginger, kola nuts, palm oil, palm kernels and piassava (palm fibres). The palm also provides the basis for home-made palm wine.

Sierra Leone is noted for its mineral wealth which has been the source of many of its troubles. It exports and produces gem- and industrial-quality diamonds, bauxite (aluminium ore) and rutile (titanium ore). In 2000, some 450,000 carats of gem-quality and 150,000 carats of industrial-quality diamonds were produced. Production of bauxite in 1994 totalled 735,000 tonnes, and of rutile and ilmenite (titanium ores), around 203,000 tonnes. Gold was also exported in small quantities.

Writing about the Sierra Leone of the 1970s, Aminatta Forna would say: 'The mining companies shadowed every nuance and change in politics in Sierra Leone and all over Africa. These were the vested interests, although the term wasn't widely used in those days: they helped shape every political outcome in ways that could not be quantified and were not even understood. There were whispers, rumours and nothing changed in countries like Sierra Leone without the mineral concessions first being negotiated.'

Diamonds were discovered in the early 1930s and in 1935, the British colonial administration granted the De Beers mining company exclusive mining and prospecting rights over the entire country for ninety-nine years. By 1937, Sierra Leone was mining one million carats annually.

However, by 1956 there were an estimated 75,000 illegal miners in the heart of the diamond area. This led to smuggling on a vast scale – mainly by Mandingo and Lebanese traders.

In the early 1950s, Lebanese smugglers began to re-route their trade through Liberia, where Belgian and Israeli diamond merchants soon established offices. Struggling to keep their control of the trade, De Beers set up a buying office in Liberia's capital Monrovia in 1954. In 1955, the colonial administration scrapped the De Beers nationwide monopoly, confining its operations to just two fields. The following year, a scheme was introduced under which both mining and buying licenses were granted to indigenous miners. It seemed like an example of benign colonial rule, but since these licenses could be traded, inevitably many ended up being owned by Lebanese merchants.

The diamonds in Sierra Leone are close to the surface in alluvial soil and consequently 'mining' consists of simply digging holes a few metres deep and panning in the mud and water with a circular mesh sieve called a *shake*

shake – there is no need for any of the elaborate mining equipment required in South Africa. In 1972, the third largest diamond in the world was discovered in the Kono fields. In 1994, an enormous Sierra Leonean 172-carat diamond was sold at auction for £1.57 million.

The diamond capital of the country is Kenema, which is about 330 km east of Freetown. Kenema used to be the timber trading centre of Sierra Leone but now Hangha Road, the main street, is lined with Lebanese diamond dealers' shops crowded with diggers. Ravaged by ruthless logging, the countryside around Kenema would be the scene of heavy fighting in the late 1990s between different factions attempting to control the diamond fields.

Despite this natural wealth, the country has the dubious distinction of being one of the poorest nations in the world. In 2000, Europeans and Americans working in Sierra Leone were surprised to see the boxes and containers they had discarded as rubbish collected up from refuse heaps to be used for storage and failed to understand the desperation that drives some honest people to petty theft.

In 2001, the country had an estimated GDP of £439.6 million resulting in a per capita income of just £91.30. Life expectancy for men is thirty-seven years and for women forty years. The country has an illiteracy rate of 68.6 per cent.

With this wealth of history behind them and obvious disadvantages and assets, the population of Sierra Leone approached the prospect of independence and nationhood with the excitement, pride and optimism that characterised all the British colonies in Africa over forty years ago.

On 6 March 1957, the British colony of the Gold Coast had given the lead when, under the charismatic Prime Minister Kwame Nkrumah, it became the independent state of Ghana. Soon the diverse peoples of Sierra Leone knew it would be their turn to accept the challenge of independence.

Chapter 3
Independence

Fambul tik kin behn, boht i nohba brok.
The family tree may bend, but it never breaks.

At midnight on 27 April 1961, the flag of the colony of Sierra Leone, spot-lit against the tropical night, was slowly lowered at a ceremony at Government House in Freetown. The governor, immaculate in his white uniform, snapped a salute as he watched it descend.

The flag was a microcosm of the history of the country to date: a Blue Ensign with a shield in the blue field. In the top part of the shield was the Union flag as it had been prior to 1801 – incorporating only the crosses of St George and St Andrew. The lower part of the shield was divided into halves by a vertical line. On one side was a liberated slave seated on the seashore with a ship in the offing; on the other side, on a golden ground, was a green palm tree. Underneath was the motto '*Auspice Britannia Liber*' – 'Free under Britain's protection'.

The crowds watched with growing excitement as simultaneously a new flag with horizontal bars of leaf green, white and cobalt blue was raised in its place. The green stood for agriculture, the white for peace and the blue for the Atlantic Ocean. As it reached the top of the flagpole, fireworks crackled and exploded in the sky, drowning out the cheering.

The British colony was history. Sierra Leone was now an independent nation.

The constitution of 1961 extended the franchise to women. It was a time of optimism. The national anthem 'High We Exalt Thee, Realm of the Free' reflected these aspirations.

As with all former African colonies, the departing British administration left behind a working society that was a miniature mirror image of the United Kingdom. One surviving feature of the colonial administration is the division of the country into provinces. The Freetown Peninsula is the Western Province, the coastal plain to the south is the Southern Province, the northern plain and inland mountains constitute the Northern Province and the interior with its diamond fields to the south-east is the Eastern Province. These provinces might not reflect the tribal areas within the country but would prove useful in future plans and operations within Sierra Leone.

At the time of its independence, the country had a sophisticated, educated middle class, with merchants and traders mostly living in the Western Province and Freetown. The British had established a parliament, an independent judiciary and armed forces answerable to that parliament. They also bequeathed the Sierra Leone Brewery to the young nation. Planning had begun before independence in 1957 and by 1962 it was producing the local Star Beer along with European beers and stouts.

Following the elections of 1962, Margai remained prime minister. It would take a mere five years for the government to begin to unravel and be destroyed by the corrosive mixture of tribalism and corruption seemingly so endemic to Sierra Leone and the rest of Africa. Corruption has always existed in Africa, but it is seen by the more successful individuals as a means of support for their extended families and circle of friends. It is summed up by an enigmatic West African proverb – 'The palm tree casts a long shadow'. Politics offers the best opportunity to give preferment and benefits to one's extended family and consequently no politician would willingly relinquish such power. In Sierra Leone, people would joke, 'Our political leaders never resign – they run away.'

However, at the time of independence, to many it seemed that the country was on a heady race into nationhood. In 1963, Sierra Leone joined the Organisation of African Unity (OAU) and a year later, along with Liberia and Guinea, set up the Mano River Union (MRU) and, probably under pressure from the Lebanese community, broke diplomatic ties with Israel.

The March 1967 general election proved to be a pivotal moment in Sierra Leone's political history. On the eve of the elections, the opposition APP under Siaka Stevens made political capital out of Margai's proposals for the establishment of a single-party state and a republican constitution. The largely mismanaged electoral process heralded prolonged disagreement over the winner. Inconclusive results, which gave the APP thirty-two seats, the SLPP twenty-eight and six to independent candidates, forced the governor general to declare that Siaka Stevens should form a new government, much to the chagrin of the SLPP.

This unsatisfactory chain of events prompted the intervention of Brigadier David Lansana, the commander of the Sierra Leone Army, who ordered the arrest of both the governor general and Stevens on the grounds that a new government could not be formed prior to the announcement of definitive election results.

Lansana's plan was to restore Margai to power. However, junior officers arrested Lansana and established a National Reformation Council (NRC) led by Colonel Juxon-Smith. In 1968, non-commissioned army officers overthrew the NRC junta and invited Siaka Stevens to form a government.

In 1938, the Chinese Communist leader Mao Tse-tung wrote in *Problems of War and Strategy* the much-quoted aphorism 'political power grows out of the barrel of a gun'. Power in Sierra Leone was certainly growing out of the barrel of a gun, but guns would soon destroy governments and replace power with chaos. As a young girl, Aminatta Forna lived through this time. Her description of the erosion of civil liberties and human rights in *The Devil that Danced on the Water* reads like the *Machtergreifung* – the Seizure of Power, the takeover of Germany by the Nazis after the elections of 1933.

'People say they didn't notice,' she wrote, 'never saw what was happening to their neighbours, knew nothing of the arrests, the burning houses, the children shot at dawn, failed to spot the prime minister's growing power, glimpsed nothing of the shadows drawing in around the edges. People were rendered blind, deaf and dumb and pleaded ignorance. How could they have stood up against what they didn't even know was happening?'

Sierra Leone was declared a republic on 19 April 1971 and Stevens was sworn in as executive president on 21 April. Opposition to the government was gradually eliminated; in elections held in May 1973, the APP was unopposed and Stevens was re-elected president. He purged the army of its senior Mende officers and replaced them with loyal Temne northerners. However, morale sank and wages, ammunition and equipment dwindled. In 1971, he had also established a special paramilitary force from Internal Security Units 1 and 2 and renamed it the State Security Division (SSD). To the canny population of Freetown, the SSD, which was made up of men from Guinea, became known privately as 'Siaka Stevens' Dogs'.

Members of the SLPP were put on trial for treason. The traditional governing institutions of the state, particularly the state security apparatus, were subverted to serve the private interests of the APP.

The Stevens era was characterised by unbridled corruption, mismanagement, nepotism and extortion. Courting popularity, he turned diamonds and the presence of De Beers into a political issue, tacitly encouraging illegal mining. In 1971, Stevens effectively nationalised the De Beers operation, with all important decisions being made by himself or his close associate Jamil Mohammed, a Lebanese businessman.

From a high of over two million carats in 1970, legitimate diamond exports dropped to 595,000 carats in 1980 and then to a mere 48,000 in 1988 as illegal trading eroded the official figures. In 1984, De Beers sold its remaining shares to a company controlled by Jamil.

In 1975, Sierra Leone signed a trade and aid agreement with the European Community and helped to form ECOWAS, the Economic Community of West African States – the regional political and economic union.

In 1978, following an election campaign during which Mendes fought Temnes and there was a death toll of over 100, Stevens won again, was sworn in for a new seven-year term and declared a new constitution making the country a one-party state. The APP was now the only legal party in Sierra Leone. In the early 1980s, the country suffered an economic slowdown as sagging export revenues left the government unable to pay for essential imports.

In 1980 Sierra Leone hosted the OAU summit and a year later the ECOWAS summit, in a gesture aimed to assert the country's national identity.

In the summer of 1982, war visited Freetown in an unusual form when the cruise liner SS *Canberra* put into Freetown to refuel. The *Canberra* had been reconfigured as a troop ship and was carrying the 3rd Battalion Parachute Regiment and 40 and 45 Commando of the Royal Marines, part of the British task force sailing south to liberate the Falklands, which had been occupied by Argentina. The *Canberra* tied up at Queen Elizabeth II Quay – with a maximum draft of 9.9 m and no restriction on berthing length, this was the only berth that could handle the big ship.

Aboard the *Canberra*, BBC reporter Robert Fox recalled the stop: 'It was a sticky, overcast day. A couple of nubile English girls, inexpertly escorted by their father, had come down to the refuelling jetty to wave at the troops.

No one was allowed ashore except the party carrying mail and dockyard workers from Vosper Thornycroft ... On the side of the liner away from the jetty the troops were doing a roaring trade with the bumboats. Knives, skins and spears were traded with the slender figures in the hollowed-out tree trunks serving for canoes; the currency was empty polythene water and chemical containers. Some of the superior canoes offered monkeys and parrots. But the barter was brought to an end on the order of the medical staff. They said the skins carried a risk of anthrax and rabies. As the attentions of the frustrated traders became more persistent, the water-hoses were turned on them from the liner.'

Stevens retired in November 1985, aged eighty, and the following January Major-General Joseph Saidu Momoh, who was from the minority Limba tribe and head of the army, was sworn in as president. He placed even greater responsibility for the country's economy in the hands of Jamil Mohammed. A coup attempt was suppressed in March 1987, and in November the president declared a state of economic emergency as the country's inflation was now among the highest in Africa. Diamond smugglers were robbing the country of 90 per cent of its gem revenue. Jamil had been forced into exile after the failed coup and Israeli 'investors' with connections to the Antwerp diamond trade, and to the Russian and American crime families, now became involved with the government's diamond enterprises.

In 1990, Sierra Leone hosted the ECOWAS summit and, crucially, provided a military base for the ECOMOG force that was attempting to end the civil war in Liberia. However, this would antagonise the dissident leader Charles Taylor.

In 1991, as if the country's woes were not enough, the Revolutionary United Front (RUF) began fighting Momoh's corrupt government and would continue to fight the military regime of his successors. Their brutality would mark them out even in the cruel world of Africa.

The RUF had been established in Liberia in the late 1980s by Foday Sankoh, a disaffected army corporal. Sankoh began his political career in the 1970s as a critic of widespread corruption in the country's military and political elite. He lost his job as a TV cameraman for these anti-government views and was briefly imprisoned. Increasingly radicalised, Sankoh joined other Sierra Leoneans in Libya, where Colonel Muammar al-Gaddafi was sponsoring revolutionary movements. It was here that

Sankoh met the Liberian dissident leader Charles Taylor, who was also training in 'revolutionary tactics'.

While the terrible social, political and economic conditions in Sierra Leone in the early 1990s certainly demanded change, the RUF lacked a strong political agenda and was largely motivated by the ambitions of its opportunistic commanders. The country's widespread poverty and unemployment, however, meant there was no shortage of potential recruits and the organisation's ranks were swelled by idle and violent youths from Freetown's slums.

Sankoh, with his grizzled beard and genial exterior, would exercise control through fear, rewards of drugs and alcohol and a strange paternalistic relationship with his young fighters. Many of these fighters were illiterate children, some as young as seven, who had been kidnapped and press-ganged into loose formations that were dignified with the title 'Small Boys Unit' (SBU). A mixture of coercion, drugs, the exhilaration of war and a kind of anarchic freedom made them formidable and terrifying fighters.[1]

The murderous cruelty that characterised the fighting in Sierra Leone was the product of a short life expectancy, fear of what might happen to the perpetrator if he or she did not join in with the atrocities and a desire to enhance or retain standing within a group. This produced gang members who were known for inflicting some particular type of cruelty.

Sankoh's response to criticism was to deny stories of atrocities, although he was fond of quoting the saying 'when a lion and an elephant are fighting, the grass is going to suffer'.

Sankoh was known to his infant soldiers as 'Papa'. After completing his training in Libya he fought with Taylor's National Patriotic Front before establishing the RUF and crossing over the border into Sierra Leone in 1991. During the following years, the RUF overran Sierra Leone's mineral assets and established control over much of the east of the country. The conflict was in effect an extension of the civil war in Liberia. Taylor had encouraged the creation of a rebel movement in Sierra Leone to force President Momoh to withdraw from ECOWAS and tie down ECOMOG, which was becoming embroiled in Liberia's civil war.

ECOMOG had first been deployed in Liberia in 1990 to halt factional fighting in the capital, Monrovia. ECOMOG was initially made up of some 4,000 troops from Nigeria, Ghana, Guinea, Sierra Leone and The Gambia.

Its role was at times controversial, particularly when it effectively became a faction in the war, preventing Taylor's forces from entering the capital.

This policy was changed, however, and the Nigerian commanders began co-operating with Taylor when it was clear that he was leading the major force in the country. ECOMOG had been instrumental in ensuring security during elections won by Charles Taylor. It is a bitter irony that in August 2003, landing in driving rain, ECOMOG would be back in Liberia, this time to ensure the smooth departure of Taylor and to keep the peace between his forces and rebels in Monrovia.

Once the RUF was created, Taylor ensured a constant supply of arms and for the remainder of Momoh's rule the RUF mounted a sustained rebellion against the central government in Freetown. Economic centres, especially the diamond-mining areas in the south-eastern and south-western regions of the country, became the main targets.

Libya provided the arms and training. Weapons shipments to the RUF were dispatched in Libyan Air Force (LAF) freighters from Tripoli to the Burkina Faso airport at Ouagadougou. They were then shipped to Robertsfield airport in Liberia. The bulk of the materiel reached the RUF's two main operational headquarters in the extreme east of Sierra Leone at Kailahun and Pendembu by helicopter, again with the help of the LAF. Helicopter air-drops were also being made to Daru, Yengema, Koidu and several RUF strongholds in the interior to the immediate west of the Kambui Hills.

Other consignments reached Sierra Leone by road after crossing the Moro River, which separates Liberia and Sierra Leone, at any one of a number of points including Mano, Bomaru or by ferry at Bombohun. Logistically, it appeared that the RUF had established an efficient, well-oiled transport system that would not have worked as well as it did without the agreement of President Taylor. Burkina Faso and Côte d'Ivoire also played an important covert role in the supply line, with weapons distributed direct from Bobo-Dioulasso in Burkina Faso to Monrovia in Liberia, or through north-west Côte d'Ivoire, and finally into Sierra Leone.

The RUF was able to pay for its supplies via the transit of diamonds through Liberia. These gems would become known as the notorious 'Blood Diamonds'.

In an attempt to secure his power base in 1991, Momoh drafted a new constitution providing for a multi-party system in Sierra Leone. He increased the numerical strength of the army by recruiting drug addicts, thieves, unemployed youths, rural and urban drifters and hooligans. He also used the military services of the newly formed anti-Taylor coalition in Sierra Leone, known as the United Liberian Movement (ULIMO). Momoh was unpopular in Sierra Leone and was seen as a puppet of his own ministers. His pusillanimity earned him the nicknames Josephine Momoh and *Dandogo* – the Limba for 'Fool'.

In April 1992, a demonstration by soldiers complaining about unpaid wages quickly turned into a coup as troops commanded by Lieutenant Solomon Musa occupied several government buildings. By 29 April 1992, Momoh was in exile in Guinea-Conakry and Captain Valentine Strasser was heading up a government made up of a group of young officers. It was rumoured that the youthful Strasser had been chosen as leader because he spoke the clearest English and therefore was best suited to broadcast the first communiqués to the world.

Strasser's government, the National Provincial Ruling Council (NPRC), reduced street crime (which was so bad that it caused the UN to list Sierra Leone as the world's worst place to live in 1992) and lowered inflation from 115 per cent to 15 per cent. This allowed the country to receive over £165.5 million in global aid packages. Strasser, who at age twenty-five had become one of the world's youngest heads of state, was criticised for restricting freedom of the press, executing political enemies and the continuing ravages of the civil war. In 1994 he endorsed a two-year transition to multi-party democracy, with elections scheduled for May 1996.

During 1994, the RUF escalated the guerrilla war. By early 1995, when the RUF captured an economically vital rutile mine, the guerrillas controlled most of the countryside. Government forces, notwithstanding military support from Nigeria and Guinea and the allocation of three-quarters of the national budget to the war, appeared unable to check the RUF.

By January 1995, the RUF had overrun the three most important mining sites in the country. These included a number of leased concessions in the Koidu diamond area, the Swiss-owned Sierra Ore and Metal Company's (Sieromco's) bauxite mine at Mokanji and the US/Australian-owned Sierra Rutile Ltd operation at Gbangbatok. In addition to closing down Sierra Leone's principal foreign revenue earners, the RUF raised its international profile by threatening to execute seventeen Western hostages.

In April 1995, with the RUF reported to be only 35 km from the capital,

Strasser lifted the ban on political parties and formed a national commission for reconciliation. The fighting had forced thousands of rural Sierra Leoneans to flee their homes and by March 1995 it was estimated that more than 900,000 were refugees; 150,000 were in Guinea, 90,000 in Liberia and more than 600,000 in camps inside Sierra Leone. At least 5,000 people had been killed in the fighting since 1991.

In January 1996, a military coup by Defence Minister Julius Maada Bio removed Strasser from office.[2] Elections followed shortly afterwards and, despite continued violence, in March the veteran politician Ahmad Tejan Kabbah of the SLPP was voted in as president following a two-round contest. International observers declared the election 'as fair as you would expect in this part of Africa considering all the circumstances.'

Kabbah was born on 16 February 1932 and educated in Sierra Leone and the UK. He began his career in public service in 1959, first as a district commissioner for the British colonial administration and then, following independence, as a senior civil servant in Sierra Leone. He then took up employment with the UN Development Programme, serving in New York, Tanzania and Lesotho until around 1993. It was while he was in New York that he became friends with another West African diplomat based at the UN headquarters – Kofi Annan. After he was elected president of Sierra Leone in March 1996, Kabbah continued negotiations with the RUF for a ceasefire against a background of sporadic fighting.

In 1998, the British public would become aware of Sierra Leone when the activities of Sandline International were picked up by the media, highlighting the role and activities of private military companies (PMCs) in the country. At the time, although comparisons were made with the Reagan administration's Iran Contra arms scandal, the Sandline operation was entirely different. The details of the Sandline operation are discussed in more detail in Chapter 4, but it had its roots back in May 1995 when Strasser had contracted the South African PMC Executive Outcomes (EO), based in Pretoria, to assist in the war against the RUF.

However, even that was not the first time that foreign troops had been hired to fight in Sierra Leone. In 1995, Major Bob Mackenzie, an American Vietnam War veteran of the 101st Airborne Division who adopted the *nom de guerre* McKenna, was already working with fifty-eight men of Gurkha Security Guards Ltd, leading and training forces in Sierra Leone.

Mackenzie had been medically discharged from the US Army after he was severely wounded in Vietnam, losing large amounts of muscle tissue in one arm. Despite these injuries, he passed selection for C Squadron of the Rhodesian SAS. He was to die in action on 24 February 1995 when a patrol of Sierra Leone soldiers he was leading located an RUF camp; in the fire fight, the Sierra Leonean officer was wounded and his soldiers ran away. Mackenzie was wounded and captured giving covering fire as he and a former British Army NCO attempted to move the officer to safety. A group of nuns held by the insurgents said they had seen Mackenzie brought into the camp and testified to his ultimate fate. The RUF fighters killed and ate him, beginning with his liver since they believed that this would enable them to take on the courage of the warrior they had killed.

Executive Outcomes' origins lie some six years before Mackenzie's death, during the last days of the apartheid government in South Africa. ANC leader Nelson Mandela requested that President F. W. de Klerk disband the South African Defence Force (SADF) Special Forces to prevent a possible right-wing Afrikaner coup against the ANC, which some Afrikaners in the SADF saw not as a political party and the future elected government but as their long-time enemy.

Among the units to go was the elite SADF 32 Battalion that had fought in Angola against Cuban, Angolan and Soviet forces. Others included the ethnically mixed police counter-insurgency unit *Kovoet* (Crowbar) that had operated in Namibia, all four Reconnaissance Regiments and the shadowy Civil Co-operation Bureau (CCB).

In 1993, former SADF officer Eeben Barlow, who had served with both 32 Battalion and the CCB, was approached by Heritage Oil with a request for him to organise a group to assist the Angolan government to recover oil exploration equipment that was now in territory held by the rebel group UNITA (*Uniao Nacional para a Independencia Total de Angola*). Barlow recruited a group of experienced South African ex-soldiers and policemen from the disbanded special units and gave it the innocuous name Executive Outcomes (EO). They recovered the equipment, the client was delighted and EO was in business. EO was subsequently contracted by the Popular Movement for the Liberation of Angola (MPLA) – the government in Angola – to counter the UNITA rebel movement.

In April 1995, an EO team came to Sierra Leone with the blessing of Valentine Strasser. In return, the PMC was guaranteed £840,000 a month in profits from the Kono diamond mines. Once in-country, EO employed the Kamajor militia movement which had been established in 1994 and consisted mostly of traditional hunters from the Mende territory in the south and east of the country.[3] EO also brought in two of South Africa's most highly decorated former SADF air force pilots.

It took EO less than a fortnight to clear the coast of rebels, killing hundreds in a succession of precision helicopter gunship strikes that caused the rest to flee. A few weeks later, an EO force of eighty-seven men, accompanied by squads of government soldiers, drove the rebel army out of the Kono diamond fields 300 km into the interior. By early November 1995, EO-supported forces had captured Kailahun and made progress towards retaking the Sieromco and Sierra Rutile mines.

EO operated two Mi-17 transport helicopters, communications equipment and night-vision equipment. Other assets included small arms and ammunition, light and heavy machine guns, plus 60 mm, 82 mm and 120 mm mortars, RPGs, two BMP-2 tracked APCs and a number of short-wheel-based Land Rovers on which EO had mounted either 12.7 mm or 14.5 mm heavy machine guns.

An Mi-17 maintenance team was based at Lungi Airport and one of two Andover aircraft was permanently on standby at Lungi for emergency casualty evacuation. Meanwhile, EO leased Boeing 727s from Ibis Air for personnel transport to and from South Africa. Belorussian personnel manned Mi-24E 'Hind' gunships, which were bought by the Sierra Leone government in early 1995. These crews (probably five) were engaged in armed reconnaissance and in support of Mi-17-borne infantry assaults.

Though there were only between 150 and 200 men in-country, the EO team was a formidable and well-balanced force. Their operations not only defeated the RUF but provided security, enabling many internal refugees to return home.

EO had begun training parts of the Sierra Leone Army (SLA) in April 1995. New recruits and serving members of the SLA were formed into company-sized units and given six weeks' training before being deployed as a unit against the RUF. EO-trained units, operating independently of EO advisers, were now regularly closing with the RUF and inflicting serious losses.

Elections were held in March 1996 and Kabbah became president. He agreed to keep on the foreign PMCs and local affiliates. Under Kabbah, EO's training programme for the Kamajors intensified and the militia became an increasingly important force, both politically and militarily.

In co-operation with ECOMOG, EO continued to fight the RUF, defeating them overwhelmingly in a number of battles, and by August 1996 the RUF proposed peace negotiations. After Kabbah took office in April, EO's contract was renegotiated downward to £685,000 per month. As a result of pressure from the International Monetary Fund (IMF) on the government to cut spending, Kabbah proposed without consultation to reduce EO's fees to £391,000 per month, even though the IMF thought EO's charges were reasonable. EO subsequently explained both to the Kabbah government and the IMF that it could not make such cuts, but did, however, agree to lower its fees to £503,000 per month and add the shortfall to already substantial arrears, an arrangement that continued until EO left Sierra Leone in January 1997. When it departed, the government still owed EO £10.882 million.

Kabbah's government and the RUF signed a peace agreement in November 1996. An important provision was that EO would leave Sierra Leone by January 1997. EO management was reported as saying, 'Of course we will go but, rest assured, in less than a hundred days the RUF will welsh on the deal.' Opposition to the government would in fact come from a different quarter: Kabbah had antagonised the army by drafting a plan for its reduction, and the army was also angered by Kabbah's increasing reliance on the Kamajors for security.

A violent military coup on 25 May 1997, led by a group of disaffected SLA junior officers loyal to Major Johnny Paul Koroma, ended the sixteen-month period of democracy in Sierra Leone.

Koroma, a graduate of the Royal Military Academy Sandhurst and an officer in the Republic of Sierra Leone Military Forces (RSLMF), was loyal to the earlier regime of his fellow officer Valentine Strasser. In April 1996, after Kabbah had become president and replaced the discredited Strasser, Koroma was arrested for plotting to overthrow the new government. Koroma's trial, however, never took place. The officers who launched the coup released him from jail after eight hours of fighting. They then seized power in the city, aided by prisoners (some of them officers awaiting trial after earlier alleged coup attempts, but mostly common criminals) who had also been sprung from Pademba Road Prison.

Koroma was remembered at RMA Sandhurst for his reply to a question about prisoner handling. The officer cadets in his syndicate group had earlier heard a lecture on the Geneva Convention and the rights of prisoners of war. However, when asked what he would do with prisoners captured after a platoon attack he replied, 'I strangle them like chickens straight away!'

The syndicate and instructor roared with laughter – but remained unsure as to whether this was actually a joke.

Koroma accused Kabbah of being 'nurtured on tribal and sectional conflict', and cited the government's failure to end the war with the RUF and low pay as reasons for the coup. The US ambassador to Sierra Leone, John Leigh, was probably closer to the mark when he said that the coup's organisers were simply 'out to line their own pockets'.

Koroma, known by his initials as 'J. P.', promoted himself to lieutenant-colonel and took control of the new Armed Forces Revolutionary Council or Armed Forces Ruling Congress (AFRC) regime. Kabbah fled to Guinea by helicopter and the AFRC made the fatal move of inviting the RUF to share power and form a combined junta. Koroma became deputy leader of the RUF and the resulting disastrous regime would only finally be evicted from Freetown in 1998. Outside military observers of this unholy union of soldiers and RUF rebels coined a new word: the SOldiers and reBELS became Sobels. They rampaged through Freetown in an orgy of looting, rape and murder.

Nigeria initially sent 700 troops and two naval vessels that had been part of the ECOMOG operation in Liberia to bolster the Nigerian ECOMOG forces already based in Sierra Leone under the command of Major-General Timothy Shelpidi. Intervention by the ECOMOG forces provided some stability but failed to remove Koroma from power. At that time, ECOMOG's action was supported by the UN and the Organisation of African Unity (OAU).

The only area of Freetown that looked as if it would be spared the brutalities of the RUF and AFRC was the Aberdeen Peninsula. Access to the peninsula was possible only by a causeway from Murray Town or the coastal road along the 500 m-wide peninsula running south to Lumley Village. If effective road blocks were manned at these access points, the area could be kept secure. On the peninsula was the Bintumani Conference Centre and hotels including the prestigious Mammy Yoko, plus a number of restaurants and bars.

On 2 June 1997, the Sobels responded to a Nigerian naval bombardment by four warships by besieging the Mammy Yoko Hotel, which was full of foreign nationals who had fled Freetown and was being guarded by a company of Nigerian ECOMOG soldiers. At least twenty-nine people would die in the fighting that day and a further forty-two were wounded. By a happy coincidence, Will Scully had returned to Freetown and was in the city when the coup began. This highly experienced soldier proceeded to lead the roof-top defence of the hotel with weapons provided by the ECOMOG soldiers. With a GPMG and belt of 7.62 mm link around his shoulders and accompanied by British Army Major Lincoln Jopp of the Scots Guards, Scully was caught on film by a Reuters TV camera crew. Jopp, immaculate in tropical camouflage uniform, was in-country heading a small British Army team training Sierra Leone Army officers. Eventually Jopp had to withdraw from the battle after he was wounded by shrapnel from an exploding RPG7 rocket. Scully, a lean figure in civilian clothes, moved skilfully around firing short bursts with the GPMG at concentrations of Sobels in the grounds below the hotel.

'That's what I want,' cried a delighted Nigerian colonel who was also on the roof with ECOMOG soldiers.

'That's what I do,' Scully replied laconically.

A 'Hind' D flown by the rebellious Sierra Leone Army strafed the hotel, which had already been hit by RPG7 rockets and small arms fire, but eventually Peter Penfold, the urbane and patrician British high commissioner, negotiated a temporary ceasefire with the AFRC.

Penfold was no stranger to challenging diplomatic posts. From 1975–78 he had served in Addis Ababa in Ethiopia and from 1984–87 in Kampala in Uganda. Prior to his posting to Sierra Leone he had been special advisor on drugs in the Caribbean.

In Freetown in June 1997 it was shaping up to be, in the words of Wellington describing the battle of Waterloo on 18 June 1815, 'a near run thing'.

As chaos increased, the 1,894 men of the 22nd US Marine Corps Expeditionary Unit commanded by Colonel Sam Helland, aboard the amphibious assault ship the USS *Kearsarge* (LHD 3) commanded by Captain Michael Wittkamp, were ordered to take up station offshore by US Secretary of State Madeleine Albright. In addition to the Marine detachment, the *Kearsarge* had aboard twelve CH-46 Sea Knight helicopters, four CH-53E Sea Stallion helicopters, six AV-8B Harrier attack aircraft, three

UH-1N 'Huey' helicopters and four AH-1W Super Cobra helicopters. It had already mounted one evacuation operation for US citizens, but if these assets could be committed again, this powerful and well-balanced force could be instrumental in ensuring a safe evacuation from Freetown for the remaining foreign nationals. However, the US Navy and Marine Corps were now hampered by complex rules of engagement in what was not seen as a formal war zone.

Before the complete collapse of order in Freetown, the French had stationed the frigate *Jean Moulin* (F 785) offshore and their evacuation operation had been, as Will Scully observed, 'typically minimalist': a Zodiac inflatable with a small crew immaculate in tropical white uniforms had nosed in to the beach, the officer had stepped ashore and produced a laptop computer with a direct data link to the warship and the French nationals had been processed on the beach and taken out to the warship.

Although evacuations of some British and French nationals had taken place, as the situation deteriorated in Freetown more expatriates made their way through the town to the walled Mammy Yoko Hotel.

With the pressure now on, it emerged that Peter Penfold, who was in contact with both the US warship and the foreign nationals trapped in the Mammy Yoko Hotel, was forcing the hand of US command. From the British High Commission in the Wilberforce district of Freetown he had looked north across Aberdeen Creek and watched the rebel advance on the Mammy Yoko Hotel. He explained to US command that the evacuees would assemble on Lumley Beach near the hotel for the US Marines to transport them to the *Kearsarge*.

Scully wrote of Penfold: 'He was an experienced diplomat who had seen similar situations before but was nonetheless gambling on forcing the United States into action on moral grounds and the only way to make them react was precisely if we were attacked on the beach in open ground.'

This gamble paid off and eventually more than 1,200 foreign nationals were evacuated. The Marines and crew of the *Kearsage* ran a highly efficient operation, moving in on 3 June to fly the evacuees off the beach close to the Cape Sierra Hotel.

It earned Penfold praise from British Labour Prime Minister Tony Blair. The British High Commissioner, a keen supporter of Kabbah, flew out of the country with him and would subsequently become an important player in the politics of Sierra Leone.

Reviewing the intense day's fighting that took place on Monday 2 June 1997, Will Scully would say, 'Post-combat trauma, so favourite a topic among journalists and a ready excuse among so-called veterans claiming mental damage, has no place in this calm and rarefied state in which the mind has been improved and strengthened by the experience, expanded and empowered by the extreme tensions. This was strength of spirit, amounting to faith, like steel hardened by fire. I had never felt better.'

Back in Freetown, the Sobels looted the Mammy Yoko, blew up the hotel safe and dismantled the basins, lavatories, air conditioners and carpets.

'I couldn't pay people to clean it out so well in that short a period of time,' commented the American owner Roger Crooks, who received a commendation from the US State Department for his help in the evacuation. Crooks had worked closely with Scully in the defence and evacuation of the hotel.

The few things left in the hotel disappeared in 1999 when the Sierra Leonean government used the Mammy Yoko to house disarmed RUF rebels. The ex-combatants removed roofing tiles to use as bedding and stripped the wiring from the walls, finishing the job they had left incomplete two years before.

'Oh, well,' said Crooks at the time in an interview with Andrew Maykuth of *The Philadelphia Inquirer*, 'the wiring was having faults anyway.'

Crooks is one of the many foreigners who has been drawn to Sierra Leone and has helped to shape the character of the country. 'I've been all over Africa, and I find Sierra Leoneans the easiest people to get along with,' he said.

In 1995, the Sierra Leone government, in a desperate effort to raise hard currency, had begun auctioning state assets. Crooks had worked in the oil industry and was interested in the national refinery, but he ended up winning a long-term lease on the Mammy Yoko Hotel.[4]

Despite the destruction that followed the 1997 incursion, the hotel named after the Sierra Leonean heroine would still prove to be a shrewd investment.

Chapter 4
'No Living Thing'

Ohl krai du foh behrin.
Any kind of crying will do for a funeral.

No country recognised the Koroma regime and in 1997 the UN Security Council unanimously passed the British-sponsored Security Council Resolution (SCR) 1132 imposing an arms and oil embargo on the country. In Whitehall, the British government drafted an Order-in-Council which gave UN SCR 1132 force in British law. It was not debated in Parliament and consequently its drafting was virtually secret. The Order-in-Council (Statutory Instrument 1997 No. 2592) proved to be a clumsy interpretation of SCR 1132 since it prohibited the export of arms to anyone in Sierra Leone, not just the rebels.

All bilateral and multilateral aid to the country was suspended, causing severe problems for the new regime since Sierra Leone was by this time almost entirely dependent on foreign aid. ECOMOG warships and gunners covered the approaches to Freetown in order to intercept or engage ships attempting to break the blockade.

On 2 September, Sierra Leone radio reported that Nigerian troops had killed several fishermen and damaged their trawlers when they had fired into the Atlantic Ocean in order to prevent ships from sailing into Freetown.

On 4 September, at least fifty people were killed and a further forty were injured when Nigerian gunners shelled two container ships in Freetown. A barrage before dawn was also reported to have hit a busy dockside marketplace.

Three days later, paramilitary policemen and a port official were seriously injured when a Nigerian aircraft attacked and strafed an embargo-breaking ship docked in Freetown.

On 12 September, two people were killed and a further two wounded when Nigerian aircraft strafed the Sierra Leonean vessel *Norvisco* and attacked the Kissi Terminal. It was estimated that a total of fifty people were killed during the previous week in Nigerian air-strikes on Freetown. Some 200,000 people were estimated to have evacuated the city because of these attacks.

Both sides suffered slight casualties on 22 September when troops loyal to the Sierra Leonean military junta traded artillery fire with Nigerian soldiers in Freetown. This fighting was reported to have continued for about forty-five minutes.

At the end of the month, seven civilians were killed when Nigerian aircraft bombed the Port Loko district, 60 km from Freetown.

The air attacks continued on 7 October: at least two government soldiers and two civilians were killed and an additional twenty-eight people were wounded when a Nigerian jet bombed the military junta's headquarters west of Freetown. Reportedly, there was to have been a meeting at the base including J. P. Koroma, the chief of the defence staff and other senior military personnel. The same target was hit by air-strikes a day later.

On 16 October, Nigerian jets bombed and silenced a television and radio transmission centre at Leicester Peak, 10 km west of Freetown. There were no reports of casualties. A day later, hundreds of civilians fled Freetown as a result of several days of attacks by Nigerian aircraft and shelling from Nigerian troops across the estuary from the airport at Lungi.

Under its new illegal regime, Sierra Leone was suspended from the Commonwealth in January 1998. Deposed President Kabbah appealed to the international community and ECOWAS to restore him and his government to power – by force, if necessary.

From Guinea, Kabbah opened discussions with Indian-born banker Rakesh Saxena, then living in Canada and wanted by the Thai authorities for alleged financial fraud. British Foreign Secretary Robin Cook would describe Saxena as 'an Indian businessman, travelling on the passport of a dead Serb, awaiting extradition from Canada for alleged embezzlement from a bank in Thailand.' Saxena offered to provide up to £5.5 million to fund a counter-coup in return for exploration concessions in Sierra Leone's diamond, bauxite and gold fields. Lieutenant-Colonel Timothy Spicer, a retired Scots Guards officer who had served with distinction with the British Army in Northern Ireland and the Falklands and who was now the head of the PMC Sandline International, was contacted and commissioned to make an intelligence assessment of the situation.

Sandline already had a foothold in Sierra Leone in 1998, since the UN employed the Sandline subsidiary Lifeguard Security. Lifeguard had been doing invaluable work protecting several commercial sites in the country including a diamond mine, an industrial plant and the important Bumbuma Dam. The guards were armed and deployed in small parties of between twelve and thirty men.

Lifeguard operated a Russian-built Mil Mi-17 helicopter. The helicopter could carry twenty-eight passengers and was used to ferry men between Freetown and the sites inland. This rugged transport helicopter was flown by two South African pilots – Juba Joubert and Neil Ellis – accompanied by Fijian ex-22 SAS soldier Fred Marafano.

Ellis had the unusual distinction of having had three SA-7s fired simultaneously at his helicopter in southern Angola while he was on active duty with the South African Air Force.

Marafano was known and respected by his former SAS colleagues. Will Scully recalled meeting him in Sierra Leone in 1997: 'Fred Marafano was a big-boned, powerful Fijian with a broad honest face and years of SAS experience training and fighting all kinds of friends and enemies in rough places all over the world. A fearsome fighter with fists or weapons, he nonetheless had a great sense of humour and always developed immense enthusiasm for the people he worked with.'

Spicer was adamant that Sandline would only work for a government and consequently although the funds might come from Saxena, Sandline would be contracted by Kabbah, the elected head of state of Sierra Leone. The package that Spicer called Project Python would include a command and control group to work with the Kamajors and liaise with ECOMOG, the provision of helicopter support as a 'force enhancer', a shipment of weapons to enable ECOMOG to arm 8,000 loyal Kamajors and perhaps a special force unit. The total cost would be in the region of £5.5 million.

In May 1998, Sandline was reported to have obtained 35,560 kg of small arms from Bulgaria. The weapons were flown to Lungi International Airport, which was still under ECOMOG control and was the only airport in the country capable of handling large transport aircraft. From there the weapons would be distributed to the Kamajors.

At this point the law caught up with Saxena and he was arrested in Vancouver having paid only some of the promised funds. Sandline had received about £840,000 but were committed to Project Python.

As the story became public, the British government asserted that the Sandline operation was in breach of the UN arms embargo, an embargo that had actually helped Koroma to stay in power. Supposedly, it was also a violation of the British government's promise to pursue a foreign policy with 'an ethical dimension'. In its defence, Sandline said it was convinced that it had been given the go-ahead for the exports by the Foreign Office. It appears that this was true since, after questioning Spicer, HM Customs and Excise said it could not find enough evidence to prosecute Sandline.

At this point, British High Commissioner Peter Penfold became involved. He had escaped from Freetown and was now staying in the same hotel as Kabbah in Conakry in neighbouring Guinea. A career diplomat, he was privy to Kabbah's plan to use Sandline and had passed the details on to the Foreign Office. To Kabbah and Penfold, the UN arms embargo applied only to the illegal Koroma government and thus Sandline was cleared to go ahead. Graham McKinley, the former defence attaché in Freetown, was questioned by intelligence officers about Project Python. McKinley said that Penfold would not have agreed anything with Spicer without informing London.

In his book *An Unorthodox Soldier*, Spicer recalled, '... all these actions – including the arrival of the arms shipment – were known to the Foreign Office, whatever they chose to deny later. They knew quite specifically what we were going to do regarding arms shipments and military intervention, for at that meeting on 19 January 1998 – the one arranged after Peter Penfold's visit to our offices on 23 December 1997, where we had shown him the draft contract – we briefed them fully on what we were about to do – and they said "fine".'

Interviewed by the BBC after his retirement, Penfold said, 'They [the Foreign Office] also had a copy of my reports that I sent, dated 2 February, clearly showing that arms and equipment were part of this agreement. I also attached a number of documents which had issued from the Foreign and Commonwealth Office, which clearly showed that, from reading these documents, the understanding of the Foreign and Commonwealth Office was that the sanctions did not apply to President Kabbah.'

A report was later released by the Foreign Affairs Select Committee, headed by Donald Anderson MP, which criticised the government's handling of the affair. MPs would report that the confused Foreign Office policy was the result of 'dealing in half-truths – a dangerous commodity'.

Jane's Intelligence Watch Report of 20 May 1998 stated: 'MI6 alerted the Foreign Office on five occasions that UK suppliers were shipping weapons to Sierra Leone, in violation of a UN embargo, Foreign Secretary Robin Cook revealed yesterday. The warnings were issued between October 1997 and March 1998, contradicting Cook's previous testimony that the Foreign Office had no knowledge of the affair until a UK parliamentarian exposed it in March 1998. A Customs and Excise investigation into the matter has decided not to prosecute Sandline International. Sandline admits to shipping weapons, mostly AK-47 assault rifles, to forces in Sierra Leone, but it claims it acted with the knowledge of the Foreign Office.'

Meanwhile, as the fighting escalated in Sierra Leone, the UN refugee agency said that some 1,400 people had reached Guinea by sea. More were expected soon as tens of thousands of civilians fled their homes. One report said that fifty people fleeing the fighting drowned in a river north of Freetown after their boat capsized. Local police said the boat struck a rock during bad weather. The Nigerian Navy patrolling offshore discovered that there was money to be made from offering 'protection' to the refugee boats.

The French charity *Médicins Sans Frontières*, one of the few aid organisations left in Freetown, said it had very little food and that the main civilian hospital was running out of drugs. The hospital had been overwhelmed by the numbers of wounded people, mostly injured by shrapnel.

On Wednesday 11 February 1998, local newspapers reported that twenty-five corpses had been taken to a mortuary in Freetown. Earlier reports said that at least twenty-five people, including a dozen civilians, had been killed since fighting broke out.

In the light of the chaos, the vicious fighting between the Nigerian forces and the RUF and Koroma loyalists and the atrocities committed by the RUF against civilians, many observers commented that the only bad thing about the EO and Sandline operations in Sierra Leone was that they were discontinued. Working with groups like the Kamajors, they would have produced a low-cost solution for the problems of Sierra Leone before they got out of control.

As several British newspapers noted, the actions and inaction of the British government had a strong whiff of hypocrisy about them. The British broadsheet newspaper *The Independent* commented, 'We are invited to believe that, to adapt an old joke, Mr Cook has been treated by his staff as a sort of political mushroom – kept in the dark only to find himself now covered in the rich manure of political embarrassment.'

Cook, while undoubtedly an intelligent and experienced politician, had a restricted circle of friends within government and had not managed to increase it with the rather cavalier attitude he exhibited to his post.

In a TV interview, Cook compared himself to an earlier Labour foreign secretary, the formidable Ernest Bevin. 'The story goes,' Cook said, 'that Ernest Bevin, on his first weekend, was left with five red boxes and a note saying: "Foreign Secretary, we thought you would like to do these five red boxes over the weekend." And on Monday, when the staff came into the private office, they found the five red boxes in the same place with a note in his handwriting: "A kind thought, but sadly erroneous." I'm happy to say that nobody's ever tried to present me with five red boxes, but ever since I heard that story I have recognised that you can be a successful foreign secretary if you focus on the big questions, not necessarily if you finish the paperwork.'

But now the British government was embarrassed, feeling that its 'foreign policy with an ethical dimension' had been compromised. The Sandline operation was investigated in an inquiry that began on Monday 18 May 1998 and was headed by Sir Thomas Legg, a retired senior civil servant. He savaged the Foreign Office for 'systematic failures of communication' but cleared ministers of deceit. The Foreign Office, which had twice been sent details of Project Python by Penfold, escaped extreme censure. The lone diplomat Penfold, however, was blamed for sanctioning the arms import and questioned by Customs and Excise. He was not charged and returned to Sierra Leone to complete his tour of duty.

Hansard, the official record of proceedings in the House of Commons, reported the following on 2 March 1999: 'Amendment by Mr Robin Cook welcoming the decision of the Foreign Affairs Select Committee in its Report on Sierra Leone (HC 116, 1998–99) to commend the resolute support which the British Government is giving to the restoration of democracy in Sierra Leone and endorses the conclusion of the Legg Inquiry that no Minister had given encouragement or approval to any breach of the arms embargo in Sierra Leone and congratulating the Government on accepting all the recommendations of the Report of the Legg Inquiry and on the steps it has since taken to modernise management in the FCO [Foreign and Commonwealth Office].' This amendment was agreed with no call for a vote. It was a rather smug conclusion to the controversy generated by Project Python.

In Freetown, however, when Penfold returned following Kabbah's restoration, he was hailed as a hero who had supported the country and helped to bring back democracy and stability. Carried shoulder high by crowds through the streets of the capital, he later remarked, 'Here was a white man being carried through the streets of this black African capital, thirty years after their independence, with so many Union Jacks being flown. There were probably more Union Jacks than when Queen Victoria was there.'

With wonderful British understatement he added, 'It was a very unusual situation. I found it very moving.'

In 2002, when Zainab Bangura, the Sierra Leone presidential candidate in the Campaign for Good Governance, was interviewed by the BBC, she said with cheerful candour that she believed that Robin Cook panicked when the Sandline operation became public. 'If he had been a smart politician like Tony Blair he'd have said, "What is the problem here? We support this country, these people, and they are in the right and they won so what is the problem?" I think if that had been done earlier on, it could have saved all this embarrassment. I think he did it basically to save himself from all the embarrassment.'

In his official London residence, No. 10 Downing Street, Prime Minister Tony Blair had vented his exasperation to his aides when the story had broken in 1998 using language very similar to that of Zainab Bangura: 'For God's sake, the good guys won.'

Let the last word on the Sandline affair come from Will Scully in *Once a Pilgrim*: 'This "scandal" highlights the eternal gulf between actor and critic, between those with balls enough to work in places like Sierra Leone and those who stay safely at home and pass judgement.'

The restoration of the 'good guys' had begun in February 1998 when Nigerian-led forces under the auspices of ECOMOG mounted a two-pronged assault on Freetown. Largely ignored by Whitehall and the Foreign Office was the fact that Nigeria was no paragon of democratic rule, being controlled as it was by corrupt and manipulative military dictator General Sani Abacha.

On 10 February, Brigadier-General Abdulwane Mohamed, the ECOMOG chief of staff for Sierra Leone, stated that ECOMOG troops were engaged in an all-out offensive and had advanced into the outskirts of Freetown. At least twenty-five people, including a dozen civilians, were reported to have been killed in fighting between Nigerian and junta troops in the suburb of Kissy.

A day later, ECOMOG troops were reported to have captured Queen Elizabeth II Quay, the main seaport and ferry terminal.

For three hours before dawn on 12 February, the Nigerian-led intervention force and junta troops exchanged artillery fire. ECOMOG troops finally entered the centre of the capital later in the day, encountering minimal opposition.

General Sani Abacha maintained that his forces were trying to restore the country's elected government to power. However, many thought that Nigeria's quest for regional domination was the main reason for the invasion, as well as being a way of controlling Sierra Leone's diamond deposits. Nearly 750,000 civilians were trapped between the RUF and ECOMOG forces in the centre of Freetown and many thousands had to flee the capital.

On 13 February, Nigerian forces captured the presidential state house in Freetown. Fighting continued for several more days, with many casualties. By 22 April, Koroma was reported to be besieged in the village of Kongo Wawoh, close to Kayima, and he eventually fled to Liberia.

In the light of the ECOMOG victory, Press Association journalist Ian Stewart received a request from the New York office to write a story on the theme 'Africa standing up for democracy'. Stewart's reaction was: '*Bullshit*, I thought. This is one African military thug flexing his muscles to impress another military thug.'

Kabbah returned to office in March 1998 and declared a state of emergency. With fighting continuing in many areas, the UN brought in emergency aid.

Arriving at Lungi Airport to cover Kabbah's return, journalist Stewart had his first encounter with Dr Julius Spencer, Sierra Leone's minister of information. 'I spotted a mature-looking man, perhaps in his fifties, with a goatee and a loose, oversized floral shirt. He wore cargo-pocketed army pants and had green rubber sandals on his feet. An assault rifle was propped up next to him ... Young women flanked him on both sides. One wore a miniskirt and a tight, lime-green tube top. Her hair was chemically relaxed and dyed blonde. Her Day-Glo, three-inch platform shoes matched her form-fitting top. The other woman wore a long evening dress with spiked high heels. Her lips glowed with glossy red lipstick.'

At first appearance, Spencer might have looked like any other hedonistic African politician. He would, however, prove a loyal ally for Stewart when, following an ambush, his prompt actions would save the young Canadian journalist's life. Later in 2000, the minister would be uncompromising in negotiations with the West Side Boys.

By December 1998, a new crisis had gripped Sierra Leone, partly caused by domestic politics. As Kabbah reconsolidated his position, he was under considerable domestic pressure to act tough. Indeed, many argued that the May 1997 coup was due, at least to some extent, to the president's indecisiveness.

Kabbah decided to prosecute the AFRC/RUF rebels, but this move had legal and political ramifications. Under an agreement signed in Conakry in October 1997 between ECOWAS and the RUF/AFRC junta, the latter promised to relinquish power to Kabbah in April 1998, in exchange for which all the members of the junta would be free from prosecution. This arrangement, however, could not be effected because ECOMOG forces had removed the junta before the date set by the Conakry Agreement. Was Kabbah in law obliged to respect the agreement, especially the clauses about legal immunity?

The weight of public opinion in the capital was that the president was free to prosecute the AFRC conspirators, especially as he had not been reinstated under the terms of the Conakry Agreement. Many felt that punishing the coup plotters would deter others, while giving their president the strongman image they wanted. Kabbah went along with this and twenty-four military officers, including a woman, were tried, condemned to death and, despite appeals from the UK and other international bodies, publicly executed.

A press release issued by Dr Julius Spencer on 13 October 1998 giving the reasons for the executions made ghastly reading:

State House has announced that following the sentencing of the former military officers on Monday 12th October 1998 and even before, over 99 per cent of the people of Sierra Leone have expressed the view that the law of Sierra Leone should take its course. The people of Sierra Leone are normally mild, kind and God-fearing people. For them to be overwhelming in their demand for the full implementation of the law with regard to the condemned former military officers is a clear manifestation of the extent of the atrocities committed by the AFRC/RUF junta. The trials which are now over gave the people the opportunity to hear evidence from victims and eye witnesses which confirmed what the people already knew.

There are many examples of atrocities committed, but these are a few of the gruesome atrocities committed by the AFRC junta. An eighty-six-year-old woman was carried to a field where her only son, who had been brutalised, was lying helpless in the hands of his captors, saw them open his chest, cut off part of his heart and stuff it into her mouth. Her son was subsequently decapitated and his head was given to her and she was forced to breast-feed the decapitated head. The inhabitants of the township where she lived were told not to admit her to their homes after they had burnt down her own house ...

Above all, throughout their trial, these people showed no remorse and were even making plans to escape from prison. The remnants of the AFRC/RUF are still callously amputating, decapitating, maiming and killing innocent civilians.

Sankoh, who had earlier been repatriated from Nigeria where he had been held in custody, was found guilty of treason and condemned to death. However, the execution of the officers and the death sentence passed on Sankoh triggered renewed fighting, hardening the rebels' attitude and increasing their passion for revenge. Subsequently many thought that Kabbah had been rash, especially as it was obvious that the balance of military power favoured the rebels. At the time that he was reinstated, the insurgents still retained considerable strength. Dislodged from the capital, they had moved to the hinterland, where they were able to reconsolidate. Indeed, one of the reasons why ECOMOG refused to continue pursuing them was because of the relative strength they were believed to have in some areas outside Freetown. It was this military strength that the RUF/AFRC harnessed to launch a renewed attack against Freetown in December 1998.

Another reason why the fight was going out of ECOMOG was the death of General Abacha, which meant the loss of the most important external supporter of the Kabbah government. Abacha, it was rumoured, had died in somewhat bizarre circumstances while attempting to demonstrate his sexual potency. Although Abacha's successor, General Abubakar, did not withdraw Nigerian troops from Sierra Leone, it was clear that the conflict meant less to him. Indeed, the rebel and junta forces calculated that Nigeria under Abubakar was unlikely to respond with the kind of military force that had been characteristic of Abacha.

By this time, ECOMOG was tired and many of its soldiers saw no justification in showing any commitment to the conflict in Sierra Leone. It had spent more than seven years in Liberia (an operation they had thought would last for a few weeks at the most) and many Nigerians saw dangers in the continuation of any open-ended commitment in Sierra Leone. Morale was low because the soldiers had not been regularly paid and the lack of co-operation from Sierra Leonean forces added to their diminished interest in the conflict. Many saw no justification for dying for a cause that was seen as outside Nigeria's immediate interest.

Some officers did not like the policies of the ECOMOG commander, General Maxwell Khobe, whose position in Sierra Leone had become somewhat controversial. He went in as the leader of the peacekeeping force but was later made the country's chief of defence staff to oversee national security. This gave him a free hand and access to opportunities and privileges, which he allegedly refused to use to benefit other officers and junior ranks. He was also seen as receiving all the glory while other officers and their troops, who were doing the 'dirty work', languished without recognition. Some officers in the Nigerian Army thus allegedly wanted to sabotage the mission. Indeed, after the entire crisis was resolved, Khobe confirmed that those officers whose inaction accounted for the crisis were under interrogation.

ECOMOG was using conventional tactics against a guerrilla organisation, but as Vietnam had demonstrated nearly twenty years earlier, air-strikes, for example, had very little military effect on rebels. Thus they were never really weakened enough to be unable to organise a co-ordinated response. In addition, the fact that the rebels were more familiar with the local terrain and had mingled with the local population gave ECOMOG little chance to respond with any credible counter-offensive.

Finally, as was the case with Liberia, ECOWAS was far from united about what should be done in Sierra Leone. Some members saw Nigeria's actions in the country as an unnecessary over-reaction. Liberia and Burkina Faso were known to be against ECOMOG to such an extent that Nigeria threatened to take retaliatory measures against Liberia if it continued to sabotage the military operation in Sierra Leone. Other ECOWAS members maintained only a weak commitment to the peacekeeping initiative. In such a situation, it was difficult for the peacekeeping efforts to be effective.

With all this in mind, the AFRC/RUF junta launched an attack, first on Waterloo, about 30 km from Freetown, and later on the capital. They met little resistance; within days of entering the city suburbs, the rebel force had hijacked the initiative from ECOMOG. The regional peacekeeping force had to fight a sustained battle, with reinforcements being sent from Nigeria, before the rebels could be dislodged.

The RUF and AFRC had disguised themselves as refugees and had passed ECOMOG checkpoints unnoticed to penetrate the Freetown peninsula. Although the rebels had given warning of an impending attack, ECOMOG was expecting a direct military assault that the regional force would have no problem repulsing. By managing to bypass checkpoints and penetrating the capital before attacking, the rebels had the advantage of surprise and ECOMOG was forced to respond to a strategy it had not anticipated.

The RUF's success was due in part to them taking a leaf from the government's book and using diamond-revenue-hired mercenaries, especially from Ukraine and Burkina Faso. In addition to giving direct military assistance, these mercenaries were believed to have assisted the rebels in overhauling their tactics and strategy. With the additional strength provided by the mercenaries, the rebels were able to threaten ECOMOG's control of the capital.

Kabbah, a number of government ministers and UN officials were forced to seek the protection of the ECOMOG headquarters near the airport. The ceasefire that was eventually agreed was conditional on the release of Sankoh, but peace talks were inconclusive and Sankoh remained in custody.

This was the time of the ghastly Operation 'No Living Thing' launched by RUF General Sam 'Mosquito' Bockarie in which he ordered that 'everyone is to be killed down to the last chicken'.

Such was the character of the war that it remains unclear whether Sam 'Mosquito' Bockarie was also Sam Maskita of Kaidu. Bockarie had been given the nickname 'Mosquito' because, like the insect, his attacks were unexpected and always painful. He was notorious in Freetown in 1997 when frightened refugees described him to Will Scully. According to the refugees, 'He wore black-rimmed glasses without glass which gave him an insectlike appearance, pieces of mirror were plaited into his hair and he was permanently high on ganja. Two women wearing dresses made of the same material as men's fatigues accompanied him everywhere, shrieking and dancing; he was convinced he could fly and was indestructible.' This person may have been Bockarie, but it is likely that this description was a composite of several of the terrifying RUF gang leaders ravaging Freetown at that time.

The names of earlier RUF offensives spoke for themselves: Operation 'Burn House' gave way to Operation 'Pay Yourself'; then came Operation 'No Living Thing'. It was Bockarie who conceived the hideous terror tactic of cutting off the hands and arms of civilians who were thought to be pro-government.

Amputations had been practised by the Belgians in the Congo when it was their colony. Plantation managers would cut off the hands of workers who didn't bring in enough rubber. In Islamic Sharia law, convicted thieves have their hands amputated. In the 1970s and 1980s, Mozambique's Renamo rebels also carried out amputations and in Uganda, the Lord's Resistance Army has amputated ears and tongues. But nowhere have amputations been inflicted on the same scale as in Sierra Leone.

The number of amputations started increasing markedly during the 1996 election campaign in Sierra Leone. The RUF saw it as a way of punishing people for voting. One of the slogans in the election campaign had included the exhortation 'let's put our hands together to create a new future'. Without hands, the RUF reasoned, a man or woman could not vote for the government.

The atrocities were often planned and premeditated. Victims and witnesses describe well-organised operations to round up civilians who were later executed, attacked with machetes or raped. On several occasions, rebels gave advance warning that atrocities were to be committed later.

Witnesses describe the existence of distinct units known for committing particular crimes, like the 'Burn House Unit', 'Cut Hands Commando' and 'Blood Shed Squad'. Some of these squads had a trademark way of killing, such as the 'Kill Man No Blood Unit', whose method was to beat people to death without shedding blood, or the 'Born Naked Squad', who stripped their victims before killing them. The closer ECOMOG forces got to rebel positions, the more these squads were mobilised and sent on operations.

Corinne Dufka of Human Rights Watch, interviewed by Netherlands Radio World Report, said, 'I often heard this story: a man had his hands amputated; he would scream at the rebels, "Just kill me. You've killed me already. Just kill me. Finish me off. Just kill me." And some of them would chase after the rebels with their bleeding stumps, just urging the rebels to kill them. The rebels would then come around and cut off another part of their body and that usually was either the ear or the mouth or the tongue because they were protesting.'

Atrocities were sometimes perpetrated within the context of games, in which the element of terror was maximised through the use of deception or teasing. Victims were sometimes given a choice as to how they wanted to be killed – by gunshot, machete or being burned alive – or were forced to listen to the rebels arguing over what atrocity to commit against them. Employing a tactic they had used in past offensives, the rebels sometimes dressed up in ECOMOG uniforms, trying to illicit a favourable reaction, and would then catch pro-government civilians who would later be punished.

Because ECOMOG was a largely Nigerian-directed force, Nigerian civilians were also targets during Operation 'No Living Thing'. Among the interviews conducted by Human Rights Watch is an account of the death of a Freetown-based Nigerian businessman called Mr Ben:

When they'd decided to cut off his hands, Mr. Ben started pleading, saying he was a businessman, and shouted, 'I beg you don't cut my hand, Oh Jesus, Jesus.' Then the axe man said, 'If Jesus himself comes here I'll amputate his hand as well.' Then they ordered him at gunpoint to put his right hand face up on a table and they hacked it off with an axe. And then his left hand. The rebel then put his hands in Ben's blood and walked over to his wife, who was sobbing, and smeared it on her face. He told her if she continued crying he'd kill her.

As this was happening, Ben's brother started yelling, 'God, what have you done to my brother?' So they pulled him out and cut off his two hands as well. Then they pulled out the third one who started screaming that he wasn't a Nigerian, but was from Cameroon, but they cut off his hands as well. Then they sprinkled more petrol on Ben's brother, I think he even had tribal markings, and set him on fire. His hands were hanging off his arms and he was on fire screaming, 'Please don't kill me.' They let him burn for five minutes before a commander let some of us put the fire out with dust.

For Mani, a forty-eight-year-old Liberian, the name of Sam Bockarie would haunt him for the rest of his life. He described to Human Rights Watch seeing an RUF commander order the execution of seven civilians on 21 January and then single him out for amputation:

The commander, who introduced himself as a Liberian, then ordered everyone but me to stand to one side and said, 'I'm going to kill you all, so say goodbye to the world.' He kept them there begging for three minutes and then at 7.03 p.m. – I looked at my watch – ordered another rebel to open fire on them. Then, the same Liberian said, 'I'm ordered and paid by Sam Bockarie not to spare anyone and that is why I have killed. You saw it with your own eyes. But now I am ordering your hand to be cut.'

He ordered me to lay face down in the road and called forward a rebel with an axe who then hacked off my hand. It was hanging off limp and bleeding and when I saw it I started to cry. The rebels just walked away.

After the fighting had ended, journalist Ian Stewart encountered Masseh Mokangi, a nine-year-old boy who had the biceps of a well-developed teenager. When the RUF took control of his village, he joined a group of child soldiers initially working as a porter before he 'graduated' and, machete in hand, wandered the streets accosting people. They were already doomed once he had selected them but were offered the choice of 'a long-sleeved shirt or a short-sleeved'.

They could be amputated at the wrist or the elbow.

Stewart would write grimly in *Freetown Ambush*, 'The more I had learned about Sierra Leone's rebel war, the more I had realized that it was a war against children: the amputees, the children of adult amputees, the children drugged and forced to carry out the amputations. Sierra Leone is a nation whose next generation has been destroyed.'

Incredibly, after the brutality and terror of Operation 'No Living Thing', Kabbah and Sankoh signed a formal ceasefire agreement in May 1999. US President Bill Clinton and the formidable Secretary of State Madeleine

Albright had pushed for Sankoh to be included in the 7 July Peace Accord that was intended to end the eight-year civil war. Signed in Lomé, the capital of Togo, it envisaged a power-sharing government and amnesty for the rebels, who would hand over their weapons to a UN force. J. P. Koroma was made chair for the Commission for the Consolidation of Peace in Sierra Leone. The majority of the AFRC forces would be reinstated into a new British-trained SLA. Sankoh was delighted by the intervention in the negotiations of the US presidential envoy, the Reverend Jesse Jackson, and even more so by a telephone call from President Clinton urging him to commit to peace. 'What rebel leader gets called by the president of the United States? I only got that call because I fought in the bush for so many years,' he boasted later. He also received a personal visit from Madeleine Albright in Freetown as part of the coalition government.

Kabbah dedicated the Lomé Peace Accord to the children of Sierra Leone and in a poignant gesture had four-year-old Memunatu Mansaray from Kissy stand beside him at the ceremony. At the age of two and a half, the RUF had amputated her right arm at the elbow.

Confronted by this victim of RUF cruelty, Sankoh's speech at the ceremony included words of staggering insincerity: 'Because of this violence within our society, another violence was born and it has taken a high toll. Many have died, while others have been injured like the one you saw here this evening. For all the dead, injured and maimed, we express our deep regret and implore their pardon. We are confident that together we are going to turn over this page of tragedy and suffering of our history, and look forward to a new era of opportunities in order to build a greater Sierra Leone, moulded by a better generation of Sierra Leoneans, where every one has his place.'

Sankoh took time off during the negotiations to enjoy the social scene in Lomé and *The Ghanian Chronicle* reported rather coyly that:

... Corporal Foday Saybana Sankoh also had long eyes, and a soft heart for the good things of life, including the irresistible, alluring Togolese women.

Reliable sources in Lomé say that such irresistible magnetic attraction finally tantalised Foday Sankoh into an amorous relationship with a Togolese black beauty which ended in a traditional wedlock.

Our sources gave the name of this smashing beauty as Mademoiselle

Bataba Victoire, a graduate from the University of Lomé.

The sources said while Foday Sankoh was busily delivering ultima-tums at the negotiation table with President Tejjan [sic] Kabbah's official delegation, he found time to secretly present the customary drinks to the family of the lady as part of the traditional marriage ceremony.

It is not reported what his existing wife Fatu Sankoh, a formidable woman who held dual US and Sierra Leonean nationality, made of this relation-ship.

Sankoh became chairman of the Strategic Resources Commission, giving him responsibility for the management of the diamond trade. Anyone wishing to mine diamonds had to go through this commission to obtain a licence – any evaders would, he said, suffer 'the full consequences of the law'.

As one observer put it, 'It was like giving the fox the keys to the hen house.'

Between 1997 and 1998, the value of official annual diamond exports by Sierra Leone had halved to £16.5 million. In the same period, diamond exports by neighbouring Liberia – a country that possesses relatively few diamond fields – had risen dramatically to £165.7 million. Sierra Leone's unstable neighbour had become a conduit for smuggled 'Blood Dia-monds'.

On 13 July 1998, the UN Security Council had established the UN Observer Mission in Sierra Leone (UNOMSIL), with an authorised strength of seventy military observers, for an initial period of six months. The number of military observers actually deployed, however, was only forty-one. The secretary-general named Special Envoy Francis Okelo as his special representative and chief of mission, and Brigadier-General Subhash C. Joshi (Indian Army) as chief military observer. In accordance with its mandate, the mission monitored and advised efforts to disarm combatants and restructure the nation's security forces.

This was an impossible mission, however, because there was no disar-mament or restructuring taking place. Fighting continued, with the rebel alliance gaining control of more than half the country. Unarmed UNOMSIL teams, under the protection of ECOMOG, documented reports of atrocities and human rights abuses committed against civilians, but they had neither the mandate nor the resources to stop them. The

Security Council was kept informed of the activities of the mission. In December 1998, the rebels began an offensive to retake Freetown and in January 1999 overran most of the city. This led to the evacuation of UNOMSIL personnel to Conakry in Guinea and the subsequent downsizing of the mission's military and civilian personnel.

As world attention focused on Kosovo in former Yugoslavia, Freetown-born freelance cameraman Sorious Samura returned to Sierra Leone from Britain and covered the RUF attack. Taken prisoner and threatened by the RUF, Samura managed to escape and during the next few days, while fighting raged between rebel and ECOMOG forces, he took his handheld camera and captured on video the fighting and some of the atrocities committed randomly by both sides.

The result was the immensely powerful documentary *Cry Freetown*. It would earn him the Rory Peck Award and the Mohammed Amin Award for work by freelance cameramen in news and current affairs. No one had won both awards before. The film was shown on British, French and South African television but rejected by US television networks because they felt that the images were too graphic.

In an interview after his documentary had been screened, Samura said, 'In this madness my job was to record the history happening in my country, when random roadside justice was the order of the day. Personally I felt that this was the only way people would be able to see what was happening in Sierra Leone. When they see the truth, the real pictures, the brutality. It was a very dangerous thing to do at the time.'

In late October 1999, troops for a new UN force began arriving in Sierra Leone. They would make up the UN Mission in Sierra Leone (UNAMSIL), which would oversee the ceasefire between the forces loyal to Kabbah and Sankoh.

Theirs would initially be a thankless task. According to UN SCR 1270 (1999) of 22 October 1999, UNAMSIL's mandate was as follows:

(1) To co-operate with the government of Sierra Leone and the other parties to the peace agreement in the implementation of the agreement.

(2) To assist the government of Sierra Leone in the implementation of the disarmament, demobilisation and reintegration plan.

(3) To that end, to establish a presence at key locations throughout the territory of Sierra Leone, including disarmament/reception centres and demobilisation centres.

(4) To ensure the security and freedom of movement of UN personnel.

(5) To monitor adherence to the ceasefire in accordance with the ceasefire agreement of 18 May 1999 through the structures provided for therein.

(6) To encourage the parties to create confidence-building mechanisms and support their functioning.

(7) To facilitate the delivery of humanitarian assistance.

(8) To support the operations of United Nations civilian officials, including the special representative of the secretary-general and his staff, human rights officers and civil affairs officers; and to provide support, as requested, to the elections, which were to be held in accordance with the present constitution of Sierra Leone.

The night of 31 December 1999 was grimly quiet for the people of Sierra Leone. At midnight, a mere five-minute fusillade of fire with red tracers streaking into the sky from positions manned by Nigerian troops marked the dawn of the new millennium. The Sierra Leone police had forbidden the usual holiday parades with men in devil masks and costumes made from hundreds of crown bottle tops threaded on string. In any case, a dusk-to-dawn curfew kept most civilians inside with their doors locked and since Sierra Leone had been largely without power for months, many of these homes were darkened.

At dawn on 1 January 2000, President Kabbah spoke to the nation on state-run radio, predicting that things would get better: 'Those who have inflicted pain and suffering on others, let them repent. And those who have suffered, forgive, so that we can have genuine reconciliation to rebuild our country.'

But to the people, the optimism that had followed the deployment of UNAMSIL had evaporated; they looked back over seven months and wondered why they had once had such high hopes of the men in blue helmets.

Chapter 5
UNAMSIL
The International Dimension

Nyangga de slip, trohbul de go wek am.
The louse sleeps, trouble wakes it.

In October 1999, the UN had established UNAMSIL, the UN Mission in Sierra Leone, to oversee the implementation of the Lomé Peace Accord. The first UN peacekeepers for the 6,000-strong force included Kenyan and Indian battalions, who began taking over from ECOMOG. Additional troops from Bangladesh, Ghana, Guinea and Nigeria arrived during the following weeks.

This UN mission had to succeed. The Ghanaian-born UN Secretary-General Kofi Annan knew President Kabbah personally. Ghana and Sierra Leone were both member states of the Commonwealth (Sierra Leone having been reinstated in the Commonwealth when Kabbah returned to power). The large number of soldiers from African states within UNAMSIL reflected a desire to see Africans solving African problems. In reality, the national mix would highlight the differences in leadership and training between troops from different nations. Some African UN troops would be superb while others would become victims of RUF bullying.

Air cover and mobility were provided by four Ukrainian-crewed Mil Mi-24D attack helicopters and five Mil Mi-8 transport helicopters (one of which would crash in late 2001), three Mil Mi-26 heavy transport helicopters and two Sikorsky S-61N helicopters leased from civilian contractors.

In accordance with UN SCR 1289 of 7 February 2000, the UNAMSIL mandate was revised to include the following tasks:

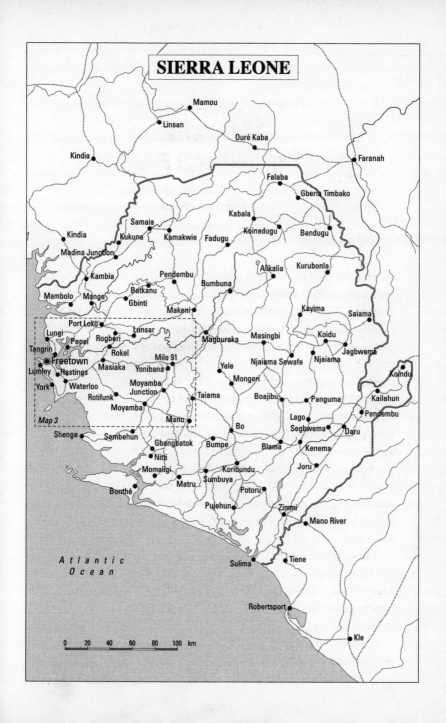

(1) To provide security at key locations and government buildings, in particular in Freetown, and at important intersections and major airports, including Lungi Airport.

(2) To facilitate the free flow of people, goods and humanitarian assistance along specified thoroughfares.

(3) To provide security in and at all sites of the disarmament, demobilisation and reintegration programme.

(4) To co-ordinate with, and assist, the Sierra Leone law enforcement authorities in the discharge of their responsibilities.

(5) To guard weapons, ammunition and other military equipment collected from ex-combatants, and to assist in their subsequent disposal or destruction.

In particular, the UN Security Council '... authorises UNAMSIL to take the necessary action to fulfil ... [its] tasks ... and affirms that, in the discharge of its mandate, UNAMSIL may take the necessary action to ensure the security and freedom of movement of its personnel and ... to afford protection to civilians under imminent threat of physical violence'.

The UN force was commanded by Major-General Vijay Kumar Jetley (Indian Army). His would not be a happy command even though he appeared to have been given a freer hand than many UN commanders. In September 2000, it was reported that the UN planned to remove Jetley and his deputies in 2001. The reason given was that the strength of UNAMSIL was increasing from the original force of 13,500 to 23,000 and this would therefore become a three-star (lieutenant-general) command appointment.

The replacement would also, however, give the UN a break since Jetley had accused his deputies of noncooperation. In a letter to the UN in May 2000[1], he had claimed that, 'The Nigerian army is interested in staying in Sierra Leone due to the massive benefits they are getting from the illegal mining of diamonds.' He went on to add that the West African troops had reached a tacit understanding with the RUF 'of non-interference in each other's activities'.

Jetley also accused his senior deputies of cultivating the RUF leadership – 'especially Foday Sankoh, behind my back' – and alleged that his Nigerian deputy had 'been in constant touch with Foday Sankoh throughout this crisis. He has probably compromised a lot of my operational plans'.

Although Nigeria had formally ceded control of the military operations to the UN in October 1999, for some time afterwards its troops still formed about half of UNAMSIL and took initial responsibility for the security of the mission, so many observers felt that Jetley's accusations were not unfounded.

Earlier in the year, on 24 February 2000, about 300 RUF fighters armed with AK-47s and RPGs had prevented the deployment of Indian and Ghanaian UN troops in the Bendu district in the east of the country. On 14 March, the RUF prevented a UNAMSIL unit that included 100 Indian troops from advancing to Kono and its diamond fields in the east.

In March 2000, the Zambian government began deploying an 800-strong infantry battalion to UNAMSIL. At almost the same time and providing a good indication of what was to come, UN peacekeepers in Sierra Leone responsible for disarming combatants were being stripped of their weapons by rebel forces. Equipment seized in ambushes included four armoured personnel carriers (APCs), several rocket-propelled grenade (RPG) launchers, at least 110 assault rifles and communication equipment. The porous Liberian border allowed RUF leaders like Sam 'Mosquito' Bockarie and Sam Maskita to train and organise groups of RUF fighters with impunity.

On 4 April, RUF fighters were reported to be looting homes in the towns around the Rokel River and Bunce Island in the Port Loko district. However, eight days later UNAMSIL reported that more than 22,500 combatants had surrendered weapons. These included 7,474 from the Civil Defence Forces, 5,590 from the AFRC and Sierra Leone Army and 1,463 from militias. These figures looked impressive, but they were illusory since only 4,227 weapons were handed in by the RUF.

As of 15 April, according to the National Committee for Disarmament, Demobilisation and Reintegration (NCDDR), only 5,000 weapons had been handed in by Sierra Leonean belligerents, who reportedly numbered about 45,000.

On 17 April, the NCDDR attempted to correct matters by opening four new camps – two of which were in the central RUF-held towns of Makeni and Magburaka. However, instead of speeding up the process, this move heralded the end of RUF disarmament for a period of one year. On 2 May 2000, RUF forces attacked the UNAMSIL positions at Makeni and Magbu-raka, killing four Kenyan soldiers. Three more Kenyans were wounded and about fifty other UNAMSIL personnel were captured. By 4 May, the number of reported UN hostages had increased to ninety-two, and by 5 May to over 500. A Zambian contingent that was taken hostage also lost thirteen APCs.

Among the British observers deployed to monitor the disarmament, demobilisation and reintegration (DDR) operation was thirty-three-year-old Major Andrew Harrison, a Parachute Regiment officer and veteran of Northern Ireland and the first Gulf War. He was based at Kailahun in the most easterly part of the country.

The DDR operation was going smoothly until the RUF Ceasefire Monitoring Committee member requested a meeting with the UN team leader and Harrison. Accompanied by Indian soldiers, they met with twenty-three-year-old 'Lieutenant-Colonel' Martin George at his headquarters. At the meeting, the RUF made a 'peaceful protest' – in the insane world of Sierra Leone this meant that around fifty armed RUF fighters stormed into the building and overpowered the group.

The RUF said that Harrison and his companions would be held because the UN was holding ten RUF 'deserters' at Makeni. After a 'cat and mouse' experience of being released and then detained again, Harrison plus a four-man helicopter crew and a Russian naval officer were moved to Giema, an RUF stronghold close to the Liberian border. They were told that if anyone attempted to escape, the remainder would be executed. In light of this, the team agreed that they would only attempt a collective escape. Harrison knew that there was a satellite telephone back at his base in Kailahun, and the remaining staff were indeed able to contact Freetown and brief them on developments.

The UN team was moved back to Kailahun and found that their house had been ransacked in their absence. Bluffing the RUF guards, Harrison said that he was going to see Lieutenant-Colonel George. He made contact with the RUF leader and persuaded him to allow the hostages to visit a nearby UN base manned by Indian troops, so that they could wash.

Once inside the base, Harrison knew that he and his companions would be protected by over 100 Indian Gurkha soldiers. Harrison did not know until later how fortuitous his move had been, since around that time, in a contact near Lungi Airport, the 16 Air Assault Brigade Pathfinder Platoon[2] attached to 1 Para for Operation Palliser had killed RUF fighters probing the position. As a British officer and soldier in the Parachute Regiment,

Harrison would have been an obvious target for revenge. (See Chapter 6 for details of Operation Palliser.)

The UN team was to remain with the Indians for two months in their 500 m-square compound. The RUF made constant demands that the white soldiers be handed over. Harrison was able to e-mail his family and the UN HQ during the siege.

Supplies of food and medicines at the UN base finally began to dwindle and on the evening of Friday 14 July Harrison was told that an operation would be launched to extract the UN team and Indian casualties. It was co-ordinated by a Special Forces liaison team that had remained behind in-country after Operation Palliser. This team would later be invaluable when preparations and plans were being made for Operation Barras. (See Chapter 8 for details of Operation Barras.)

In Freetown, UN spokesman Hirut Befecadu said that for a fortnight the RUF had refused to allow the UN to send rations to the besieged group, and that the onset of torrential rains had raised the threat of disease. She continued, 'With a distress signal received from Kailahun regarding the dwindling food and medical stocks, there was no alternative to a military option.' Commanded by Major-General Jetley, the appropriately named Operation Kukri (the kukri being the Gurkhas' weapon of choice) was launched to extract the men and evacuate them to Daru.

The distinctive *thump* of Chinook rotor blades broke through the sound of drumming rain at dawn on 15 July as two RAF helicopters flew in to lift out the team and nineteen casualties. Simultaneously, backed by Mil Mi-24D helicopter gunships and artillery, the Indian troops broke out. Troops from India, Nigeria and Ghana covered the overland withdrawal by the Indians, who suffered one killed and several wounded but who also inflicted casualties on the surrounding RUF fighters.

Back in the United Kingdom, Harrison's family had publicly criticised the government for not doing enough to secure his freedom. On being told of his release, his wife Caroline said, 'We are absolutely delighted and relieved that Andrew and the others are safe. We are looking forward to resuming normal family life.' She had earlier accused the government of abandoning her husband to the rebel forces and had petitioned Parliament to take military action to get him out.

Robin Cook welcomed Harrison's release: 'I am delighted that all the UN military observers, including Major Harrison, are safe and well. We now look to all sides to allow all the UN peacekeepers unhindered access to all places of safety.'

Harrison was not the only British officer serving as a UN military observer (UNMO) to be detained by the RUF. In April 2000, four UNMOs were based in the town of Makeni in the north-east of Sierra Leone: Major Philip Ashby (Royal Marines), 30; Major Andrew Samsonoff (Light Infantry), 26; Lieutenant-Commander Paul Rowland (Royal Navy), 31; and Major David Lingard (New Zealand Army), 37.

Some 2,000 RUF fighters were established in that area, and the UNMOs had enjoyed a reasonable relationship with the rebels until some fighters voluntarily disarmed without the permission of their commanders. The RUF commanders saw them as deserters and demanded that the weapons be returned, claiming that they had been 'stolen'. On 1 May, around 200 RUF fighters surrounded a DDR camp near Makeni and a fire fight followed.

Scotsman Ashby, who had been in the area longer than the other officers, explained later that 'some of the information we were getting from local civilians was that hostility was directed mainly at us, first of all for being British and secondly for being involved in the disarmament process'.

The four UNMOs took shelter in a walled compound defended by seventy lightly armed Kenyan soldiers. The Kenyans came under several night attacks with small arms and RPGs and the group decided that they should break out and escape to save the Kenyans from further attacks.

Prior to the breakout, Samsonoff contacted his commanding officer, Lieutenant-Colonel David Wood MC, by satellite phone. The colonel gave advice that might seem obvious, but which the Light Infantry officer knew was the key to the operation: 'Remember: this is real. It's not an exercise.' Samsonoff commented later that after the initial tension of an escape, it can be easy to switch off during an evasion.

Their faces blackened with charcoal, the four men scaled the wall of the Kenyan compound at 03.00 hours with the intention of leaving the town during the night-time RUF curfew. Their minimalist escape kit consisted of water, simple rations, map, compass, global positioning system (GPS) and first-aid kit. They reasoned that the saving in weight would allow them to move faster.

Ashby later described the early stages of the escape: 'For the first few hours the adrenalin was pumping and we were very relieved to actually get out of a bustling market town. It was fair to assume that anyone we saw on the streets was actually in the RUF. We saw several people on the way out – whether they saw us I'm not sure but I'm six foot four, and I'm a gangly white man and I'm sure they would have realised I wasn't a local.' Fortunately, before relations with the RUF had deteriorated, Ashby had visited the town regularly on his morning runs and consequently knew routes past the RUF positions.

They planned to move through the jungle by night and lay up in thickets by day to avoid discovery. Before setting out on their journey, Ashby had contacted his wife Anna in the UK by satellite phone. She alerted British officials that the group were making their escape attempt. The plan was to remain in contact with military officials during the trek, but the phone's batteries died after twenty-four hours.

The group reached a friendly village (probably known to them from UNAMSIL intelligence briefings) and a teenage guide was provided to take them to a more secure area. The guide was showing symptoms of malaria and had an open stomach wound. Despite these ailments and his flip-flop footwear, he moved rapidly through the jungle and scouted out villages. While he chatted and shared a cigarette with the locals, the group topped up their water bottles. Since they were now moving by day they made good time. When they parted with the youthful guide they gave him money for surgery for his wound and a thanks payment for his village.

Ashby recalled later, 'We did at one stage come to a friendly village where we bought every radio battery in the village and with the help of our naval officer, who is a fully qualified nuclear engineer, we attempted to improvise a battery – but sadly it didn't work.' Lieutenant-Commander Rowland had wired the batteries in series and in fact a brief signal emitted by the phone was picked up by the British electronic monitoring team in Sierra Leone.

On 12 May, they arrived at Mile 91 which was held by Guinean UN troops, and here Philip Ashby was able to phone his wife to tell her that the group was safe. She in turn passed the information on to the HQ in Freetown and the group was picked up by helicopter.

After their rescue, Ashby said, 'Our main problem was lack of water. It's still the dry season here and although there were rivers marked on our maps, in practice they were in fact pools of stagnant water. We've been drinking some unusually coloured water, shall we say. Our feet are all quite sore and we've got a plethora of exotic insect bites and we're all suffering from prickly heat and a bit of sunburn, but apart from that we're all fine.'

On 6 April 2001, the MoD announced that Major Philip Ashby, RM, would receive the Queen's Gallantry Medal. The citation read: 'He and his team were confined within a Kenyan army location, which was under sporadic attacks from the RUF. Major Ashby led the other two British and a New Zealander officer on a breakout from the location. The escape was successful, and after three days with little food and water, the four eventually reached friendly territory. Major Ashby displayed considerable leadership, exceptional coolness under pressure and considerable bravery in leading this party out of a very difficult position.'

This was in the future, of course, and when his group actually reached Mile 91, the town was under threat from the RUF. They were pleased to learn that remobilised Sierra Leone soldiers, as well as a local militia called the West Side Boys, were moving towards the town to assist in its defence.

About a month earlier in a speech to his followers in the town of Segbwema, the RUF leader Sankoh had revealed that he was still planning to seize political power. On 18 April, an RUF spokesman admitted that the organisation was involved in illegal diamond mining in the Kono district.

May was a bad month for UNAMSIL. On 1 May, at least seven UN soldiers were kidnapped by former RUF fighters from their base at Makeni, 140 km north-east of Freetown. On 2 May, at least five Kenyan soldiers were kidnapped at Magburaka in central Sierra Leone. In the east at Kailahun, twenty-eight people including two UN helicopter pilots were kidnapped. In justification for these actions, the RUF claimed they were in retaliation for the deaths of six of its fighters killed in clashes with the UN at Makeni. In reality, this disarmament centre had been attacked by the RUF and four Kenyans had been killed. At Magburaka, the Kenyans also lost three soldiers to RUF attacks.

The RUF was testing the resolve of UNAMSIL and finding that some national formations were prepared to fight, while others unsure about the rules of engagement for a force that was meant to undertake peacekeeping duties were an easier target.

On 4 May, operations hit a grim low when over 200 Zambian soldiers were captured by the RUF in central Sierra Leone. A day later, RUF fighters were seen driving through Lunsar, about 100 km east of Freetown, in captured UN vehicles and wearing UN uniforms. On 6 May, the RUF took another 226 Zambian troops prisoner near Makeni. A UN official admitted

that 110 UN soldiers and observers were being held captive in Ma...
Kailahun.

The catalyst for the violence appears to have been the withdrawal
last of the Nigerian ECOMOG forces at the end of April. The Nigerian...
fought violence with violence, and their withdrawal meant that the UN
force operating under strict rules of engagement was virtually powerless to
deal with a highly aggressive RUF.

In May 2000, the civil war showed further signs of renewal when the
RUF took UN peacekeepers hostage and advanced on Freetown. On 7 May,
the capital was described as 'tense' as hundreds of former AFRC fighters
assembled in front of Koroma's office to defend the city.

On 8 May, the RUF was reported to have halted its advance towards
Freetown and to be pulling back towards Makeni. Up to seven people were
shot dead by RUF guards after 10,000 government loyalists marched on
Sankoh's house to demand the release of UN hostages. Several small children waving stumps of amputated hands or arms were among the
protesters at his gates. In a report for *The Guardian* newspaper, journalist
Chris McGreal wrote:

Thousands of people joined the 'peace demonstration' to Sankoh's home
on Wednesday to demand his rebels release about 500 UN peacekeepers
being held hostage in the interior. The protesters carried placards
reading 'We want peace' and chanted, 'Sankoh, Sankoh, you have a bad
mind.' As the demonstration snaked through the city it grew in size.
Many shops and businesses closed in solidarity with the march, or
because they feared its consequences.

The protest was a remarkable act of defiance against the RUF's savage
leader but as it drew close to his home, the crowd grew tense and bunched
together, as if to seek protection in numbers. Those at the front stopped
just a few metres short of the gate. For ten minutes they lobbed slogans.

Then some in the crowd switched to stones and breaking windows.

The gunfire that suddenly rattled from the house was unrestrained. It
was not to deter. It was to kill. Some of the rebels inside were seen with
rocket-propelled grenades. The crowd turned and pounded a retreat as
screams competed with the endless thud of firing. Some were killed exe-
cution-style as the rebels emerged from the house to shoot men in the
head at close range.

Demonstrators complained afterwards that the UN peacekeepers who had been guarding the house, in part to keep an eye on Sankoh's whereabouts, did nothing to protect the unarmed crowd.

When the crowds later returned and stormed Sankoh's headquarters, they found it a shambles. Among the rubbish and jumbled furniture were large numbers of discarded hypodermic syringes. These had probably been looted from hospitals and medical centres and confirmed the conviction that many of the youthful RUF fighters were drugged.

Sierra Leone Army Command confirmed that two Ukrainian nationals – mercenaries, it was assumed – were with Sankoh when his Freetown house was attacked. One was killed and the other escaped to Liberia using a rebel network.

As the situation deteriorated rapidly, Sankoh and his fellow RUF ministers failed to escape from Freetown, but incredibly the RUF leader managed to disappear. UN forces admitted that they had lost track of him after his HQ had been sacked. UN spokesman David Wimhurst said at a press conference: 'We'd like to know where he is.'

It was not until over a week later that Sankoh was instantly recognised in Freetown by Kaba Sesay, a fifty-three-year-old Muslim resident. It was dawn and Sankoh, with a towel wrapped around his head as a disguise, was approaching the house from which he had disappeared nine days earlier.

'I was going to pray with my son when I saw him in front of me, on the path,' said Sesay. 'I knew who he was, but he said: "I am Foday Sankoh. Don't be scared. Will you help me? I need a taxi to take me to the Nigerian High Commission."'

Instead of calling a taxi, Sesay contacted a well-known figure in the neighbourhood – an armed ex-soldier known as 'Scorpion'. It was Scorpion who made the arrest that ended the nationwide search for the rebel leader. 'Today, I am a hero. Today the Scorpion catches the lion. The war is finished,' Scorpion shouted, as crowds chanted 'Scorpion, Scorpion'.

Sankoh's mysterious disappearance after his guards opened fire on the demonstrators outside his house had spawned a host of rumours regarding his whereabouts. It emerged that he had spent the whole period in a shack a mere 100 m from his house. When he reappeared he was accompanied by a single armed guard, who was injured as the arrest was made. According to one account, Scorpion shot the bodyguard and the round passed through his body and hit Sankoh's foot. The shooting attracted a crowd who recognised the bearded Sankoh and stripped the RUF leader naked.

Scorpion articulated their anger: 'He is an animal, so he should be naked like an animal.'

Naked, Sankoh was bundled into a car and taken to the compound of Johnny Paul Koroma and from there to the Sierra Leone Army HQ. When Sankoh arrived there, Keith Biddle, the British inspector general of Sierra Leone's Police Authority, requested help from the British Army as an angry mob gathered outside the HQ. A Lynx helicopter landed and transported Sankoh, who was strapped to a stretcher, first to HMS *Argyll* for treatment to his foot and then to an undisclosed UN location.

On 13 May, towards the end of a memorial service for nineteen people killed by Sankoh's bodyguards during the demonstration outside his HQ, the choir in the Siaka Stevens Stadium in Freetown was joined by the vast congregation in a low, rumbling chant: 'No more Sankoh, no more Sankoh.'

Even at this late juncture, the Reverend Jesse Jackson angered many Sierra Leoneans by suggesting that Sankoh might still have a positive role to play in the country.

Sankoh might be in custody, but the RUF remained a potent and threatening force in the jungle villages only a few kilometres inland from Freetown.

In May 2000, the RUF broke the ceasefire, but former AFRC leader J. P. Koroma stayed loyal to the government and increased his standing when on 7 May he broadcast a call-to-arms to defend Freetown. For the terrified population there was the prospect of more brutal assaults by the drunken, drugged men and murderous children of the RUF.

It was against this background that the British government decided that UK and other foreign nationals should be given military protection if they wished to leave the country.

It was time to send in the Royal Marines and Paratroops.

Chapter 6
Operation Palliser
Intervention by Air and Sea

Trehnkman noh de fehn palava.
A strong man doesn't provoke arguments.

On Sunday 7 May 2000, the internal conflict in Sierra Leone took on a new character when the United Kingdom launched Operation Palliser and deployed a task force to evacuate British, EU and Commonwealth passport holders from Freetown.

The operation began with about 200 men from the 1st Battalion Parachute Regiment (1 Para), the lead element of the task force, securing Lungi International Airport. A British Army spokesman in Dakar in Senegal said that about sixty civilians had been transferred to Lungi from Freetown aboard Russian- and Ukrainian-piloted UN helicopters. A further 500 Paras were due to deploy overnight in and around Freetown as the West African state lurched towards renewed civil war.

In the United Kingdom, 1 Para had been held at five days' notice to move (NTM) as part of a joint rapid reaction force (JRRF) since 1 September 1999. On 2 May 2000, the majority of the battalion had only just returned from Easter leave.

Within the battalion, A Company had initially been the envy of their fellow 'Toms'[1], having deployed on 30 April 2000 to Jamaica on Exercise Red Stripe, named after the popular and potent local beer. They were hosted on this overseas training exercise by the Jamaican Defence Force. Now that the battalion seemed likely to be deployed operationally, *Pegasus*, the Parachute Regiment journal, commented, 'The morale of A Company in Jamaica wavered when it was realised that a speedy deployment was in the offing and that our distance from West Africa would almost certainly preclude participation.' The company made the most of the exercise in the

Caribbean, improving basic and advanced jungle skills – their day in Africa would come.

Meanwhile, on Friday 5 May 2000, the rest of the battalion was alerted for a possible non-combatant evacuation operation (NEO) in Sierra Leone. The battalion's shortfalls, including the absent A Company, were made up from D Company 2 Para under Major Andy Charlton, bringing it up to strength as a battle group (BG).

The first indication that an operation was in the offing came with a telephone call at 07.30 hours on Friday 5 May to the home of the battalion second in command (2 IC). The battalion orderly sergeant had received an urgent message for the commanding officer (CO), Lieutenant-Colonel Gibson, or his 2 IC to telephone the station duty officer LAND command – the HQ at Wilton, Salisbury, formerly known as HQ UK Land Forces. The 2 IC hurried into work in order to call the deputy assistant chief of staff G3 operations LAND Command to learn that the battalion was to be alerted for deployment to Sierra Leone.

After an initial introduction to the LAND Command lieutenant-colonel who for the next forty-eight hours was to become the battalion's point of contact there, a twenty-five-minute conversation followed during which the 2 IC worked hard to 'sell' 1 Para as the solution to the problem. The potential rivals were Special Forces and the amphibious ready group (ARG), based on 42 Commando Royal Marines, embarked on HMS *Ocean* in Marseilles. They could reach Sierra Leone waters in twelve days. At this stage, the emphasis was very firmly on contingency planning for the use of the spearhead lead element (SLE) – troops on immediate standby for operational deployment – as one of a number of options being considered.

However, to some extent the 2 IC of 1 Para did not need to 'sell' the battle group. The MoD had already compared the capabilities of the ARG and 16 Air Assault Brigade, of which 1 Para was the infantry battalion component. The Brigade was a new formation assembled in September 1999 with the amalgamation of 24 Airmobile Brigade and 5 Airborne Brigade with 9 Regiment Army Air Corps[2]. As an air-manoeuvre brigade, it was a uniquely flexible and powerful formation within the UK Order of Battle designed to secure or open points of entry for other land or air elements. The Paras nicknamed the Brigade's new diving-eagle insignia 'The Demented Budgie'.

Planning continued fitfully at 1 Para throughout 6 May. Initially, there was doubt that the contingency planning at the permanent joint head-quarters (PJHQ) at Northwood in north London would develop into an operation, but as the day progressed the possibility increased.

A veteran airborne soldier explained the dilemma facing PJHQ: 'Though the ARG would be fully self-sufficient in combat service support (CSS), including ammunition and medical assets, it would take over a week to get there. 1 Para, as spearhead lead element (SLE) at twenty-four-hours' NTM, could have lead elements on the ground in some thirty-six to forty-eight hours at a push, but with very limited CSS. The situation seemed to be deteriorating fast in Sierra Leone. The ARG might be too late. A stitch in time ...'

The sequence of events was as follows:

At 10.30 hours on Friday 5 May, the 2 IC 1 Para received a follow-up telephone call explaining that the situation in Sierra Leone was confused and deteriorating as the RUF advanced on Freetown.

At 17.10 hours, the 2 IC was informed that the operation would be called 'Palliser'. Lungi Airport was judged to be vulnerable.

At 14.00 hours on Saturday 6 May, the CO held the first full orders group (O Group) with all the supporting commanders invited to be present. Colonel Gibson introduced the meeting and then handed over to the intelligence officer (IO), who gave a background briefing on Sierra Leone.

A Zambian battalion, part of UNAMSIL, was reported to have surrendered to the RUF. There were fears of a general collapse of UNAMSIL, the capture of Freetown by the RUF and a threat to the safety of the 1,300 entitled persons (EPs), who included UK citizens working in the city. The RUF looked as if it was planning a repeat of Operation 'No Living Thing'. The British cabinet had met the previous day, but at that moment did not wish to take unilateral action that might precipitate the collapse of UNAMSIL.

The battle group received a formal notice to move from LAND Command, who wanted to know how quickly they would be ready to emplane. It was becoming very clear that the situation in-theatre was deteriorating rapidly. The meeting broke up in turmoil as officers rushed to telephones to alert their units to the new timescale.

Nearly 170 years earlier, the Prussian military philosopher Karl von Clausewitz had caught the spirit of the moment writing in his seminal treatise *Vom Krieg* (*On War*): 'It is better to act quickly and err than to hesitate until the time of action is passed.'

At 16.15 hours on 6 May, the CO directed the battle group to deploy to the operational mounting centre (OMC) – a former airfield at South Cerney, Wiltshire. Shortly afterwards, at about 17.00 hours, a message came from LAND Command directing the battalion to move to the OMC at best speed. The barracks and mess halls at South Cerney not only provide accommodation and food, but the hangars are large covered areas in which troops can be assembled and briefed in private and under cover.

The night was spent on battle preparation for the forthcoming operation. Ammunition arrived, the boxes were opened up and the contents distributed to the Paras, who sat filling magazines and stowing them in their ammunition pouches.

Major Charlton, commanding D Company 2 Para, had, like the rest of the company, come straight from Easter leave. While he was driving from his home in London, the other 209 officers and men had travelled from France, Greece, Spain, Scotland, Northumberland, Wales and the West Country as soon as they heard about the possibility of a deployment. They had reported to Meeanee Barracks, Colchester, and then travelled down to the OMC. Charlton recalled later that they were eager for news and keen to get going.

The battle group was tasked to secure Lungi Airport as a forward operating base (FOB) and to conduct an NEO of the entitled persons. It was shaping up to be a classic airborne operation with all the strengths and weaknesses of 'light infantry'.

Airborne forces have very limited CSS or conventional combat power, and the umbilical cord is an intermittent and tenuous air bridge. An assumption of isolation is made from day one of air insertion. Airborne forces, therefore, thrive on making do with very limited resources, rapid decisions and taking risks. Optimally, they should be inserted directly at the point of crisis to 'hold the ring' before something with more punch is sent in to reinforce them – something like the ARG. The use of 1 Para was appropriate at Freetown both doctrinally (securing a point of entry) and practically under the circumstances: they were to act as a 'fire brigade' to immediately gain a degree of control over a crisis situation.

The Paras and later the Marines would be the high-profile element of Operation Palliser. What was less well known at the time, although the media in Freetown did pick up some indications, was that the operation was the largest regular Special Forces deployment since Operation Granby in the first Gulf War. In total, two Sabre Squadrons from 22 SAS along with the Regimental HQ and CO, an SBS troop and Chinooks plus C130s from the Joint Special Forces Aviation Wing (JSFAW) were deployed to Sierra Leone.

The first leg of the journey for 1 Para was a six-hour flight from RAF Lyneham, Wiltshire (which is a couple of kilometres from the OMC) on 7 May to Dakar in Senegal in the luxury of RAF TriStars. The former French colony to the north of Sierra Leone would be invaluable in Operation Palliser and subsequently in Operation Barras. For a city in the tropics, Dakar, on the Cap Vert peninsula on the western fringes of Senegal, is cool, refreshed by onshore Atlantic breezes.

The Paras were driven out to a French Army camp near the airport to the north of Dakar. It was here that the advance party of C Company group were 'quietly herded to one side to await developments'. The officers of battle group HQ declined the offer of lunch and wine at the French garrison officers' mess and established communications with PJHQ and UNAMSIL in Freetown. Writing in *Pegasus*, C Company reported that the men still at Dakar would recall the update from the intelligence officer which stated that 'reports of 4-5,000 rebels concentrating to the north are overestimated'. Even so, it 'was effective in focusing the mind'.

In the late afternoon of 7 May, the C Company advance group of 102 troops crammed into one C-130 Mk1, took off from Dakar (now designated the forward mounting base – FMB) and were inserted into Lungi Airport at 19.15 hours on Sunday 7 May. At this stage, it was unclear whether Lungi had been deserted by UNAMSIL or even overrun by the RUF and according to C Company in *Pegasus*, taking no risks, the company 'completed the first operational TALO [tactical air-land operation] for many years, much to the surprise of the Nigerian and UN forces at Lungi.'

The soldiers of C Company also recalled that, 'Despite the oppressive heat and humidity, our initial impression was that the country was very beautiful but very poor. The local population and resident UN troops were very happy to see us. This was evident in every village patrolled throughout the operation.'

In New York, the UN announced that the British task force would secure not only the airport, but assist UN troops in defending the part of town that included the UN headquarters at the Mammy Yoko hotel.

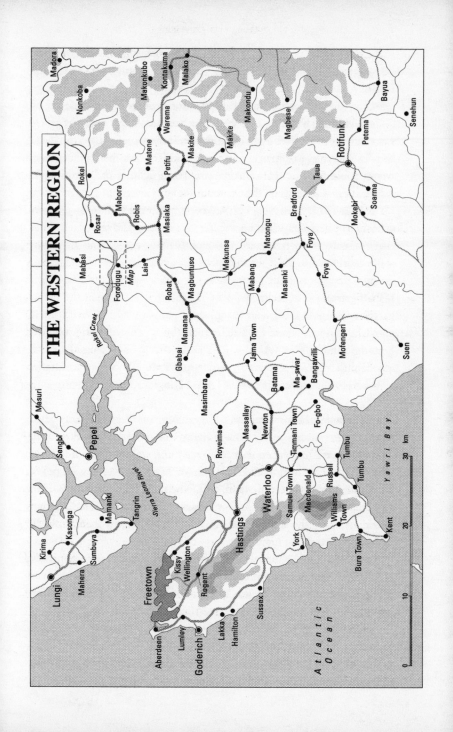

The following morning at 10.30 hours, the CO and his tactical HQ group flew from Dakar to Lungi, now the forward operational base (FOB).

D Company 2 Para had waited at Dakar for a couple of hours, sitting by the airfield in the harsh African sun, their frustration and desire to get on with the job growing with the increasing heat. Eventually they convinced the pilot and chief loadmaster of a C-130 Mk1 Hercules that the transport aircraft could accommodate 101 paratroops in fighting order with light equipment and were off on the two-hour flight to Lungi.

The balance of the battle group was complete at the FOB by 23.30 hours on Monday 8 May, sixty-four hours after the battalion had received the first telephone call.

The tasks for 1 Para battle group were:

(1) Establish an HQ at Lungi Airport
(2) Secure Lungi and Aberdeen Peninsulas
(3) When ordered, secure the British high commissioner's residence and compound
(4) Establish an evacuee assembly area (EAA) at the UN HQ – the Mammy Yoko Hotel – and an alternative EAA at Lungi Airport

Also on Monday, Major Charlton had begun to conduct a company-sized fighting and clearance patrol from Lungi, 13 km to the south of Freetown, towards Tagrin Point ferry port where a reception area for a seaborne evacuation from Freetown could be secured. With 10 Platoon at point, commanded by 2 Lt Duncan Mann, the 100 men of D Company moved off.

As the patrol advanced, Charlton was summoned to the battle group tactical HQ over the combat net radio. When he arrived there, Colonel Gibson was waiting for him.

'How long,' asked Colonel Gibson, indicating two CH-47 helicopters, 'will it take you to get your company into those two Chinooks?'

The major knew that he was being offered both a challenge and an opportunity. 'Four to five minutes,' he estimated.

'Correct answer,' replied the colonel. 'Get over to Freetown and secure the evacuation around the Mammy Yoko Hotel.'

That evening at 19.00 hours, the company was inserted on to the Aberdeen Peninsula by two CH-47 Chinook helicopters of No. 7 Squadron

RAF to secure the peninsula and the EAA at the UN HQ. The D Company group moved into the gutted Bintumani Conference Centre close to the Mammy Yoko Hotel on Man of War Bay. It was a good position overlooking the whole of Aberdeen, the western edges and approaches into Freetown and the sea approaches from the Lungi Peninsula. The soldiers would live in the deserted halls and rooms of the former conference centre for three weeks. Temperatures could go up to 35°C and tropical storms with strong onshore winds whipped through the empty windows of the gutted centre.

In these diverse weather conditions, Charlton admitted that he had a special respect for the attached 1 Para Support Company 81 mm mortar detachment under Corporal Glencross. These stoic men were in open weapons pits dug in near the conference centre.

There was no running water, no mosquito nets and the men slept on the concrete floors. The troops had deployed in webbing with full day sacs to save space and weight; their 35 to 45-litre day sacs or patrol packs would probably have contained their helmets, some basic rations, a 'brew kit' for making hot drinks, socks, a radio and/or battery, CWS night sight, ammunition and a poncho, bivvy bag or poncho liner. Bergans (rucksacks) containing the bulk of their kit were to follow. To save space, many had put their mosquito nets into their Bergans. In the oppressive tropical heat, it was vital for the troops, who at this stage were not acclimatised, to travel as light as possible; carrying a Bergan long distances would have produced heat casualties. Aircraft space on the initial inload was also very limited. Fresh water was flown over from the battalion echelon in Lungi. Water provided by the Nigerian UNAMSIL Company camped near the conference centre was accepted gratefully but boiled and treated with purification tablets before it was drunk.

In London, the MoD said that the British troops did not expect to engage the rebels, but they did not rule out bolstering the UN operation or securing the airport until 3,000 UN reinforcements had arrived. An official said: 'After the evacuation we do not know how this will develop.'

Announcements on the BBC World Service and warnings spread via the warden system run by the British High Commission advised the estimated 500 British citizens in and around Freetown to assemble at collection points throughout the city. It all seemed like a replay of June 1997.

'At the main evacuation point, the Mami [sic] Yoko beach hotel, there were two lines at the gate,' wrote journalist Chris McGreal. 'The Brits and the Others. Officially the hotel is the UN headquarters in Freetown, but entry was very much controlled by British officials. Outside, squaddies told people which line to get into. The Brits' line included European Union citizens, those from the Commonwealth, so long as it was a country with a recognisable name, and Americans. The rest, mostly Lebanese, were left to shout denunciations about discrimination. It did them no good, but they were all afforded a degree of protection if not promised evacuation. The Mami [sic] Yoko is on an isthmus in the far west of the city. The only bridge is guarded by Indian soldiers in a large white tank.' (The white tank was in fact a BMP-2 APC.)

Most of the evacuees were hoping to cross to the relative safety of Lungi International Airport, which was being protected by the 1 Para battle group. Among those waiting at the gate of the hotel was Alan Webster, who had been working in Freetown. 'I packed this bag two days ago because I guessed this was going to happen,' he said. 'I don't want to leave the country. I just want to go to the airport and see what happens. They are very unsafe, these people. You cannot predict them at all.'

During the night, as UNAMSIL and Sierra Leonean patrols drove through the city, hundreds of British citizens poured into the hotel, clutching passports and packed suitcases, and waited to be taken to safety. A Sierra Leonean woman waited in the hotel courtyard with her nine-year-old daughter, who was a British citizen. The woman said that rebels had killed her husband and four of their children the year before by forcing them into their home and setting it on fire.

Chris McGreal reported:

For now, Freetown's streets are controlled by what passes for a government army – partially trained, partially disciplined and partially concerned with who it kills. But the fear is not eased by the mass evacuation of foreigners spearheaded by Britain. United Nations and British troops are in abundance for now. They tear through the city in four-wheel drives with blue stickers and Union flags, offering a fleeting twinge of security. But people wonder who they are here to protect, and whether they will go when all the whites have been got out ...

Groups of government soldiers and Kamajor militiamen loyal to the government cruised the streets punching their fists in the air and promising the RUF a drubbing if they want another fight. They seemed to feel they had got the better of the day's battles.

A group of young Sierra Leonean officers offered reassurances with protestations of how well they had recently been trained by the British Army. The rebels would not get the better of them this time, they said. But then a group of government soldiers went swinging by on the back of a lorry, bandannas wrapped around their heads and beer bottles in their hands.

They were barely distinguishable from the rebels. It would be a bad evening to be mistaken for an RUF sympathiser.

It was the men from D Company 2 Para who were dealing with the line of 'Brits and Others'. Major Charlton looked back with pride on the way his soldiers dealt with situations during the first night, when the rules of engagement would have permitted them to open fire. 'That is not to say that on a number of occasions weapons were not cocked ready or that an elbow or carefully aimed Size 8 [boot] were not deployed but no shots were fired and 278 EPs were evacuated from the Mammy Yoko hotel on 8/9 May.' Experience in Northern Ireland had taught the soldiers that confrontations could be defused without bloodshed.

Close to the hotel was a football pitch and helipad from which evacuees were shuttled across to Lungi. The hotel had a perimeter wall with two gates that allowed the Paras to control access.

The 1 Para battle group's operations were settling into a steady state by the close of Friday 12 May, seven days after they had received the first call. The battle group was deployed as two groups, the majority around Lungi Airport, while D Company held Aberdeen Peninsula.

Charlton secured the permission of the Nigerian UNAMSIL sector commander and the Freetown police commissioner to operate mobile and foot patrols outside Aberdeen and deeper into Freetown. The Paras had two WMIK Land Rovers, a Pinzgauer truck, a UN Land Rover and two command post vehicles (CPVs) donated by the British High Commission. Mobility was enhanced and response times became quicker. Patrols reached out as far as the amputee camp where the Paras were confronted by victims of RUF brutality, many of them children.

At Lungi, B Company was deployed 3 km north of the battle group to block RUF infiltration and attacks on the airfield. The Company commander sited 4 and 5 Platoons forward to block the two roads leading to the airfield. Along with 6 Platoon, they patrolled the local villages and surrounding jungle with a high profile intended to deter the RUF and reassure the civilian community. A large Company HQ element formed a mobile reserve.

C Company spent three weeks as the operations company with one platoon on fifteen minutes' notice to move (NTM) and one platoon on one hour NTM. The third platoon guarded the company position at the Mahera Beach Hotel.

'Life in the hotel grounds,' they would later write in *Pegasus*, 'was far healthier than in the overcrowded airport where facilities became stretched as more and more UN troops and equipment arrived. Other Companies seemed to think we were living at Club Med, but this is far from the truth and more a case of "first come, first served" and . . . we arrived first.'

It soon became possible to scale down the NEO effort. By 12 May, 353 EPs had been evacuated, followed by sixty-five Senegalese nationals the following day. However, 453 registered EPs decided to remain in Freetown.

Five days later, Sergeant Stephen Heaney of the Pathfinder Platoon would win the Military Cross for his part in a night-time fire fight with a large group of RUF. It was a typical RUF probe, testing the mettle of the new force in Sierra Leone.

The citation for Sergeant Heaney's MC said that while his men were patrolling at the Lungi Loi road junction near the airport, they were confronted by a forty-strong rebel force and a fire fight developed. The RUF had approached the Pathfinder position and opened fire after being challenged. Under fire, Heaney pressed forward, calling for mortar fire to illuminate the enemy position. He then directed his men's fire on the rebels, killing four, and after ten minutes the remainder were forced to withdraw. At the time, Captain Cantrill RM, the OC of the 42 Commando Reconnaissance Platoon who was attached as an LO, was No. 2 on the 51 mm mortar and provided illumination during the action.

At first light, it was confirmed that four rebels had been killed in the initial contact. No injuries were sustained by the platoon; however, one civilian had been shot in the chest. She was treated by the platoon's patrol medic and evacuated by helicopter.

After a search of the contact area and a clearance patrol, the platoon recovered a variety of weapons and ammunition including an RPG launcher and rockets. Local villagers also reported having seen up to a further ten dead rebels, bringing the unconfirmed total to fourteen.

C Company took over the Pathfinders' position at Lungi Loi to give the platoon a break after ten days in this forward position. The day after the RUF attack, the rebels were back again, entering Freetown to make a reconnaissance of the company positions. 'Fortunately they were recognised by the locals and severely dealt with by the resident Nigerian troops who appeared to have a slightly different view on handling prisoners,' commented *Pegasus*. Blindfolded and with their wrists tied, the RUF men were put in the back of a local vehicle with a banner attached to the canvas roof that boasted the slogan 'Senior Man'. They were probably relieved to be guarded by Corporal Picuard and Private Gray of C Company.

At Lungi Airport, the support company deployed its valuable assets where they would be most effective. The anti-tank platoon, with thermal imaging (TI) Milan infra-red adaptor (MIRA) sights for its Milan anti-tank missiles, took over a rather rickety water tower and the control tower. From these vantage points they were able to cover most of the approaches to the airfield and adjoining beach. They had one battle, albeit with nature, in the shape of a plague of African black hornets. The control tower was also used by the snipers under Colour Sergeant Tonks, while others worked forward with B Company.

In addition to the detachment deployed with D Company, the mortars under Colour Sergeant Scullion had detachments on the airfield and with the Pathfinders at Lungi Loi. Though they fired a considerable amount of ammunition, principally illumination rounds, they also fired high explosives for 'training purposes'.

Airborne support for the first phase of Operation Palliser had been provided by twenty-one C-130 Hercules and four TriStar tasks used to deploy 1 Para; these aircraft were supplemented by civilian air charters. Eight Hercules remained deployed in Dakar for ongoing tasks and a daily resupply from the UK. Joint Helicopter Command (JHC) Chinooks remained in-theatre and were available to support British or UNAMSIL operations. On the ground, small detachments from the Tactical Communications Wing and Tactical Medical Wing were in-theatre to support elements of the air transport and JHC assets.

Looking back on the lessons from the first phase of the operation, an experienced retired officer commented, 'It is no good having high readiness forces if people insist on them having to acclimatise for fourteen days before becoming operational in a theatre. If you have the time, of course, use it to acclimatise before insertion. Palliser showed that troops can, if needs must, operate immediately, providing the limitations are understood: their loads must be minimised, they need lots of water, they must be fit, they must be disciplined in environmental health and supervised at every level, and commanders must know their limitations. That means that you need to train at doing this.'

In the American Civil War, the dashing Confederate General Nathan Bedford Forrest had characterised his victory over the garrison at Murfreesboro in 1862 as a result of arriving 'firstest with the mostest'.

In Operation Palliser, if the Paras had been 'firstest', then the amphibious ready group (ARG) based around 42 Commando RM, commanded by Lieutenant-Colonel Andy Salmon, would arrive with the 'mostest'. A key element for the 'mostest' was the ARG Logistic Task Group with their vehicles and communications equipment.

When the crisis had begun, the ARG had been on Exercise Ambrose Hill at the Canjuers training area in southern France. At 02.00 hours on 5 May, it was warned off for possible operations in Sierra Leone. A hastily convened O Group cut short the training and by 05.30 hours on 7 May, the force was re-embarked and on its way to Gibraltar. Here the Marines fired on the ranges and zeroed their weapons while stores were loaded and by 14 May, HMS *Ocean* (L 12), the ARG flagship, was in position off Sierra Leone.

In addition to 42 Commando, HMS *Ocean* had an air group consisting of four Commando Sea King Mk4s, two RM Air Squadron Lynx Mk7s, two RM Air Squadron Gazelles and two RAF CH-47 Chinooks. *Ocean* entered service in 1999 with a complement of 285, plus a further 180 Fleet Air Arm personnel when aircraft are embarked. She can carry up to 800 Royal Marines.

In France, *Ocean*'s air group had been developing an airborne extraction technique that would have been very welcome to some of the UNMOs who had been trapped in RUF territory earlier in the year. With the acronym TRAP – tactical recovery of aircraft and personnel – this technique brought together three of the four types of helicopter on *Ocean*.

Prior to a mission, a pilot would have filled out an 'Isoprep' (isolated personnel report) form. This gives personal details known as 'the big six' –

name, rank, number, date of birth, blood group and religion. In addition, it includes a description of the pilot's physical appearance and four pieces of personal information known only to that individual – for example, the name and breed of the family dog. This would ensure that the rescue helicopter would not be drawn into an ambush by an impostor, since the downed pilot could be interrogated at a safe altitude. The completed forms were held by the air group.

On a TRAP mission, the team would deploy Lynx and Gazelle helicopters fitted with high-magnification sights. The Lynx also mounts the BAe Systems Avionics SS600 Series 3 thermal imaging equipment. The TRAP team would home in on the downed airman's SARBE distress beacon or radio and examine the area for any hostile forces. Two Sea Kings, each carrying a section of Marines, would then land to secure the area and extract the pilot or crew.

As *Ocean* was steaming south on 8 May, the aircraft carrier HMS *Illustrious* (R 06) broke off from a NATO exercise in the Bay of Biscay. Within hours of receiving a signal to head south for West Africa, she detached from the exercise and completed the 2,000 nautical mile journey (the equivalent of London to Cairo) in just four days. She had thirteen Harriers and five helicopters embarked. A further five helicopters of her air group remained aboard Royal Fleet Auxiliary (RFA) *Fort George* (A388)[3] until returning to complete the total of twenty-three aircraft on board.

Of the thirteen Harriers, seven were F/A.2 Sea Harriers belonging to 801 Naval Air Squadron based at Yeovilton, Somerset, and six were GR.7 Harriers from RAF 3 (Fighter) Squadron based at RAF Cottesmore, near Grantham, East Anglia. These aircraft were embarked as part of the newly integrated 'Joint Force Harrier', designed to optimise the deployability and interoperability of the two types of aircraft[4]. When the Harriers began flying over Sierra Leone, the pilots were pleased to know that the TRAP teams were ready aboard HMS *Ocean*.

The task force was growing into one of the largest naval forces deployed since the liberation of the Falklands in 1982. In addition to *Illustrious*, the ships involved and their commanders would eventually include: HMS *Ocean*, Captain Scott Lidbetter; HMS *Chatham* (F 87), Captain George Zambellas; RFA *Fort George* (A 388), Captain Les Coupland; RFA *Fort Austin* (A 386), Captain Dave Pitt; RFA *Sir Bedivere* (L 3004), Captain Dave Pursall; and RFA *Sir Tristram* (L 3505), Captain Ross Ferris.

The ARG landed on 25 May after eleven days of reconnaissance, surveys and monitoring of events ashore. Following the Para contact at Lungi Loi on 17 May, the 105 mm light guns of 8 Alma Commando Battery, 29 Commando Regiment RA, were lifted by Chinook into position at Petifu Junction. From here they could provide fire support or illumination if the RUF attempted another probe.

The Marines took over from the Paras and Operation Palliser moved into a new phase. The distinctive feature of the ARG's operations was their variety, which included riverine and heliborne patrols, plans for evacuation, vehicle repairs, recruit training and support for the local police.

During a river patrol on 1 June, the Marines arrested fifteen West Side Boys and recovered weapons and ammunition. For riverine operations, the men of 42 Commando had the rigid raiding craft (RRC) of 539 Assault Squadron Boat Group and the landing craft vehicle and personnel (LCVPs) of 9 Assault Squadron. In preparation for the deployment of HMS *Chatham* and HMS *Argyll* inshore to give naval gunfire support (the *Argyll* had been deployed to Sierra Leone from patrol duties), the Sierra Leone River was surveyed by landing craft from 9 Assault Squadron since the charts available dated back to the 1970s and areas had silted up.

The M Company group took over the Aberdeen Peninsula and sited check points and defensive positions. This company had WMIK Land Rovers and the machine gunners gave a fire-power demonstration that served to reassure the local population and convince RUF sympathisers that the ARG was not a force to be taken on.

The Marines patrolling into Freetown were particularly taken with a multicoloured sign painted on a building that read:

MIRACLE CENTRE

we cure

GHONORREA
PILE
STOMACH ACHE
GOITA
MAN POWER

Meet with the Rev Prince Fem
for all your problems

At their base on the Aberdeen Peninsula, Surgeon Lieutenant Barry Huxtable practised more conventional and reliable medicine, including dental checks for M Company.

By the end of the month, the advancing rebels had been beaten back by UNAMSIL and Sierra Leone forces. ECOWAS had pledged to supply 3,000 additional troops to strengthen the 13,000-strong UNAMSIL during early 2000. Three ECOWAS members – Nigeria, Ghana and Guinea – had six infantry battalions serving with the force. The UN also approved an increase in the strength of UNAMSIL to 16,000 personnel, as recommended by Kofi Annan.

On 26 May, President Kabbah said that Sankoh would be prosecuted, but later reports indicated that the Sierra Leone government was considering a plan announced by West African leaders to place Sankoh under Nigerian custody to ensure his safety. Informed observers said that any effort to prosecute Sankoh could reignite the civil war.

By 7 June, the ARG received orders for a tactical withdrawal and handover to UNAMSIL. The whole force was to be re-embarked in eight days. With the situation now stable, the VIPs began to arrive. The Commandant General Royal Marines, Major General R. H. G. Fulton, visited the ARG; Deputy Prime Minister John Prescott visited the Sierra Leone Army, which was now being trained by the British Army short-term training team (STTT); and Foreign Secretary Robin Cook flew in on 8 June.

The ARG had been away from Plymouth for nearly four months and the mail delivery, though very welcome, had been infrequent. When the force was on operations, the troops were entitled to free airmail letters – known by their pale-blue colour as 'Blueys'. They could also make a twenty-minute free phone call from HMS *Ocean* once a week.

Marine Lyndon with 4 Troop L Company, writing in the Royal Marine journal *Globe & Laurel*, recalled the frustrations of Royal Marines or 'Royal' waiting for phone calls: 'Booking a slot had to be done several days in advance, but did not guarantee you would get through. Choice words could be heard on 2 deck each night from Royal as he made his way back to his messdeck after waiting two days for a ten-minute phone slot, only to find his missus had decided to use the phone when he was trying to get through.'

In addition to the Paratroops and Royal Marines, some 120 support troops including men and women from the Royal Army Medical Corps,

Royal Military Police and Royal Logistic Corps deployed to Sierra Leone and remained after the Paras had returned home.

Flight Lieutenant Ellie Pook RAF, the UK Mobile Air Movements Squadron (MAMS) team leader, produced a memorable account of life at Lungi. 'Lungi was probably one of the most basic airports in the world; however, there were aircraft steps (whether they reached the height of a VC-10 or TriStar was irrelevant), a couple of power sets and other associated equipment. With all my kit gathered up, I was taken to the accommodation, a mere five-minute walk from the far side of the pan, past the Chinooks to the veranda in the president's lodge – luxurious accommodation with power, lights, an indoor swimming pool when it rained and a rat. It slept eight comfortably, had space for three desks, the satellite telephone worked and the medics were happy as they could hold a clinic there.

'Once the domestics were sorted out,' she recalled, 'it was on to the work bit. Up to the Joint Theatre Force Headquarters (JTFHQ) to meet various individuals, enjoy the air conditioning and marvel at the showers, cook tent, beds with built-in mosquito nets and the number of computers. Back to the "office" via the hangar to meet Mr. Khabia, the airport manager (a man who would prove to be invaluable), and other UN and RAF staff. A more comprehensive brief took place in between the transport aircraft arriving and departing. "You must carry your SA80 when you walk up to JTFHQ, the hangar and ATC. Go everywhere in pairs, curfew and stand-to at first light and handle all transport aircraft arriving and departing Lungi."

'The management challenge,' continued Pook, 'was to ensure that the boys were in a fit state to handle the aircraft and to drive the aircraft handling equipment. They had to be well rested, eat properly and drink enough to keep going but more importantly, as the locals were assisting with the driving of the tractors and tugs, that they understood the word and signals for stop!

'The aircraft and helicopter movements seemed continuous; if it wasn't ours it was the UN's. Despite being tired and wearing earplugs to block out some of the noise, the whine of the Antonov 124 engines as it taxied to its parking slot was enough to wake the dead! On top of the aircraft and helicopter movements, the phone rang at all hours and people snored or talked in their sleep and then a mosquito would buzz around your ear. Quality sleep was a rare commodity.'

The most complex period for the UK MAMS, she recalled, was the recovery of 1 Para and elements of the JTFHQ. 'Frantic load planning with changes every five minutes followed as everyone decided that they should be first out. In the end it was decided that the Paras would go first with other personnel on a fill-up basis and their equipment would be recovered on C-130s. Once that decision had been made we were able to deconflict the (RAF) aircraft flow, load plan, get a system in place for the checking and preparation of the equipment and paperwork and, along with ATC staff, devise a parking plot. Needless to say the planning proved invaluable, but when you are working and operating on the same pan as the UN you are better off just "cuffing it".

'The recovery of 1 Para and the JTFHQ was completed on time and the Royal Marines replaced the Paras, which eased our workload a little. The deployment of equipment for the Royal Anglians started, then came their personnel – they had been tasked to provide the training for the Sierra Leone Army. The recovery of the Marines and the final elements of the JTFHQ continued in between a visit by the foreign secretary, and then it was time for the team to go home, giving another team a chance to enjoy the challenges of an operational theatre.'

The resources of the ARG Logistic Task Group included a powerful Foden recovery vehicle operated by Corporal Falconer and Marine 'Windsor' Davies. This redoubtable team worked with the RAF at Lungi, where they used the 12,500 kg-capacity slewing crane on their Foden to assist an RAF ground crew lifting the main engine into a Chinook.

Looking back, Ellie Pook summed up the feelings of many service men and women who had been part of Operation Palliser: 'The work was hard, hours were long, decent sleep was non-existent, but spirits remained high despite the heat, humidity, boil-in-the-bag food, mosquitoes and constant changes to the plan. Why? We could see our contribution to the peacekeeping effort and the fact that it was appreciated – a job done well in exacting circumstances. All this based in a 12 x 12 tent with duck boards on the floor, right-angle torches and a couple of solar shower bags – a five-star luxury in a place like Lungi.'

At sea, the frigate HMS *Argyll*, which had protected the seaward flank of British forces ashore, resumed her duties as Atlantic Task Ship South, but RFA *Sir Percivale*, known affectionately to her crew as 'Percy', remained in Freetown to support the British Army training team. In the coming months, both ships would play an important part in operations in Sierra Leone.

Operation Palliser had been an obvious success, but to the UNAMSIL command the British presence was now becoming less welcome. British officers, despite being outside the UN chain of command, sat in on UN military planning sessions and assigned a full-time adviser to the Sierra Leone military in order to bring some organisational cohesion to the irregular units fighting on the government side.

Worse still, Britain was, according to UK Secretary of State for Defence Geoffrey Hoon, 'to all intents and purposes running the day-to-day operation of UN forces' in Sierra Leone.

Hoon's overstatement of the situation on the ground fuelled an intense internal debate within the British Parliament on the appropriate limits of British military engagement in Sierra Leone.

Robin Cook had told the Commons that 'Britain will not abandon its commitment to Sierra Leone', but opposition politicians warned him against embroiling troops in a lengthy conflict. Cook would not put a time limit on the operation. He said that the government would review the mandate daily. 'Our first duty is to protect the lives of British citizens in Sierra Leone and others to whom we have consular responsibility.'

Francis Maude, the Conservative shadow foreign secretary, said, 'Britain's armed forces are already stretched dangerously thin. There would be no public support, I believe, for allowing British forces to be sucked into a civil war.'

Menzies Campbell, the Liberal Democrat shadow foreign secretary, had the same fears, warning Mr Cook against 'mission creep'.

Early on Wednesday 30 May, British troops began distributing leaflets in Freetown with the insignia of the Sierra Leone Army. The leaflets explained that the British force had achieved its mission of stabilising the security situation while UNAMSIL troops arrived, and now the ARG would be withdrawing.

'The recent military successes by the government of Sierra Leone defence forces clearly demonstrate the effectiveness and cohesion that now exist,' the leaflets continued. 'The UK fully supports their increasingly impressive capability. The government of Sierra Leone defence forces and UNAMSIL are building closer co-operation in a number of areas including convoys, intelligence and inspection of troop movements.'

The leaflets also gave reassurance about the training that UK soldiers would be giving the Sierra Leone Army after pulling out: 'A strong British military team will remain to assist the government defence forces and UNAMSIL.'

But many people in Freetown said that they wanted the UK troops to stay.

At this time, with the ARG about to depart Sierra Leone, the 200 personnel of the British Army STTT remained in Sierra Leone as part of Operation Basilica. At the Benguema Training Centre (BTC) at Waterloo, over 20 km south-east of Freetown, they would put about 1,000 Sierra Leonean troops through basic training and infantry skills. These troops would become the new Sierra Leone Army (SLA) 4 Brigade. The programme began in June with a team from the 2nd Battalion Royal Anglian Regiment, 'The Poachers', who were replaced on 22 July by the 1st Battalion Royal Irish, who in turn would be replaced by men of the 2nd Battalion The Royal Light Infantry.

The British training team were to have no combat or patrol duties, but could use force to defend themselves if attacked. As part of the training package, the British government supplied the Sierra Leone Army with uniforms, ponchos, four thousand 81 mm mortar bombs and five million rounds of 7.62 mm ammunition for the surplus British Army self-loading rifles (SLRs) that were supplied to the SLA. For the 'old sweats' in the training teams, the semi-automatic SLR was a familiar weapon from their days as young soldiers. The large amount of personal equipment was necessary because the first troops who reported for training arrived with virtually nothing. They were issued uniforms, bedding, '58 Pattern webbing and even shoes – the trainers issued to recruits became prized items that were closely guarded.

Sixty men from the Assault Engineer Troop of 42 Commando assisted the Royal Engineers of 9 Squadron and worked on building the BTC for 2 Royal Anglian. Over 200 underslung loads were flown in by helicopter. The versatile Sergeant Screech of the Assault Engineer Troop also had 1,000 SLA recruits as a local labour force helping to build the camp.

With the work finished, he recalled, 'The arrival of ninety-seven trainees on two 4-tonne wagons was like a scene out of a film with them singing their war songs. Tents were erected to ensure that the Anglians kept dry as the rainy season approached, but I would have been more worried about the relatives of the four cobras we killed in the tents. The camp was now completed. We said our goodbyes and were even invited to go and fight the RUF, with the promise of ninety-seven men to start a diamond mine after the war ... thanks for the offer!'

The sappers of 9 Squadron had not only worked on the construction of BTC but had also provided the infrastructure for all the Company locations, providing fresh desalinated water, ablutions and also carrying out 'hearts and minds' tasks like rebuilding damaged bridges. The versatility of the sappers and assault engineers reached a pinnacle of professional expertise when Corporal Kev Bateman and his section built a power shower. Sergeant Screech recalled visitors to the Engineers' ablution block asking, 'You couldn't knock one of those up for us?'

The medical staff of 42 Commando assisted in the screening of recruits for the BTC. Writing in *Globe & Laurel*, Leading Medical Assistant Middleton recalled that, 'Although this seemed rather daunting, it turned out to be a quite valuable learning experience. Potential recruits were trying to join with one eye, or limbs disabled through polio or rickets and all manner of different ailments which MAs rarely see. Another interesting insight was the various gunshot injuries some of these re-joiners had suffered and how they had healed, showing little or no permanent effects, even where their joints had been involved.'

Operation Palliser had been a demonstration of military power untrammelled by the UN's rules of engagement and complex and inflexible chain of command. It was little wonder, then, that the RUF and other militias realised that the British forces in Sierra Leone were not to be provoked or humiliated. In the days before the ARG withdrew, it was reported that 300 RUF fighters had gathered to surrender but were beyond the 42 Commando tactical area of operational responsibility.

The STT got to work while in Freetown, the invaluable RFA *Sir Percivale* was a secure environment in which stores could be kept dry. Detachments were rotated through as the quartermaster's working party to protect the ship and to give the soldiers a respite from the heat and humidity as well as good food. The soldiers from the STTT had a chance to shower, get their kit laundered and sleep in cabins.

The training team from 2 Royal Anglian watched their SLA recruits improve as individuals and begin to work together in tactical formations. By the close of the tour, one of their enduring memories was the spontaneous, cheerful singing of the recruits as they marched – although in reality, despite the best efforts of the NCOs, the marching remained a very typically African shuffling jog.

Commenting on the training programme, one expatriate sneered over his evening drink in Freetown, 'Brilliant, if we get the army really smart and efficient and disciplined, maybe next time they get shirty about their pay and how little they're being allowed to rip everyone off for, the next coup will be a bloodless one.'

In reality, the Operation Basilica training programme was producing a disciplined force that had the confidence to take on the RUF in areas that had previously been 'no-go' territory.

Interviewed by Wilfred Leeroy Kabs-Kanu of the Sierra Leonean newspaper *Expo Times* at the end of 2000, Minister of Information Julius Spencer was briskly frank about the British presence in the country. 'There are only two factions in the war in Sierra Leone: the rebels and the people of Sierra Leone. If you understand the history and character of the war, you will understand this. The assistance of the British is to the people of Sierra Leone. The protestations of the RUF and their sympathisers are due to the fact that with British assistance, the legitimate government of the people of Sierra Leone is being given the capacity to defend them and defend democracy. Remember the RUF's protestations about Executive Outcomes, and their protestations about the Nigerians? Now it is the turn of the British.'

Back in May 2000, whatever the reservations expressed by British politicians, lives had been saved and stability enhanced in Freetown through the presence of British troops on the ground. But the men and women in Parliament would reduce the operation to the level of an accountant's balance sheet.

Questioned in the Commons about the cost of the operation, Defence Secretary Geoffrey Hoon replied on 26 June: 'The additional costs of Operation Palliser, the evacuation deployment to Sierra Leone which commenced on 5 May, are still being established, but it is estimated that they will amount to some £8 million. As Operation Palliser is not a United Nations operation, we do not expect to claim any of those costs from the United Nations.'

However, the speed of the deployment of 1 Para and 42 Commando to Sierra Leone meant that there was an extra unforeseen price to pay. When 42 Commando returned to their base at Plymouth, it was confirmed that two men had contracted malaria and a further four Royal Marines were under observation.

Following Operation Palliser, the MoD set up a system to monitor the health of all British personnel who had been deployed to West Africa. According to the MoD, 'This is not because we expect serious long-term problems. It is a sensible precaution in the light of the large numbers of servicemen deployed on Operation Palliser, some 4,500 at its peak, and the particular health risks prevalent in Sierra Leone. Health surveillance of deployed forces is expected to become a routine part of our arrangements in future.'

A more down-to-earth view came from Leading Medical Assistant Middleton of 42 Commando, who summed it up in *Globe & Laurel*: 'Even with a good medical brief, mosquito nets and repellent, the constant battle with one of the country's smallest residents caused much anguish and discomfort. Reports of 1 Para's malaria cases raised the awareness and utilisation of all MAs.'

The Foreign and Commonwealth Office (FCO) advice to travellers concurred with this observation in its list of tropical diseases prevalent in Sierra Leone: 'Waterborne diseases, malaria and other tropical diseases are prevalent. You should consider taking prophylaxis against malaria and using insect repellent. Vaccination against rabies and yellow fever (required to enter Guinea) are strongly advised. You should consult your doctor about these and other requirements before travelling. HIV/AIDS is prevalent. Lassa fever can be contracted in Kenema and the east. If you have travelled in this region you should seek urgent medical advice for any fever not positively identified as malaria.'

It was perhaps with all this in mind that Dr Lewis Moonie, under-secretary of state for defence, said in Parliament in the summer of 2000: 'The UK operation in Sierra Leone is an excellent example of our ability to deploy forces rapidly to meet crises worldwide. One of the lessons which we have learned from previous deployments, including the Gulf War, is ensuring adequate health monitoring of those deployed so that any longer term problems can be identified and dealt with as soon as possible. We owe it to our people to ensure that all personnel who deploy on operations do so with the right medical protection.'

Six months later, all these confident words would be tested by fourteen soldiers from 1 and 2 Para who had contracted malaria. On Monday 5 February 2001, a solicitor acting for the men threatened to take the MoD to court over its alleged failure to supply them with drugs in a timely fashion. He stated that 'in one case the MoD acknowledged that a soldier did not receive any medication at all'. It emerged that some 200 soldiers had arrived in Sierra Leone without anti-malaria tablets because of a shortage of an anti-malaria drug called Mefloquine. Mefloquine, the solicitor pointed out, needed to be in the body for at least twenty-four hours to be effective. The paratroopers were given the drug only eleven hours before they arrived in West Africa, yet they were informed about their destination thirty-six hours before they left the UK.

A spokeswoman for the MoD said that 'the Ministry's medical advice is that if taken within twenty-four hours of arrival [in malarial regions] you will be protected'.

Of the personnel who served in Sierra Leone, 112 contracted malaria and there were three other suspected cases. Yet between 1995 and 2000, only forty-seven armed forces personnel had contracted the illness. In 2000, the Liberal Democrat defence spokesman Paul Keetch was told by Geoffrey Hoon that 'the number of cases [of malaria] confirmed are within medically expected numbers'.

Mefloquine, marketed as Lariam, is an effective anti-malaria prophylactic, but not without its critics. There have been reports in the medical press of it producing unforeseen side effects such as convulsions, headaches and auditory and visual hallucinations.

While some people do get side effects, often they can be confused with the environmental effects of a new country (with no acclimatisation) and the stress of potentially going to war. The side-effects issue has also been exaggerated and possibly fabricated by some soldiers in the past as an attempt at mitigation for offences, varying from negligent discharge of weapons (NDs) and road traffic accidents to violent assaults. Whatever the truth, the side effects are a lot less severe than contracting malaria.

On the same day that the Paras' lawyer said that they would take the MoD to court, the Ministry admitted they were responsible for only one soldier catching malaria. He had not been provided with drugs until five days after arriving in Sierra Leone. However, soldiers had been taken ill on duty in Sierra Leone as stocks of Mefloquine had run low and Royal Army Medical Corps staff had been obliged to buy a less effective drug in Senegal.

Despite this, the MoD rejected the claims by the fourteen Paras, asserting that they had all received Mefloquine before departure.

It seemed a sorry conclusion to Operation Palliser, giving the impression that the government and MoD were prepared to risk soldiers' lives and health but not to offer them much support or assistance in the event of injury or death.

However, the truth of the situation was probably more complex. The malaria cases were in fact the result of several factors, including some soldiers failing to follow correct field discipline – sleeves rolled down, use of mosquito repellent, use of mosquito nets when available – and the chain of command not always policing these precautions vigorously enough. Some soldiers may have negligently failed to take drugs when told to do so, or deliberately have stopped taking them because of perceived or real side effects and not told anyone that they had done so.

As one experienced soldier observed, 'There is no doubt that more people got malaria on Palliser than should have, had all measures been taken rigorously, and had the combat service support chain worked correctly. There again, they all had a lot on their minds. No military operation has ever been faultless – or ever will be.

'The "compensation culture" does not help either,' he continued, 'because it obscures the genuine cases behind the opportunists. In addition, there is a lack of understanding generally that there is no 100 per cent protection against disease, just as there is no 100 per cent protection against a bullet. Both are occupational hazards. Luck, good and bad, is a factor of war. The one mosi that gets through, injects and takes a big drink might just be the one carrying the most virulent strain, and you might just by bad luck be more susceptible than your fellow soldiers ...'

During their tour in Sierra Leone, learning from the 1 Para experience, the soldiers of the Royal Irish conscientiously took their Lariam. While on a patrol through a rural village, a Royal Irish section was caught in a short but heavy tropical rainstorm. The villagers ran for shelter and the soldiers waited patiently in the open for the rain to cease. When the sky had cleared, the villagers emerged to ask the soldiers if it was true that the special tablets they took made them waterproof.

In June, UN spokesman Fred Eckhard reported that a company of Jordanian Special Forces, part of UNAMSIL forces holding a post at Rokel Bridge 63 km north-east of Freetown, had repulsed three attempts by about 200 RUF fighters to cross Rokel Creek by canoe. The Jordanians, who came under fire, suffered no casualties. Three months later, Rokel Creek and the Jordanians would again move centre stage in the events leading up to the capture of the Royal Irish soldiers.

On 23 July, in a drive to reopen the strategic road linking Freetown with the international airport at Lungi currently blocked by the WSB, UNAMSIL launched Operation Thunderbolt. Initially, details of the operation were scanty, but at the time the Associated Press reported that at least one peacekeeper was wounded in the fighting, while an unknown number of renegades were killed.

A more spectacular account was filed by Foday Koroma for the 30 August 2000 edition of the Freetown-based *Expo Times* newspaper which had the strap line 'Exposing Today for Tomorrow':

Lightning swept across the dark cloud and there was a heavy noise. There was a thunderbolt that saw the West Side Boys in disarray. Quickly, very quickly, they were dislodged from their Okra [sic] Hills base.

This was the picture painted of the operation carried out by the United Nations.

Peacekeepers in Sierra Leone, UNAMSIL, have tried to get rid of the nagging renegade soldiers. Everybody had hoped it was the end of the harassment, extortion and intimidation perpetrated by the self-styled West Side Boys along the Freetown/Masiaka highway.

Nobody would have thought the renegade soldiers would ever again show their faces along the highway. Some reports spoke of how the helicopter gun ship had drowned hundreds of WSB in their desperate bid to escape the wrath of the ferocious peacekeepers.

But just a few hours after the 'successful' operation, the West Side jungle boys were back at their checkpoints, doing the same things they were [always] doing. As a way of manifesting their presence, two of their commanders, including Commander Kallay, the new leader, went to Masiaka and had a tête-à-tête with the Jordanian troops stationed there. Not long after, a government-owned Road Transport Corporation bus was ambushed and the passengers were dispossessed of their belongings. The driver of the bus reported the incident to the Jordanian troops but nothing was done.

The West Side Boys are still at their Okra [sic] Hill base. This brings into question the success of 'Operation Thunderbolt'. It also heaps the question of the use of force to resolve our decade-long civil war.

Various forces have come and gone, but none have been able to end the war. From Executive Outcomes to Sandline International, from ECOMOG to UNAMSIL, the war is still on. 'The people are still suffering,' says Musa Kamara, a displaced man from Makeni.

The WSB had once again become a menace to traffic, setting up random roadblocks to extort money and goods from vehicles and pedestrians. A Freetown-based aid worker had fallen victim to one of these roadblocks. When he was interviewed by the BBC on 30 August 2000, he was terrified that members of the gang might track him down and insisted on remaining anonymous:

We had a lot of materials in the pick-up, some of it underneath plastic sheeting. They searched the vehicle and we asked if we could continue. They refused to let us go and told us to wait for further instructions. Then suddenly they put us in the vehicle and drove off the main road into the jungle. They said we were going to a village about five miles away. We stopped halfway and then they took everything from the vehicle.

We were later taken to a village about seven miles from the main road and held in close detention until about 8 p.m. that evening. After that we were taken in a boat to the group's main base in a village called Gberi Bana and that is where we were held for ten days.

In Gberi Bana, we were allowed to move around because there was no way to escape; there were guys with guns everywhere.

They had taken this village over completely, chasing out the people who originally lived there.

At the beginning, they threatened to execute us because they said the United Nations was planning to attack them. This was during Operation Thunderbolt, which was aimed at getting rid of the West Side Boys' checkpoints on the main road.

As the interview continues, his fear can be detected in the short, almost telegraphic delivery:

There were lots of the group in the area, despite the UN's claims to have secured it.

They never made any demands. They only asked that they should be allowed back in the government army and that the government shouldn't use force against them.

You know these boys are just there to cause trouble. They're very unpredictable – they could be nice one moment and nasty the next.

At the base, there were men and women – some of them very young. Their number varied.

At one point, they said they were mobilising and at that point there were between 200 and 300 armed people there. In another location, there were 60-100 people.

They have a reputation for being drunk, but actually they don't have access to much alcohol. They do smoke a lot of marijuana and they also take some cocaine. There are many marijuana plantations.

Basically they act like highway robbers; when they run out of things they seize vehicles and steal the contents.

They are capable of committing atrocities. While I was being held, six women suspected of witchcraft were executed by firing squad. They used their AK-47s.

I only heard the firing, but a colleague saw three dead bodies.

These were the men who were now holding the eleven Royal Irish Regiment soldiers and their SLA liaison officer.

Chapter 7
Negotiations

Big moht noh in masta in poh wan.
A big mouth doesn't know its master is poor.

In Britain, the realisation of what had happened had begun to dawn on the government and the MoD. Eleven soldiers from the Royal Irish Regiment and one Sierra Leone Army soldier had gone missing on Friday 25 August near the towns of Masiaka and Forodugu in Sierra Leone.

A Downing Street spokesman initially said that Prime Minister Tony Blair would be briefed on the situation on his return from holiday. However, the PM realised this was a 'complex and difficult situation' and wanted to be updated immediately. 'Whenever British forces are held against their will, anywhere in the world, it is something the government takes very seriously,' he said.

At Howe Barracks, Canterbury – the UK HQ of 1 Royal Irish – the families of the captured soldiers gathered, desperately waiting for news. It emerged that eight of the soldiers were from Northern Ireland, two from the Republic and one from Merseyside. A dedicated satellite link between the barracks and the British HQ in Sierra Leone was set up by Sunday 27 August to ensure that the families were kept up to date with developments.

The battalion had been based in Canterbury for a year and the soldiers and their families enjoyed a good relationship with the local community. A barman at the Mill House pub opposite the barracks said that the men were 'nice lads' who were proud of their regiment.

Talking off the record, a Royal Irish soldier who knew the kidnapped men said, 'They're really great guys and are well liked by everyone. They are some of the best-trained guys in the regiment. Anyone can get lost in strange and extreme surroundings.'

Talking to BBC News 24, the corporation's rolling television news channel, Colonel Stewart Douglas of the Royal Irish said that the soldiers were being treated well and that none of them had been injured. 'It is an unpleasant situation for them but they are in good spirits. It is a strong group and they are experienced soldiers . . . it won't be the first time they will have found themselves in a conflict environment.'

He added that the soldiers would have been trained for such a hostage situation and that they would be putting their 'procedures into place . . . It depends on their captors but I think it is a good sign that the captors are in direct contact with us'.

He added that the men's families were receiving regular updates of the situation since 'the families are our prime concern', and explained that 'we have a very well-developed regimental system and we are in a position to give good support to the families'.

Meanwhile in Freetown, however, Minister of Information Dr Julius Spencer described the West Side Boys as 'unpredictable bandits'.

The first contact between the West Side Boys (WSB) and the staff at Benguema Training Centre (BTC) was probably via brief exchanges over the patrol's radio.

The face-to-face negotiations that followed were headed by Lieutenant-Colonel Simon Fordham, CO 1 Royal Irish. To those who did not know him, Fordham could appear a robust, bluff and direct 'soldiers' soldier', but this gruff exterior concealed the true nature of this shrewd and very experienced officer. He brought only a small team with him for his meetings with the rebels, which took place at the top of the track leading down to Magbeni. The West Side Boys arrived fully armed and in large numbers. The Royal Irish regimental sergeant major (RSM) accompanied Fordham on one of these meetings. He observed a seventeen-year-old girl soldier put down her RPG7 and walk forward to the Royal Irish Land Rovers, turn around and walk back, pacing out the range. When she reached her RPG7, she adjusted the sights and settled down with the launcher on her shoulder to cover the British vehicles.

Unseen down the track behind Lieutenant-Colonel Fordham were two officers from the Metropolitan Police Hostage and Crisis Negotiation Unit. They advised Fordham on strategy and briefed and debriefed him before and after the meetings.

Ideally, if the negotiations were successful, the standoff would be resolved and the patrol released without any need for 'direct action' – an attack to rescue the hostages. However, preliminary plans for an attack were already being made – detailed information about the WSB and their positions was needed and would be acquired through human and electronic intelligence already operating in the area.

At a meeting on 27 August, the WSB demanded the release from detention of Foday Sankoh, who they referred to as 'General Papa', along with food and medicine, in exchange for the British troops.

On 28 August, at the UN HQ in New York, Kofi Annan reported that the soldiers would be released 'in the near future'.

A day later, the RSO was allowed to leave the jungle camp accompanied by 'Brigadier' Foday Kallay, the WSB leader, to meet Lieutenant-Colonel Fordham and the hostage negotiation team at the UN base in Masiaka. The officer assured them that the Royal Irish captives were being treated well and that no one was injured. At the close of the meeting before he rejoined his comrades he secretly handed over a map of the WSB base hidden in ballpoint pen.

The situation did indeed seem to be improving when two days later, on the evening of 30 August, five of the eleven Royal Irish soldiers were released in exchange for a satellite phone and medical supplies. The remaining six soldiers, the officers and NCOs, would not be released until the other WSB demands had been met.

Lieutenant-Commander Tony Cramp, the MoD spokesman in Sierra Leone, said that the freed soldiers were 'in very good condition' and were on their way to Freetown. He added: 'They are being looked after and they are in close contact with their families and are concerned for their colleagues. They are relaxing and calming down after what happened.'

One of the young Rangers had sustained the morale of the group with his robust Irish humour. One night at Gberi Bana, as the men looked up at the stars in the black tropical night, they spotted a satellite traversing the sky. This, the young Irishman explained to the West Side Boys, was a US reconnaissance satellite keeping watch on the imprisoned patrol, and to the amazement of the WSB and the delight of his comrades, he proceeded to serenade it with a rendition of the children's ditty 'Twinkle, Twinkle, Little Star'.

In Freetown, speaking on condition of anonymity, a Foreign Office spokesman told the Associated Press that the five soldiers were released with the help of the UN, specifically the Jordanian contingent.

Colonel Jehad al-Widyan, at the Jordanian base at Magbuntuso, said that his men were now holding back in their contacts with the militia to avoid endangering the lives of the seven remaining captives (six Royal Irish soldiers and their Sierra Leone Army LO).

On Friday 1 September, *The Guardian* carried a report by journalist Chris McGreal disturbing for readers in Britain, but not one that was news to many people in Freetown. It described how 'UN peacekeepers responsible for security in the area where the West Side Boys were operating were continuing to jointly man checkpoints with them, at which civilians are robbed and abused'.

Human Rights Watch accused the UN of appeasing the gang while entire villages were depopulated as a result of civilians fleeing in fear.

At least five UN checkpoints in the Masiaka area continued to be manned by Jordanian peacekeepers while armed West Side Boys were present or in control. A taxi driver described roadblocks at which UN soldiers sat in the shade while drunken or drugged young men wielding machetes and guns robbed drivers and abused civilians: 'If you see the West Side Boys at the checkpoint it is very bad news,' he said. 'They just point their guns in your face and ask what you have in your pockets and the UN soldiers don't do anything. I don't think they could just kill you there, because that would be too much, but you know that if they want to kill you a mile down the road the UN won't do anything, because they are so friendly with these guys.'

The West Side Boys were a group that was known euphemistically in Freetown as 'self-provisioning' – they were bandits.

When the UN launched Operation Thunderbolt and sent Nigerian troops and Indian helicopter gunships to clear the WSB from the road and press them to demobilise, some in the UN believed that the gang were tipped off that the attack was coming and withdrew to a safe area.

'I do not think collaboration is too strong a word to describe what is happening,' said a UN official who regularly drove the road to visit refugees. 'The Jordanians,' he asserted, 'are feeding those guys and socialising with them without thinking that these are the same ones who are killing people and raping girls. Some of us have commented on this inside the UN and said we can't just have our soldiers stand by and let it happen, but we are told that we have to build confidence so [that] they give up their guns and join the demobilisation process.'

Pressed by journalists in Freetown, UN spokesman Lieutenant-Commander Patrick Coker declined to comment beyond saying: 'It's not true.'

'Even the British have had close contact with the group in recent months,' wrote McGreal. He added that when the war flared up again in May, the British were so keen to find troops to defend the government that the West Side Boys were supplied with ammunition, food and medicines.

During a crucial battle at Rogberi Junction earlier in the year, a British lieutenant-colonel was reported to have directed the West Side Boys' attack on the rebels. (There were also unconfirmed reports of British Special Forces working with the WSB during this period.) However, relations soured as the renegades showed little enthusiasm for putting themselves under the direct command of the government's new army.

In June, West Side Boys had turned their guns on government troops during a battle for another town, Lunsar. The dispute was about the inflated ranks they had awarded themselves while living in the bush.

The five freed Royal Irish Regiment soldiers were flown to RFA *Sir Percivale* in Freetown for a detailed debriefing, during which they would be asked to explain how their convoy was captured and where the remaining members of the group were being held.

'They've got some serious questions to answer,' said Tony Cramp.

The soldiers described how Kallay had visited the group every day, repeatedly demanding to know why they had driven to his camp. He shouted at them, 'Explain your mission or I will shoot you!'

Several days after their capture, according to the WSB leader's chief bodyguard 'Corporal Blood' in an interview following his surrender to UNAMSIL after Operation Barras, Kallay, perhaps on a cocaine-induced paranoid low, appeared to have decided he had had enough. Six soldiers were marched to the Dead Zone and tied to wooden poles about a metre apart. The bodyguards lined up, stony-faced, pointing their AK-47 assault rifles at the captives, and awaited the order to fire.

According to 'Corporal Blood', as the rest of the Britons fell silent, the patrol commander, Major Alan Marshall, tried to reason with Kallay, who was shouting: 'I will kill you! I will kill you!'

'Even when he was tied to the stake, the major continued to speak to Kallay,' 'Corporal Blood' said. 'He was very cool. He told Kallay, "We just came to see you, to tell you to forget fighting. We did not come with any bad intentions. If you kill us, it will not be for any reason."'

The threats continued for half an hour; then Kallay relented and ordered the men back to their hut in the main camp.

Having survived Operation Thunderbolt and emboldened now by their notoriety, the WSB had returned to the main highway heading inland from Freetown towards Masiaka – a stretch of road where they had previously conducted a campaign of kidnapping, extortion and rape against passing civilians. Locals feared a fresh campaign of robbery and harassment.

Colonel Jehad al-Widyan said, 'We don't want to say anything to the West Side Boys or take any action against them because of the safety of the hostages. This incident has lifted their spirits and they have come back to the road.'

Within a few days, as the result of an almost accidental encounter with the Royal Irish patrol, the West Side Boys had become the lead news item in the UK media. They had started out with no political agenda, but now it had become exhilarating for them to be able to make demands of the British negotiators and have them fulfilled. This was a long way from stopping trucks and cars at random and robbing the passengers. It was little wonder that the youthful, aggressive and intoxicated young rebels had affected exotic names and ranks like 'Colonel Savage' and 'Colonel Terminator', while their spokesman in dealings with the British styled himself 'Colonel Cambodia'.

Titles, insignia and exotic names carry considerable weight in Africa. Idi Amin, the ruthless Ugandan dictator who seized power in a coup in 1971, took delight in wearing grandiose uniforms and awarding himself medals, including one he called the Victory Cross – which was, of course, his version of the Victoria Cross.

For the British negotiating team in Sierra Leone, the drug habits of the WSB made them particularly difficult to work with. They were adolescents with guns and attitude, and this already dangerous combination was compounded by the effects of excessive use of cannabis, which produces short-term-memory loss as well as mild paranoia. A course of action that might have been agreed with negotiators would have been forgotten by 'Colonel Cambodia' and the WSB within twenty-four hours. If cocaine was used by the WSB, its after-effects could have made them even more paranoid and forgetful.

The West Side Boys described the hostages as 'very comfortable', but British staff in Freetown now knew from the released soldiers that Major Marshall (at that time unnamed in reports) had been beaten by his captors. It would later emerge that the Sierra Leone Army liaison officer (LO) had suffered an even more severe assault. A desire to keep the emotional temperature in the negotiations as low as possible was probably the reason why the abuses that the soldiers were suffering were not publicised.

Soon after he had received the satellite phone in exchange for the first five released hostages, 'Colonel Cambodia' realised that he had a wider audience than a military radio net and called up the BBC African Service. He said that the hostages had been taken in order to get Britain to pressure President Kabbah to recognise the WSB as a legitimate group, to free their arrested leaders from prison and to form a new government with seats for their leaders.

'Colonel Cambodia' explained that the group had now fallen out with 'J. P.' Koroma, who had expressed support for President Kabbah. He said that they distrusted the government and would not disarm until their demands were met. 'We won't give up until we revisit the Lomé Peace Accord. That is the first one, and then secondly, they have to release all the AFRC detainees including our wives, our children and our brothers. Only we need an interim government. In fact, the AFRC has got a new leader. No more J. P. [Johnny Paul Koroma] because J. P. betrayed us. Now we have got another AFRC representative or a leader here, who is Brigadier-General F. Kallay.'

'Colonel Cambodia' said that the WSB had participated in the 1997 coup: 'We took over the government from Kabbah.' He said that his group had been excluded from the 1999 Lomé Peace Accord, which was signed by Mr Kabbah and RUF leader Foday Sankoh. For this reason, 'Colonel Cambodia' reiterated, the Lomé Accord must be 'revisited', and the WSB were holding the soldiers hostage as a means of securing negotiations with the government.

In a rambling interview, he repeated, 'We are holding on to them so that we'll be able to pass our requests through them to the government because the government is a government against the West Side Boys. We will hold on to them until our demands are solved.' These demands included the release of 'Brigadier Bomb Blast' and AFRC commander Santigie Kanu, whose *nom de guerre* was 'Brigadier 55', who were being held in gaol in Freetown.

In May, 'Bomb Blast' was among a group arrested after a shooting incident; he was later released, after it appeared that he had been falsely accused. In early June, he was arrested after he was involved in a fire fight with 'Brigadier 55' during which a UN soldier was reported to have been injured. The fight was believed to have started over a four-wheel-drive vehicle belonging to Foday Sankoh, which the WSB stole about the time that Sankoh temporarily went into hiding in May.

When asked by the BBC African Service how the West Side Boys came to capture the soldiers, 'Colonel Cambodia' replied grandly: 'We captured these soldiers because they entered into our area of responsibility without communicating with us or our commanders.'

The WSB would soon exhaust the batteries in the satellite phone, but as Richard Connaughton notes in *Small Wars and Insurgencies*, 'This telephone might have proved his [Kallay's] Trojan horse because, through the process of signal interception, the precise location of the bandits could be verified.' Electronic warfare specialists from the Royal Corps of Signals and possibly GCHQ Cheltenham not only located the position of the telephone, but after the broadcast to the BBC were able to switch it on and off remotely.

Following the seizure of the Royal Irish patrol, Freetown journalist Winston Ojokutu Macauley castigated the UK and Sierra Leonean governments, saying that they were 'dragging their feet' in resolving the situation in the country. Only a few months earlier, he asserted, the West Side Boys had shown no signs of following any sort of political agenda. Now enjoying international publicity, the group was making a mixture of unrealistic high-flown political demands and drawing up a shopping list of how much they could grab as ransom payments.

However, for the WSB, the seizure of the Royal Irish patrol held the seeds of the gang's destruction. By holding the soldiers hostage, the WSB had something with which to bargain. If they released the soldiers, however, the WSB would lose their leverage. The implied threat that the WSB would execute their captives kept up the pressure in the negotiations – but if they did kill the soldiers, it would guarantee the destruction of the gang in a retaliatory attack. However, the longer the WSB held the hostages, the greater the chance that a rescue mission would be launched and Kallay and the gang would be destroyed – becoming the victims of their own hubris.

As part of the negotiations, Johnny Paul Koroma wrote twice to the WSB, sending letters to them via the local Jordanian UNAMSIL troops. In his second letter, he urged the gang to release the soldiers. 'The continuing holding of people coming to Sierra Leone to assist in the peace process does not augur well. I therefore ask you that, as in the earlier the better, you free the British soldiers.'

The contacts continued between Lieutenant-Colonel Fordham and Kallay. Sierra Leone's minister of information, the tough but bookish Dr Julius Spencer, said that the government 'would not bow to this kind of pressure' by meeting the captors' demands. In Freetown, the population now looked away or at the ground as British Army Land Rovers drove by. The WSB had humiliated the British Army, the one force that the Sierra Leoneans had hoped would bring stability and security to their country.

British officials in London insisted on Thursday 31 August that negotiations were still the best course. However, they described the situation as becoming 'delicate' and 'volatile'.

On the same day that these cautious comments were being made, a message reached the 1 Para Battalion HQ at Connaught Barracks in Dover (where 1 Para had moved from what had been the Parachute Regiment's former 'home' in Aldershot) to ring Director Special Forces (DSF). At the same time, Captain Liam Cradden, the battalion's operations officer, had been informed that there was a drama in Sierra Leone and that 1 Para might soon be involved. The requirement was for a company group to support Special Forces, to be ready to move as soon as possible.

At the time, the battalion was on no formal notice to move; they had been moved out of 16 Brigade and were 'out of role' in 2 South East Brigade, a regional brigade with no operational role except for an upcoming Northern Ireland tour at the end of the year. Many officers were still unpacking kit and possessions from their military freight organisation (MFO) boxes – those enormously versatile collapsible plywood boxes that absorb books, kit and clothing.

A Company, commanded by Major Mathew (Mat) Lowe, was selected by the shrewd and experienced CO because he knew they were jungle-trained, particularly in field firing during Exercise Red Stripe in Jamaica. In addition, some of their NCOs had been on Operation Palliser and Lowe was, quite simply, the best man for the job.

When Lowe attended his first briefing at JTFHQ, he learned that he would be required to assemble a force of between 120 and 140 men. Their mission was still undefined but would be part of the hostage-rescue operation. What they would be required to do within this operation was still being addressed by the JTFHQ. In fact, at this stage the Special Forces planning group had no defined role for the company group but knew that the numbers and fire power might be useful.

Lowe worked out the structure of the company group, which would consist of the basic Company HQ and three Rifle Platoons, who would carry two L7A2 7.62 mm general-purpose machine guns (GPMGs) per section. Though the 11.65 kg GPMG is a heavier weapon than the magazine-fed light support weapon (LSW), Major Lowe felt that the ability of the belt-fed GPMG to deliver sustained fire made it better for the action that he anticipated the company would be fighting. The gun has a cyclic rate of fire of between 650 and 1,000 rounds per minute, so a platoon would be capable of delivering between 3,900 and 6,000 rounds per minute on to a target. It was with a similar weapon that former SAS soldier Will Scully had defended the Mammy Yoko Hotel in Freetown in 1997.

Pegasus recorded that the company was receiving 'a reassuringly large amount of ammunition . . . each platoon holding roughly 6,500 rounds of 5.56 ball, 6,000 rounds of 7.62 mm 4Bit, 170 grenades (L2 HE and red phosphorus smoke) and 50 bombs for the 51 mm mortar'.

The company group was configured to give Lowe the fire power to 'find and fix' the enemy – in other words, to tie down the WSB and neutralise them while the SAS extracted the hostages. Though he would assemble specialist units from within 1 Para to reinforce A Company, Lowe did not 'cherry pick' individual soldiers from other companies within the battalion because, as a company, the soldiers of A Company knew each other. They were already configured in a Northern Ireland Order of Battle (OrBat) and Captain Danny Matthews was second in command (2 IC). The ten new recruits, two weeks out of the Infantry Training Centre at Catterick in Yorkshire, remained in the company on the grounds that, as one Para put it, 'If you're good enough to join the Battalion you're good enough to go on ops . . .'

The CO also avoided destroying the coherence of the rest of the battalion by trying to 'pack' A Company with extra talent, just in case there was a requirement subsequently to deploy another company or even the whole battalion. As a result, Lowe had a very young company with an average age of about nineteen. The young men of A Company would be up against an armed gang consisting of men and women of a largely similar average age.

Valuable sub-units and formations from within the battalion were attached to the company. They might not all be deployed in the initial attack but could be flown in to reinforce the company when it was on the ground. Most of them were veterans of Operation Palliser, and if the operation expanded, an infrastructure would be in place to support further reinforcement.

The assets attached to A Company included the Patrols Platoon consisting of the HQ and three patrols, a Signals Group consisting of the main station, a tactical patrol on foot and the LO's, whose radio operators would be in contact with Special Forces and the helicopters. Accurate long-range fire would be delivered by two sniper pairs equipped with the L115A1 long-range rifle. There would be four three-man HMG sections with the Browning 12.7 mm machine gun mounted on WIMKs. The Mortar Section would give the company effective indirect fire with its HQ and three 81 mm L16 mortars, with a maximum range of 5,800 m firing HE bombs. The Regimental Medical Officer (RMO) Captain Reece Thomas was attached to the expanded Company Aid Post, making it virtually equivalent to the Regimental Aid Post and, finally, the Echelon Element was commanded by Technical Quartermaster (QM(T)) Pete Lodge, who had played a key role in Operation Palliser.

Writing in *Pegasus* at the end of 2000, the Quartermaster's Department would, with justified pride, describe their role in both Palliser and Barras. 'At the end of Ops we closed down locations and withdrew troops and stores, maintaining excellent managerial control of operational equipment and ammunition, making closure of accounts very easy. At the time of writing, QM(T) Pete Lodge and Regimental Quartermaster Sergeant (Tech) RQMS(T) WO2 Brian McVitie are the last men out of the most recent headline-grating escapade. So the REMF's [see Glossary] have done it again!'

Recalling the 1 Para QM Department, one officer, laughing at the description REMF, remarked, 'They were always well respected and we were always glad to see them.' The invaluable RQMS(T) McVitie would end up running the critical forward operating base at Dakar for Operation Barras.

The ammunition for the company group was ordered on the same day that the structure of the company group was drawn up. Since there would be no threat from armoured vehicles, the company would only carry the 66 mm LAW – an anti-tank weapon that, although obsolescent, would be very effective against buildings and bunkers[1]. Some soldiers were equipped with the rifle grenade general service (RGGS), while others would carry, slung across their shoulders, the compact haversacks containing the M18A1 Claymore directional anti-personnel (AP) mines[2]. The mines would be used to secure the perimeter against WSB counterattacks once the village had been cleared.

On Thursday 31 August, a prepared cover story was issued that the company was on standby to reinforce the UK Spearhead Infantry battalion, the 1st Battalion Grenadier Guards, a force held on standby for quick-reaction operations. The company would move to South Cerney in Wiltshire for a 'readiness to move' exercise with the Grenadier Guards.

As the Spearhead battalion, the Grenadier Guards were officially the formation that would have provided the troops for the operation. It has also been suggested that the Royal Irish, who were familiar with Sierra Leone, might justifiably have felt a debt of honour to rescue their own and might have been tasked.

The Parachute Regiment is the closest thing that the British Army has to 'shock troops'. Many who have passed 'P Company', the gruelling tests of courage and stamina required to enter 'Para Reg', have after time with the Parachute Regiment gone on to face the even tougher challenge of selection for the SAS. When they met up at the beginning of the operation, men from A Company found old friends in D Squadron SAS.

From the comfort of their armchairs, it is easy for critics to argue that selecting the Parachute Regiment for the mission reinforced an attitude that infantry in the British Army were now a 'two-tier army', encapsulated in the phrase 'the Infantry and the Fuckin' Paras'. Such critics would assert that almost any well-trained and -led airmobile infantry company could have undertaken Operation Barras. Warming to their argument, they would cite history, pointing to the example of Major-General Orde Wingate's Long-Range Penetration Force, better known as the Chindits. This force was not composed of hand-picked men but of ordinary soldiers. In 1942, the first Chindit operation was undertaken by the 77th Indian Infantry Brigade, and the second in 1944 by the 3rd Indian Division. In both the brigade and the division, British, Burmese and Gurkha soldiers demonstrated extraordinary stamina and courage fighting behind Japanese lines in Burma. Though these ordinary soldiers may have achieved extraordinary results, the armchair strategists forget how hard they had trained for this role before they were committed to Burma.

In August 2000, it was possibly the Director Special Forces (DSF) who pressed for the use of 'Para Reg'. The Parachute Regiment had exercised with 'The Regiment', as the SAS is known colloquially, and had been used as backup for Special Forces in other operations. They are consistently well trained and motivated and had experience in air-assault operations.

'To be fair,' commented one airborne veteran, 'you cannot have an organisation which carries out an additional level of selection and one that specialises in light airborne and heliborne operations and then pretend it is the same as the line infantry. Barras was tailor-made for a Para Company.'

In the summer of 1942, Martin Lindsay, a young officer with 1st Battalion The Gordon Highlanders, visited Lieutenant-Colonel Lord Lovat's No. 4 Commando at Troon. Lindsay wanted to draw out the lessons learned from Operation Cauldron, the successful attack on a German battery at Dieppe. From his interviews, he produced the excellent training pamphlet *Notes from Theatres of War, No. 11*.

Writing in the RUSI Journal (a bi-monthly publication from the Royal United Services Institute for Defence and Security Studies) many years after the war, the now Sir Martin Lindsay of Downhill, CBE DSO and a veteran of the war in North-West Europe remarked that in 1942–43 the pamphlet was 'ill-received by many regimental officers who considered that they and their battalions could have carried out this action no less successfully...' Commenting on these attitudes, Lindsay wrote, 'A CO with the necessary competence for such a specialised operation was much more likely to emerge, and be a more confident choice, from units which had been continually training in assault techniques... Such units could themselves be expected to be ready at fairly short notice.' Thus, the notion of two-tier infantry is by no means a new – or necessarily undesirable –one.

Over fifty years after Operation Cauldron, the silence of total concentration descended in the operational mounting centre (OMC) at South Cerney in the late summer of 2000 when Major Lowe stood in front of A Company 1 Para.

They were not on exercise, he explained. This was an operational deployment.

The initial briefing for A Company group's part in the rescue mission was held in the suite of contingency planning offices adjoining one of the hangars at the OMC. The 1 Para intelligence officer (IO) had come directly from the PJHQ to describe to the company the situation on the ground and what was known of the enemy.

Major Lowe had identified a planning group that consisted of himself, the three platoon commanders, operations officer (G3) and intelligence team (G2), a clerk and a signaller. He had with him a folder that listed all elements of the company group which, he recalled after the operation, would 'prove invaluable'.

Commanding a Chindit column in Burma in 1944 in World War II, Brigadier Mike Calvert had used a similar approach. Under the pressure of operations, he explained, it was sometimes easy for a commander to forget what weapons or resources were available. A quick glance at his list would sometimes throw up tactical applications for weapons that might not initially have seemed obvious.

Working through the night of 31 August, Battalion Operations Officer Captain Liam Cradden and Intelligence Officer (IO) Captain Adam Jowett had produced just such an *aide-mémoire*. Issued to all the men at the OMC, it contained details of the low-level lessons that had been learned by the battalion during Operation Palliser. It covered basic administration and cautions about hydration as well as background information on the country and people of Sierra Leone. In quiet moments at South Cerney, the 'Toms' stretched out and leafed through this informative document.

Company Sergeant Major Chiswell also worked through the night breaking down the stores and distributing them to the soldiers. At this stage, it was not known how much time and space the company would have for battle preparations once in Africa. The soldiers had already updated their inoculations, been issued Lariam and prepared their equipment for a jungle deployment. Next-of-kin (NOK) forms were updated – these gave details of the close relative who was to be contacted if the soldier became a casualty, normally a wife, sibling or parent. The two identity discs on their metal chains were checked – these gave details of the soldier's name, blood group, religion and service number. To ensure that there was no accidental breach of security, all mobile phones had been collected. The company group, backed by all the resources that the battalion could provide, was resolved and focused.

The planning group flew to Dakar on the morning of Sunday 3 September. In Dakar, the intelligence that had been gathered by SAS patrols already operating around the WSB bases was studied, along with maps and photographs of the area.

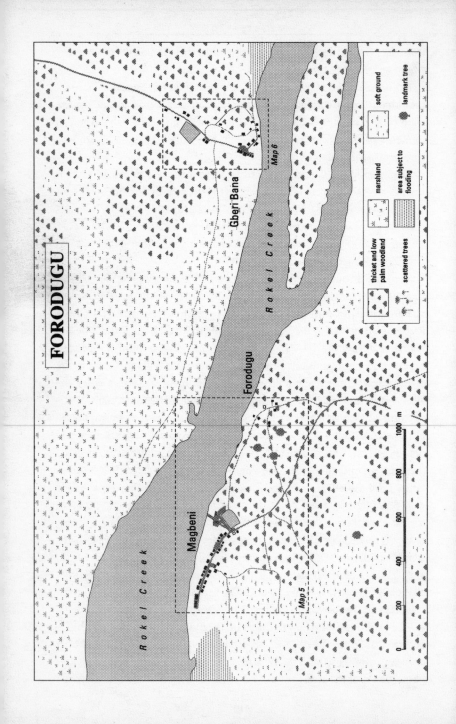

FORODUGU

Rokel Creek

Gberi Bana

Map 6

Forodugu

Magbeni

Map 5

Rokel Creek

Rokel Creek

thicket and low
palm woodland

scattered trees

marshland

area subject to
flooding

soft ground

landmark tree

0   200   400   600   800   1000 m

Peter Penfold (second from right), the British High Commissioner in Sierra Leone, who would play a crucial part in the evacuation of foreign nationals in 1997 and in the efforts to assist in the restoration of the legitimate government of President Kabbah.

All photographs are from the Fleet Photographic Unit unless otherwise credited

Major Alan Harrison, an UNMO with UNAMSIL, returns to safety in Freetown on 15 July 2000 following his extraction by RAF Chinook from Kailahun, a besieged United Nations base in the interior of Sierra Leone.
UK Land Command

Above Local people watch a 1 Para vehicle patrol. The Land Rover WMIK in the foreground mounts two machine guns, a 12.7 mm Browning HMG and a 7.62 mm GPMG in addition to the crew's weapons. *UK Land Command*

Opposite page top An exhausted Sudanese family await evacuation in May 2000. It appeared to many that but for the British intervention the RUF would again overrun Freetown. In the background is a UN Mil Mi-14 helicopter that has shuttled evacuees from Freetown to Lungi. *UK Land Command*

Opposite page bottom Corporal Bob Morgan D Company 2 Para with UN transport near Freetown. In addition to his SA80 rifle he has attached to his webbing an L2 fragmentation grenade, a smoke grenade and a radio. *UK Land Command*

The sweet taste of an individual boil-in-a-bag 24-hour ration pack pudding finds favour with a Sierra Leone youngster as a 1 Para patrol prepares a meal during Operation Palliser.
UK Land Command

Lance Corporal Nicky McDougall (RMP), serving with 16 Air Assault, cradles a child during the Operation Palliser evacuation.
UK Land Command

As 1 Para hands over to the Royal Marines, Patrols Platoon move out, bowed under the weight of their Bergans and carrying their weapons, they board an RAF Chinook at Lungi airport. UNAMSIL helicopters are parked in the background. *UK Land Command*

A Royal Navy Sea Harrier F/A2 flies an air presence mission over Freetown harbour during Operation Palliser. The grid layout of the streets can be seen with St George's Cathedral just below the aircraft.

A Royal Marine patrol from 42 Commando liaises with Kenyan UNAMSIL soldiers from KENBAT near Lungi in June 2000. Untrammelled by the rules of engagement that restricted UN operations, the British presence helped to restore confidence in Sierra Leone.

With Brigadier Richards on his right and Lt Colonel Andy Salmon on his left, Foreign Secretary Robin Cook strides along Mahera beach accompanied by camera crews and a close protection team on 8 June.

Military police from the Sierra Leone Army mount guard at the Recruit Processing Centre set up at Cockerill Barracks. They are armed with British-supplied SLR rifles and a former Soviet Bloc AK-47 and RPD light machine gun.

Having passed their medical examinations and tests, recruits at the Benguema Training Camp (BTC) roll over the top of an obstacle and double away under supervision by SLA physical training instructors.

Male and female recruits strike a determined pose during a break in training at BTC. British instructors were impressed by the enthusiasm of the soldiers, but never managed to teach conventional parade ground drill. *Author's collection*

Opposite page top Deputy Prime Minister John Prescott inspects a guard of honour at BTC. In the background are the Commander in Chief of the Sierra Leone Army and Brigadier Gordon Hughes, the commander of British Army training teams in Sierra Leone.

Opposite page bottom President Ahmad Tejan Kabbah of Sierra Leone, a polished veteran diplomat, visits HMS *Cornwall* and greets Captain Anthony Dymock. The President would give Operation Barras his complete backing in September 2000.

A Light Infantry vehicle patrol with a WMIK and soft-skin Land Rover approach a simple road block in the interior of Sierra Leone. Patrols like this helped to sustain confidence within the civilian population. *UK Land Command*

With none of the lines of a warship, RFA *Sir Percivale* or 'Percy', the support ship based in Freetown, nevertheless played an important part in Barras and in the weeks leading up to the operation.

Opposite page An RAF Chinook lands on the deck of HMS *Ocean*. The Chinook pilots with the Special Forces Flight inserted A Company 1 Para and D Squadron 22 SAS into difficult landing zones during the rescue operation.

A British Army Air Corps Lynx attack helicopter hovers near an Ilyushin transport operating with UNAMSIL at Lungi airport. Fitted with night vision sights the Lynx would provide accurate fire during Barras. *UK Land Command*

Mute testimony to the ferocity of the fire fight at Rokel Creek at dawn on 10 September 2000, one of the Royal Irish Land Rovers recovered and returned to BTC, bullet-scarred but still in running order. *Author's collection*

The village of Magbeni was identified as the objective for the company group. On the map, it consisted of twenty-nine buildings ranged along a track running parallel to Rokel Creek. Since the inhabitants had been driven out by the WSB, many of the buildings had collapsed and the jungle had encroached on the little vegetable gardens. Some of the more substantial buildings were still standing, from which it would be possible to mount an effective defence. For planning purposes, these buildings were identified by letters from the phonetic alphabet from T – Tango to Z – Zulu and the platoons tasked with clusters of buildings as their objectives. The jungle vegetation, including two-metre-high elephant grass, grew close to the central track and, like some of the buildings, offered cover for both the Paras and the WSB.

A steady stream of high-grade intelligence coming in from the SAS patrol south of the creek included information that some buildings held civilians; therefore the plan had to be modified and updated. A restricted fire line (RFL) was established so that the company could advance safely, supported by direct and indirect fire.

The major threat to any attack was a heavy machine gun (HMG) in the village that could engage helicopters landing near Magbeni or across the river at Gberi Bana. However, the HMG position was screened by buildings and jungle vegetation and it was decided that it would have to be destroyed by the Lynx attack helicopters at the beginning of the operation, using its M3M pintle-mounted 12.7 mm HMG. The plan called for the Lynx to operate in darkness at low level with the crew using night-vision goggles, hitting targets like the vehicles that were a potential threat to the Paras. The attack helicopters would engage any craft that attempted to cross Rokel Creek and any people who appeared on the banks, since friendly forces would not be in this area at that point in the operation.

At some stage in the planning process, Lowe was given the mission to 'defeat' the forces in the village. This was significant because had the company been told they were to 'destroy' the WSB in Magbeni, the gang would have suffered heavier casualties, since fewer would have been given the opportunity to run away or hide. Eventually, when the attack was underway, the West Side Boys would be defeated by a combination of Lynx attack helicopters neutralising vehicles and heavy weapons and the company sweeping through the village.

Within the planning group, there was discussion about the company's role and how the troops might be inserted. They might attack overland using vehicles like WMIK Land Rovers, Pinzgauer Turbo D (4 x 4) trucks or even, it was suggested, on quad bikes for a fast approach. However, since RAF CH47 Chinooks were in-country, as the mission became clearer an air assault seemed the best and most reliable option.

One practical mobility consideration was footwear. The men would be issued with tropical uniforms, but it was decided that since the operation was not likely to last long, they would not receive new jungle boots, which would need to be broken in and might produce blisters. Some of the younger Paras opted to wear their temperate-issue leather combat boots, while veterans of Operation Palliser and those who had participated in Exercise Red Stripe located their old jungle boots.

Despite strict operational security (OpSec) within the company group and battalion, the possibility that a rescue operation might be mounted had already filtered out to the public. HQ LAND Command had been designated the supporting headquarters. In the words of one officer, 'It started sending signals all over the place (many of them totally unnecessary) and so from the outset the deployment of the Paras was in the public domain.' Signals went to other Spearhead units about the upcoming operation that even identified the size of the formation and its role in a hostage-rescue operation.

Whether this information was leaked by accident or released deliberately as part of a negotiating ploy to be fed into the Freetown rumour mill is hard to say, but soon the British newspapers were carrying stories linking the Parachute Regiment and Sierra Leone. On Tuesday 5 September, *The Guardian* ran the headline 'Paratroopers Fly Out to West Africa as "Contingency"', beneath which the article began: 'Soldiers from the elite Parachute Regiment tonight flew out to west Africa as a "contingency", as efforts continued to free six British soldiers being held hostage in Sierra Leone, defence sources in London said . . .'

A day later, the Sierra Leone Press reported that a contingent of British paratroopers had arrived in Freetown, even as negotiators continued talks with the West Side Boys.

If the story was intended to be a piece of psychological warfare, it did not appear to have impressed the WSB. Some soldiers have said since that the low-key negotiating style employed by Lieutenant-Colonel Fordham's team convinced the WSB that they were dealing with weak people they could bully. If the negotiating team had arrived in strength with men and vehicles, it would have given them the authority of overt power in the eyes of the WSB.

Asked about the deployment of the Paras, the MoD spokesman in Freetown, Tony Cramp, said on Monday 4 December: 'This in no way signifies any imminent military action in Sierra Leone. It is just a sensible contingency measure to place troops in the region.' However, for the Special Forces, the reports that the Paras were destined for Sierra Leone were a useful cover for their deployment. 'We have not ruled out any options for releasing the captives,' Cramp continued, 'but the talks are making progress and we are hopeful that this can be ended peacefully.'

However, *The Daily Telegraph*'s Phillip Sherwell, who was based in Freetown, made some perceptive and accurate connections when he wrote:

The deployment of the paratroopers, who will wait in the Senegalese capital, Dakar, is intended to intensify pressure on the West Side Boys militia to free their captives. However, the decision to send the troops to Senegal reflects concerns about provoking a dangerous response from a temperamental militia with a reputation for brutality and banditry.

Dakar is about 500 miles, or three hours' flying time by Hercules, north of Sierra Leone. The new arrivals from the 1st Parachute Battalion are familiar with the terrain as they formed part of the first wave of British troops sent to the troubled former colony when rebels advanced on Freetown in May.

They will provide an obvious back-up for any Special Forces rescue mission.

He was right: although the Paras were an overt presence, Operation Barras was, after all, a Special Forces operation. The brigadier who was Director Special Forces (DSF), along with his small JTFHQ including CO 22 SAS and OC D Squadron, was in place in Hastings with radio links to the patrols on the ground around the WSB camps. DSF was in communication upwards with the MoD's Permanent Joint Headquarters (PJHQ) and the Cabinet Office Briefing Room (COBR), known informally by the nickname 'Cobra'. COBR is an *ad hoc* group formed by the British government to handle crises and emergencies; it is chaired by a senior minister, with junior defence and foreign affairs ministers and advisers representing the police, MI5, MI6 and the SAS. The public first became aware of its existence during Operation Nimrod, the SAS operation to liberate hostages being held by Iraqi-backed terrorists in the Iranian Embassy at Princess Gate on 5 May 1980. During Barras, the DSF would probably have been represented by his chief of staff. While the PJHQ would provide the support, it would be COBR that would take the decision whether or not to launch the operation in Sierra Leone.

A year after Barras, Richard Connaughton wrote in *Small Wars and Insurgencies* that, 'The tactical commander was almost certainly SF [Special Forces] who would have taken a significant number of his regimental officers with him. SF have a strong family bond, trusting only those whom they know and respect. There was an obvious requirement for a quasi-operational level headquarters, probably at Freetown, with channels open to PJHQ. Command of this HQ was self-selected.'

Almost from the outset of the hostage crisis, the SAS had two four-man patrols on the ground. They had been inserted from Rokel Creek by assault boat, handled expertly by a Special Boat Service (SBS) coxswain. Once in position on either side of the creek, the patrols remained hidden by day and at night infiltrated through the thick bush to monitor the movements around the WSB base positions, identify weapons and log the routine in the two camps either side of the creek. They were also tasked with identifying viable helicopter landing sites.

A few hundred metres away from Magbeni on the north side of the creek, at the end of a 4.5 km track leading from a palm oil plantation, was the cluster of huts that made up Gberi Bana. In happier times, it had been the north bank landing site for the ferry from Magbeni. Among the buildings near the road were five low mud-and-cement buildings. The dense vegetation on this side of the creek allowed the SAS patrol to move close to the buildings and identify the one that housed the British captives and the building next to it, which contained seventeen Sierra Leonean civilians kidnapped a week earlier. The other three were home to Kallay and his senior commanders.

The terrain that made this location difficult to reconnoitre and attack also made it an ideal prison. Escape on foot would only be possible to the north, but while the scrub might offer cover, there were also treacherous fingers of swampy ground running inland from the creek. With escape virtually impossible, the men of the Royal Irish had by now probably privately resigned themselves to death.

The SAS teams had concealed themselves in swamps that were in places less than 250 m from Gberi Bana. However, cover was sparse on the south side of the creek and this restricted their operations. For both patrols, it would be a test of stamina and character: surviving on the cold rations and water they had brought into their hides, they endured attacks by the diverse insect life around the river. In addition, there was the constant threat of chance discovery by the children of the Small Boys Unit (SBU) roaming the area.

This is a very demanding type of soldiering that demands a very special type of soldier.

The patrols' radio operators used burst transmission and a satellite link to send back their intelligence summaries. To save time and battery life, some of this information would have been formatted into standard operating procedures (SOPs) and sent as a simple alphanumeric code. Popular newspapers, television and films are fascinated by the idea of Special Forces soldiers going into action with a dazzling armoury of high-tech equipment. The reality was probably very different, with the two patrols relying to a large extent on their eyes, ears and even their sense of smell to gather intelligence.

Though small, the four-man patrol allows two men to be on watch while two rest and in this way surveillance can for a reasonable period be undertaken round the clock.

The hides in which they laid up during the day could have been configured in a variety ways, but most common are the 'star', 'pairs' or 'top-to-tail' configurations. The 'star' is a cruciform layout with a sentry on one arm, an observer on the other, a rest bay where one man can sleep and a rest bay where a team member can prepare food or carry out his personal administration. The 'pair' configuration has the observer and sentry side by side, Bergans and kit in a central well and the rest and administration area to the rear. 'Top-to-tail' has the sleep and administration area in the centre and the observers at either end.

In a basic observation post (OP), the sentry and radio operator/ observer maintain the watch, swapping roles roughly every twenty minutes to reduce fatigue. The third man sleeps or attends to his administration, while the fourth acts as the rear sentry. The members of the party rotate anticlockwise through the positions at hourly intervals.

On a given signal, the observer wakes the sleeper and moves under a poncho liner. The sleeper moves on to sentry duty, while the sentry takes over the radio operator/observer's position. The radio operator passes across the headset and moves on to the observation position. No equipment or weapons are moved during the changeover of personnel.

One of the four Bergan rucksacks carried by the team would hold the radio and battery as well as personal kit. All Bergans would have rations and fresh water. The other three would hold surveillance devices like binoculars, tape recorder, CWS image-intensification sights or thermal imaging equipment and spare clothes and a poncho liner.

The patrols estimated there were about 50 to 100 WSB in each village camp and among the weapons that had been identified were the twin ZPU-2 14.5 mm that had blocked the Royal Irish patrol. In addition they had 60 mm and 81 mm mortars, RPGs, Kalishnikovs, medium machine guns (MMGs), anti-personnel mines and grenades. In Magbeni, besides the Bedford 4-tonne captured from the SLA, they had pick-up trucks mounting machine guns bolted to the cargo floor. These had been dubbed 'Technicals' after the name first used by the armed clans in Somalia in the 1990s.

Unlike the battered Somali vehicles, the Sierra Leone 'Technicals' were often highly decorated. Earlier in the year during Operation Palliser, 42 Commando had been visited by a WSB 'Technical'. With a multi-coloured 'camouflage' on the bodywork, the windscreen boasted the name 'Bomb Blast', while below the front bumper were the words 'West Side Junglers'. Rather less quaint were the armed men inside the vehicle.

The three Royal Irish Land Rovers were also located in the village. These vehicles, combined with the weapons, gave the West Side Boys mobility and fire power.

It was believed that the mortars and machine guns sited in Magbeni covering the approaches from the south would also be able to engage targets in Gberi Bana across Rokel Creek. The position was defended in depth – a WSB battalion also controlled Laia Junction to the south of Magbeni. These rebels could counterattack any forces entering Magbeni and would block any overland approach.

The planning progressed in Seaview House, the British military HQ on a hillside above the High Commission in Freetown. Here, working with maps, aerial photographs and models, the DSF, OC 22 SAS, OC D Squadron and staff examined all the available options. It was a tight-knit group working on the basis that plans and intelligence were classified 'UK eyes only'.

It is only possible to surmise about the D Squadron hostage-extraction operation. It is possible that it involved two Chinooks carrying 12 fire teams who would fast-rope down at two LS close to the huts while the helicopters hovered at minimum height.

Fast-roping is a technique in which soldiers slide down ropes with only leather gloves to protect their hands and slow their descent. This method allows them to reach the ground unencumbered by karabiners or abseiling harness. The maximum number of ropes would be deployed from the rear ramp of the Chinook and up to three men would have been on a rope at the same time. The helicopter would present a fleeting target to the WSB, just visible through the fronds of the palm trees. The men would probably land in LS1 and LS2 the open areas near the huts. The four-man patrols on the ground would simultaneously be engaging any WSB who might attempt to shoot at the helicopter or kill the hostages. The pre-dawn timing of the attack made it likely that the WSB would be sleeping and that the hostages would be concentrated in one location.

As they held off the WSB and grabbed the Royal Irish, a Chinook would land on LS3 the football pitch/parade ground about 150 m north of Gberi Bana, where the Royal Irish soldiers would be picked up and flown out to *Sir Percivale*. At an early stage in the discussions regarding the rescue operation, COBR had been in complete agreement that Lieutenant Bangura, the SLA LO, would be regarded as part of the British group and his evacuation given the same priority as that of the Royal Irish.

Any prisoners, the Sierra Leonean hostages and the SAS teams would be picked up by the Chinook. It would probably have a small force on board who would secure the LS, as well as a medical team who would begin treating and stabilising any casualties. If it came under fire while landing at the football pitch, the helicopter crew would suppress it with the helicopter's miniguns.

It has been estimated that a total number of twenty-five SAS men were included in the force deployed at Gberi Bana. While conventionally Special Forces rely on stealth and speed, on both sides of Rokel Creek the Paras and SAS would put in attacks that, in the words favoured by US military theorists, would deliver 'shock and awe' to the West Side Boys.

The SAS team had sixty seconds to complete their rescue mission. After that, the shock of the assault would be over and the WSB would be expected to fight back.

An advantage for the SAS team would be that the officers and NCOs in the Royal Irish would be a disciplined group, quick to respond to orders and instructions. The unknown factor would be the reactions of the Sierra Leonean captives and also whether WSB would attempt to hide among them. As a precaution, everyone who was alive – except the recognisable British soldiers – would be secured with plasticuffs before they were flown out. They would then be delivered to the JordBat location where WSB could be identified and separated from the hostages.

As the plans were finalised, the soldiers of A Company 1 Para at the Hastings Battle Camp, some 48 km south of Freetown, concentrating on platoon and company live firing and training were isolated from these reports. The platoon commanders had laid out an exact scale representation of their objectives in the 200 m strip village of Magbeni and walked and talked their soldiers through the attack. Live firing exercises sharpened their tactical skills in an area that contained field firing ranges and consequently heard the sound of gunfire daily.

As the media began to speculate about a possible rescue operation, the MoD had sent an encrypted signal to the captain of the RFA *Argus* (A 135), which had left British waters to support an exercise off Turkey, ordering him to head straight for Sierra Leone. Two Lynx helicopters were also taken to Dakar by a C130 Hercules and then on to Lungi. The two Lynxes and the three RAF Chinooks already in the country would later be deployed to the small airfield at Hastings Battle Camp.

The men of A Company group had not arrived in Sierra Leone as a formed group, but by platoon and sub-unit. While this was good for security, it meant that now they were in-country in an improvised base at the Hastings Battle Camp, some units had managed to get in more training than others. Section and platoon commanders concentrated on live firing and rehearsing the possible sequences of attack on their objectives. As the company rehearsed the attack, the plan took shape. It allowed the planning group to establish whether the company should fight through the village in a sequenced attack or as a simultaneous assault.

Two possible helicopter landing sites (LSs) had been identified. One, at the eastern end of Magbeni, was about 100 m by 80 m – a rough football pitch close to the ferry point. As an additional navigational reference point for the pilots, about 200 m to the south-east were three large trees that stood proud of the jungle canopy. This was designated LS1.

If the Paras landed at LS1, they would have the advantage of a shock action since they would be almost on top of the village, but they would be exposed to direct fire. If their mission was to destroy the WSB, this site would put them in position to sweep westwards, driving the gang into the dead end of the village. However, they would need two Chinooks to deliver enough troops to launch the attack. LS2, to the south-west of Magbeni, looked like a grassy area with a belt of jungle between the grass and the village. The SAS reconnaissance had revealed that the grassland was marshy, but it was still regarded as a viable LS. What clinched the choice was that A Company would initially have only one Chinook allocated to insert troops. Once these men were on the ground, the helicopter would turn around and bring in the balance of the company group. It was going to be a sequenced attack launched from LS2.

The rehearsals in the tropical heat confirmed that the Paras would need to fight carrying minimal equipment – ammunition, water and first-aid field dressings only. However, even this basic equipment – similar in concept to the 'Raiding Order' worn by Commandos in World War II – would weigh a minimum of 9 kg and many men would opt to carry more.

The soldiers would wear helmets and combat body armour – though the weight would make them sweat and consequently dehydrate, it was reckoned that the price was worth it since hopefully it would still be relatively cool during the pre-dawn attack. Prior to the operation, there was considerable debate about whether the armour should be worn since it was feared that men could become heat casualties, particularly those carrying radios and weapons like the GPMG or the 12.7 kg barrel, 11.6 kg base plate and 12.3 kg mounting of the 81 mm L16 mortar. The GPMG gunners would probably have 600 rounds of belted ammunition and their No. 2 would carry a further 200 rounds, along with rifles and magazines.

The combat body armour would give protection against 1.10 g fragments travelling at 445 m/s and hits by rifle fire at longer ranges. In the fighting that would follow, the decision to use the armour would be more than justified.

As A Company group pressed on with detailed training for its mission, in London the MoD was still unable to explain why the Royal Irish had turned off the main road so far from the BTC. The Ministry said they were surprised that the soldiers had disappeared into the bush – but they were not surprised that the men had lunched with Jordanian UN peacekeepers before the journey that ended with them being captured.

General Mohamed Garba, the Nigerian commander of UNAMSIL, said that the soldiers had failed to tell the UN about their activities and disputed the British account of the kidnapping. He agreed that the soldiers from the Royal Irish Regiment were captured while deep inside militia-held jungle, but denied that they had met the Jordanian troops.

Around this time, two SAS negotiators were reportedly sent to assist the team headed by Lieutenant-Colonel Fordham. One of them was a thirty-four-year-old sergeant with D Squadron who was also tasked with reconnaissance and intelligence gathering. In the guise of a Royal Irish Regiment major, he joined the difficult negotiating process.

According to the popular British newspaper *The Mail on Sunday*, a senior military source said: 'This sergeant is one of the top soldiers in the world. His record is astonishing. He joined the SAS from the Royal Engineers in 1990 and he is now a key member of A Squadron.' In total, the SAS sergeant made five visits during the negotiations near Magbeni.[3]

HMS *Argyll's* medical officer, Surgeon Lieutenant Jon Carty, had come ashore to join the negotiating team, to treat the remaining hostages should they be released or, if the situation deteriorated in the volatile atmosphere, to provide primary casualty care. Carty recalled, 'I was obviously very excited to be given the opportunity to put my training to use, but I soon realised how challenging this was going to be.'

Though the news was out that the Paras were in Sierra Leone, Brigadier Hughes, the commander of British Army training teams in Sierra Leone, insisted that the emphasis should still remain on the negotiations. However, Hughes, who had begun his career in the British Army with the Royal Signals, added that the use of force to end the hostage crisis was clearly an option.

The Occra Hills, the area where the hostages were being held, had been surrounded at a distance by UNAMSIL forces to prevent the West Side Boys from moving their captives. However, the press reported ominously that military sources said that a raid would not be easy given the terrain and the gang's knowledge of the area.

Pressed about the possibility of direct action, Tony Cramp said only that the Army was 'planning for every contingency'. One British newspaper noted that in addition to the STTT staff, there had been an unspecified number of SAS soldiers in Sierra Leone before the hostage crisis developed. In Freetown, newspapers like *Awoko Tok Tok, The Democrat Concord Times* and *Standard Times* began calling for action to help restore confidence in British forces.

Freetown-based journalist Foday Koroma wrote scathingly in the *Expo Times*: 'When the British soldiers fell into the hands of the West Side Boys, Britain ruled out the use of force to free them. Can somebody figure out why? Well, this is it: Britain knows that any false move will endanger the lives of their nationals. Yes, their lives are very precious. What about the ordinary Sierra Leonean that bears the brunt any time force is used against the rebels? Is his life so worthless that nobody cares a hoot what happens to him? That should not be the case.'

Emboldened by their success and new status, the WSB launched attacks against neighbouring armed groups. It was reported that they used the captured Royal Irish Land Rovers and that Kallay was dressed in a British uniform. The *Irish Examiner* gave more detail in a report on Friday 8 September: 'Members of a band of maverick fighters holding six British soldiers hostage in Sierra Leone clashed again yesterday with a pro-government militia further inland, military sources and transport officials said.'

BBC correspondent Lansana Fofana reported that the fighting between the WSB and members of the Gbethis and Kapras – pro-government militias which formed part of the Civil Defence Force – lasted for an hour and took place on the highway between Masiaka and Mile 91. Reuters quoted military sources as saying that fighting between the West Side Boys and the Gbethis militia continued along the main highway, adding that the road had been closed east of Kontakuna. A Road Transport Corporation official in Freetown said, 'No bus service will be available today because of continued fighting between the Gbethis and the West Side Boys.' Villagers along the highway complained of continued harassment by armed militiamen.

Forfana continued, 'They cited particularly the West Side Boys, who often abandon their jungle base to forage for food and in the process steal chickens and goats as well as whatever food they lay hands on. Apart from stealing foodstuffs, the militia boys also extort monies from villagers and reportedly rape teenage girls.'

There were fears that the Gbethis and Kapras would counterattack the West Side Boys and that this would put the lives of the Royal Irish hostages at serious risk. The northern-based Gbethis and Kapras, along with the Donsos (Konos) and Tamaboros, were part of the Sierra Leone Civil Defence Force loyal to the Kabbah government, which also included the Organised Body of Hunters in the west and the Kamajors in the south and east.

Relatives of the WSB who made two visits to the riverside base said they wanted to bring both the West Side Boys and the hostages back to Freetown. One relative said that the negotiation delegation had offered the West Side Boys bread, sugar and powdered milk, but no money. In a country as impoverished as Sierra Leone, these gifts were a significant gesture. 'They assured us that they will soon come out of the bush after they release the remaining British hostages,' the relative said. She added that the fighters wanted Britain and the Freetown government to guarantee immunity from arrest for the gang if they did this.

One mother, Juliet Sesay, said they had appealed to their sons, saying that the British were in Sierra Leone to help the country. The West Side Boys responded that they had nothing against the British but that the abductions had finally brought attention to their demands. The WSB then said that they wanted Britain to guarantee them safe passage out of Sierra Leone and to provide them with an education abroad like that offered to Valentine Strasser.

The scheme was put to British officials by Johnny Paul Koroma after the relatives returned from a visit to Gberi Bana. 'Some of them want to get out of the country,' he said. 'They want to study in some vocational institute so that when they come back later they will be useful to the country. I think the bottom line is fear. We will talk to the British, we will talk to the government, to guarantee their security.'

An escape to a British university seemed very unlikely for the West Side Boys, but it was possible that another African country might be persuaded to accept Kallay and his followers for some kind of training programme as a contribution to peace in Sierra Leone.

'We've not specified any country at all,' Koroma said. 'Wherever they want to send them; it might be Nigeria, it might be Ghana or Zambia, it might be any country in Africa. It is not necessarily Britain.'

The West Side Boys wanted those fighters who were not sent abroad to be guaranteed places in the Sierra Leone Army, now in training with the British STTT.

British officials declined to comment while negotiations continued, but the proposals could have indicated that the West Side Boys had backed away from their original demand for the release of their leaders and other comrades from prison and were seeking a way out of the hostage crisis. Such a deal, it was felt, would also have the attraction of removing the violent and maverick WSB from the vicinity of Freetown.

Kallay told relatives he feared that if he freed the British captives, his fighters would be vulnerable to attack by the Sierra Leone Army or UN forces. His elder brother, Maxim Sesay, said that the leader was seeking assurances from the British for his security and that the West Side Boys were looking for international recognition. 'I wasn't able to see him but I was able to send a message to him with a West Side Boy and I told him he should release the British soldiers,' Sesay said. 'In his answer to me he told me he has no confidence in the government and he wants international recognition, that is why he took them. They were taken so the British government would come to their rescue and he would get international recognition.' He added that the authorities had arrested some of the West Side Boys and that '[Kallay] himself is afraid because of what he has done.' Sesay said that his brother had told him that the hostages would be released – 'but with conditions'.

In an attempt to reassure the hostage-takers, Sierra Leone's attorney-general said that he had no plans to prosecute the West Side Boys for holding the soldiers captive. However, in rumour-filled Freetown it was said that the government was split on the issue.

In London, Tony Blair and Robin Cook were directly involved in the events, discussing the problem in consultations with Chief of Defence Staff (CDS) General Sir Charles Guthrie during a series of Cabinet Committee meetings. The sixty-two-year-old general brought considerable experience to the discussions. Commissioned into the Welsh Guards, he had served with the SAS in Aden, the Gulf, Malaysia and East Africa and with the Welsh Guards in Cyprus, Germany and Northern Ireland.

His appointment as CDS in April 1977 by Michael Portillo MP, the then secretary of state for defence, did not go down smoothly within the armed services since he was replacing another soldier, Field Marshal Sir Peter Inge. It confirmed the collapse of what was called, in language that could have come from the Victorian satirical songwriter W. S. Gilbert, 'Buggins' turn' – the system of rotating the top job through the three services. Pressed about his choice, Mr Portillo replied that the appointment had been made 'entirely on merit'.

By the first week of September, defence chiefs had warned the UK Cabinet that the rebels' threats to kill the hostages had to be taken seriously, citing the mock executions as evidence. They also feared that the rebels might move or split up the hostages. Kallay had said that if his demands were not met he would take the Britons further inland, implicitly suggesting that they would be handed to the RUF.

In Sierra Leone, Tony Cramp said, 'There were further meetings yesterday and it is felt that things are moving forward. Things are still positive and we remain confident of getting them out through dialogue and talking. We are moving forward. We are not complacent about it but we are still confident.'

As British attention was focused on resolving the hostage crisis, a story broke that provided a very unwelcome distraction. One of the female recruits who had just completed the STTT training programme was identified as having been implicated in atrocities including abductions, murders and amputations. The woman had allegedly been given the nickname 'Cut Hands' as a result of her actions during the brutal January 1999 attack on Freetown, where she reportedly abducted children and forced them to kill or to hack off limbs.

Eighteen-year-old Suffice Makagia, who had been with the gang led by 'Cut Hands' for a year, said, 'Sometimes she made us shoot and kill everyone we saw but she always saved some people for us to amputate.'

Tony Cramp said that the army was taking the allegations seriously. He explained that there was a process established to screen those entering the training programme, but that it had been set up during an emergency. 'It is run by the Sierra Leonean Army and we advise on it. It's coarse. The screening process was put in place when the security of Sierra Leone was in jeopardy. When the situation stabilises, the aim will be to put the proper screening process in place. It will include everyone, even those already in the frontline ... With regards to this individual, obviously we didn't know about her. We have now got the information and will deal with it appropriately.'

As the pressure increased in the hostage crisis, Surgeon Lieutenant Jon Carty was relocated to RFA *Sir Percivale* to act as triage officer. He recalled: 'My role changed along with the emphasis of the operation. I was told that within the next forty-eight to seventy-two hours, an operation to extract the hostages would be initiated. Since the resultant casualties would be treated in *Sir Percivale*, I was moved there to assist with medical support.'

Carty's role meant that he would be the first point of contact for all casualties and was responsible for deciding on their initial treatment. To assist with this, a casualty clearing station was established in a sea-freight container on the jetty alongside *Sir Percivale*. The Royal Marines detachment aboard HMS *Argyll* was put ashore to provide a secure cordon for RFA *Sir Percivale* and the helicopter landing site on the jetty.

Although air traffic at Lungi Airport had increased dramatically in August, HMS *Argyll*'s Lynx was still the only UK aircraft available, and was consequently in demand for everything from passenger transfers to movement of stores. However, given the increased threat to British forces, Corporal Nick Tryon from *Argyll*'s Royal Marines detachment was embarked to 'ride shotgun' for the aircraft and crew. Lieutenant-Commander Jones, the pilot of the Lynx, said, 'I was very pleased to have Corporal Tryon on board, particularly in such a potentially hostile operational environment.'

Not only was *Argyll*'s Lynx still operating in a variety of supporting roles – including reconnaissance, casualty evacuation and transfer of personnel – but *Argyll*'s flight deck was also used as a temporary overnight base for two Army Mk7 Lynx AH helicopters that had been brought to Sierra Leone to support Operation Barras. They had arrived in Freetown in a C130 Hercules and, having been assembled at Lungi Airport, were flown directly to the ship.

Chief Petty Officer (CPO) Taff Hopkins, the Flight's senior maintenance rating, said, 'This was not a straightforward procedure. A great deal of preparation had to be carried out to work out whether both aircraft could be accommodated on the deck simultaneously as this was something that had not been tried before.'

Petty Officer Paul Phillips was on deck as flight deck officer when the first aircraft landed. He said, 'This was a completely unique experience. I noticed as the first aircraft landed across deck, by the hangar, that there was a problem with her starboard engine.' It quickly emerged that the aircraft had suffered a single engine failure, but before the problem was investigated, the deck was prepared for the second aircraft, which landed at the rear of the flight deck.

Argyll's flight maintenance team quickly got to work on the damaged engine. CPO Hopkins said, 'We had little choice but to change the engine.

Although we had a spare on board, this was for a Naval Lynx and consequently we had to get exceptional approval to fit it.'

Time was short and, with the help of a Royal Electrical and Mechanical Engineers (REME) team ferried out from *Sir Percivale* by *Argyll*'s seaboat, the new engine was fitted overnight in just seven hours. The aircraft was ready to play its role in the operation, as planned, at 04.30 hours the following morning.

On his sixth visit to Magbeni, the SAS sergeant, armed with only with a Browning 9 mm pistol, joined what were in effect last-ditch negotiations.

The decision to launch the rescue operation was taken on Saturday 9 September, after 'Colonel Cambodia' insisted that the WSB would hand over the six remaining British captives only once a new interim government had been formed.

As one British official put it: 'We were being strung along.'

Earlier demands by the WSB for a generator, outboard motors and supplies including cigarettes, the negotiators now decided, were simply delaying tactics. 'It became clear that Kallay had no intention of releasing the men,' the British official said. 'That view was borne out after the raid. The hostages later told us that they were sure they would be executed if we did not rescue them. There was no way they were going to be allowed to walk away.'

British Prime Minister Tony Blair had been contacted again on the Saturday afternoon and updated at his official country residence at Chequers, and told that the raid would start at first light on Sunday morning. He had already given permission to mount the rescue several days earlier when he was at the UN Millennium Summit in New York, but he once again gave it his endorsement. In London, COBR gave the operation the go-ahead.

In Freetown, President Kabbah had already given the JTFHQ carte blanche to conduct an operation against the West Side Boys at a time of their choosing. A major from the British Army Legal Corps who had flown out with the Joint Task Force HQ had brought along a document giving authorisation from the Sierra Leone Police for the operation against the WSB. Keith Biddle, the inspector general, had signed it on behalf of the Sierra Leone Police, and at that point the action against the WSB became a military rather than a police responsibility. In earlier discussions about how the Sierra Leone operation should be described in the document, the epithet 'camp raid' had been suggested and quickly dismissed as sounding rather frivolous.

In the darkness at 05.00 hours on Sunday 10 September, on the airstrip at the Hastings Battle Camp at the southern end of the Freetown peninsula, the young paratroopers of A Company 1 Para were formed up in their sticks. They talked quietly, unconsciously running their hands over their equipment, using touch to make the final checks.

In the Mk7 Lynx AH helicopter, the crew and gunners made a final visual check of their weapons and controls using their night-vision equipment. The troopers from D Squadron checked their weapons and fast-roping equipment.

Aboard the CH47 Chinook Mk 3 helicopters, the pilots of the Joint Special Forces Aviation Wing (JSFAW)[4] began the start-up sequence.

Keys were inserted into the master ignition switches and turned to the 'battery' position. The start buttons for the auxiliary power units were pressed to provide hydraulic pressure to the start motors of the main engines.

Gloved hands moved the engine condition levers to the 'ground idle' position, releasing the pressure to the starter motors and initiating the engine ignition sequence. Fuel flowed into the combustion chambers of the engines and, ignited, the Avco Lycoming T55-712 turboshafts began to build up to self-sustaining speed.

The darkness filled with noise and swirling dust.

The men picked up their weapons and, stooping, filed aboard the helicopters. In the subdued red lighting they moved down the cavernous interiors. With weapons and equipment to hand, they settled themselves into the canvas seats as comfortably as they could.

The Chinook pilots released the rotor brakes and advanced the engine condition levers to 'flight idle'. The engines accelerated to flight speed; with the rotors running at flying speed, the pilots eased the collective controls and one by one the big helicopters lifted off. Flying with night-vision goggles (NVG), the pilots had a green luminescent picture of the jungle visible below them. The GPS positions of the landing sites had been programmed in for an exact touchdown.

In the thundering darkness of the fifteen-minute flight, the young Paras and SAS Troopers were alone with their thoughts. Like Olympic athletes, the officers and NCOs were rehearsing in their minds the first moves once they landed and how they hoped the operation would develop.

Probably for all of them, their deepest thoughts, almost a prayer, were those of all soldiers going into action: if I'm killed – OK, but make it quick and painless; if wounded – don't let me be crippled; but above all, whatever happens, don't let me let my mates down.

Operation Barras[5] was on its way.

Chapter 8
Operation Barras

Yu du mi, a du yu: Moses' law.
You do unto me, I do unto you: Moses' Law.
'An eye for an eye and a tooth for a tooth.'

In the pre-dawn darkness of Sunday 10 September 2000, Mohammed Kamara, like all the West Side Boys, was unaware of the presence of the SAS patrols in the jungle around him. Moments before gunfire erupted around the huts as the patrols attacked at 06.40 hours, above the sound of nocturnal insect life Kamara detected in the distance the distinctive thudding beat of rotor blades as the Chinooks approached low over Rokel Creek. The big helicopters were so low that as they swung off towards their designated LSs, the downblast from the rotors ripped off the rusting corrugated iron roofs of the huts bordering the river and sent the tattered sheets careering across the jungle scrub.

It was a time for snap decisions.

Kamara, who two days later walked into a UN base to surrender, took one that would save his life: he ran and took cover in the swamps.

The Lynx gunship equipped with night-vision equipment swept in first. 'The helicopters were almost on the water,' Kamara said. 'They fired again and again until there was no more shooting.' By the time he emerged more than four hours later, many of his comrades were lying dead in the smoking wreckage that had been Gberi Bana and Magbeni.

Timing is essential in any military operation, but in Barras, it meant the difference between success and catastrophe. In negotiations with Lieutenant-Colonel Fordham, Kallay had repeatedly threatened to kill the hostages if he heard helicopters approaching his jungle bases.

As the Chinook carrying the SAS hostage-snatch and fire teams swept in and hovered above the palms in the half-light of dawn, the West Side Boys at Gberi Bana opened fire.

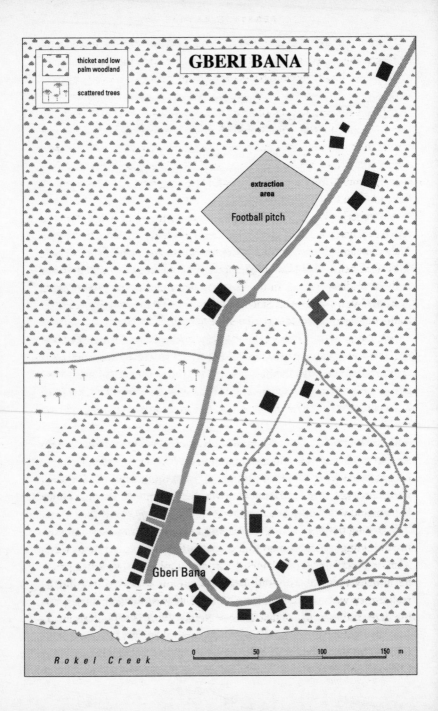

GBERI BANA

thicket and low
palm woodland

scattered trees

extraction
area

Football pitch

Gberi Bana

Rokel Creek

0   50   100   150   m

'Corporal Blood' later described the attack: 'We never experienced anything like this ... We saw the soldiers coming down to the ground. I fired my RPG two times, but both times the helicopter balanced [swerved] and I missed.'

It may have been bad shooting by 'Corporal Blood' or superb flying by the Chinook pilot – who would demonstrate his skills again a few moments later – but the teams were now down safely and the helicopters swung away out of range. Had Blood hit the helicopter with an RPG7 rocket, it could have been fatal – as would be seen in similar attacks on US helicopters in Iraq three years later.

Moments before the West Side Boys started firing at the helicopters, the SAS patrol lying up about 55 m from Gberi Bana had burst from the jungle. They went straight for the huts where the British and Sierra Leonean captives were being held and 'discouraged any interference' until the main body of soldiers arrived. In the fire fight that followed, only two people escaped alive from the West Side Boys' huts, where Kallay was subsequently found hiding under bedding and bodies.

'We didn't even realise we'd got Kallay,' said a British officer after the raid. 'Those who fought, we killed. Those who surrendered, we captured. It was only later that we identified him.' At the time, it would probably have been easy for the two men from D Squadron who discovered Kallay to have killed him, but he did not resist and his capture would be a profound psychological victory.

Among those killed was 'Mammy Kallay', who was made of more heroic stuff than her husband and died gun in hand. The news of her death was later greeted with delight by the former Sierra Leonean captives. 'She was a wicked, wicked woman,' said a man who had been held in their jungle hideout and was being made to undergo military training.

Watching from his hut, WSB prisoner Emmanuel Fabba saw SAS men blast buildings apart with 40 mm grenades fired from their M203 rifles. Kamara described seeing shapes descending rapidly from a helicopter – he initially thought they were bombs. Only on second glance did he realise they were the fast-roping SAS team. It was probably during this initial ferocious exchange that Trooper Bradley 'Brad' Tinnion was fatally wounded, hit by a 7.62 mm round that passed through his body, exiting through his shoulder. Under heavy fire, his colleagues dragged him to the Chinook and treated him as well as they could before he was evacuated.

He died shortly after reaching the medics aboard RFA *Sir Percivale*.

It was his first operational mission with the SAS.

One SAS trooper recalling the violent fire fight said, 'It was a bit like "Gunfight at the OK Corral"'. Within twenty minutes, the SAS had liberated the British hostages and were back aboard the Chinook. From there, bar a brief touchdown to pick up Major Lowe and the men from A Company who had been injured in the simultaneous attack on Magbeni, they were flown to *Sir Percivale* for medical checks and the start of the debriefing on their mission.

In Freetown, officers at the JTFHQ could hear the gunfire over their radios as contact and casualty reports came in over the nets.

It was now 07.00 hours.

As the Royal Irish were being rescued, across Rokel Creek at LS2 near Magbeni the other Chinook was inserting two platoons and the HQ of A Company 1 Para who had packed into the helicopter. Though they knew the LS would be marshy, it was still a surprise when the first two soldiers jumped down from the rear ramp of the helicopter and plunged into a chest-deep swamp. The reeds growing on LS2 had looked like grassland in aerial photographs and though the map showed areas of permanent or seasonal marshland to the south and west, the terrain around LS2 had looked viable. The SAS patrol had seen water through the grass but due to a combination of lack of cover and almost impenetrable secondary growth they had been unable to get close enough to the LS to establish the depth of the swamp.

What should have been a sprint to the tree line became a 100–150 m slog through mud and grass with weapons held high towards higher ground and the fringe of palms and scrub bordering the western end of the village, which could be seen faintly in silhouette.[1] 'It was a massive pain in the arse, but it wasn't unforeseen,' remarked an officer after the action.

This was a moment when the section commanders demonstrated their leadership potential. With fire coming from the village, the young corporals shouted encouragement to their sections and urged them to spread out and push towards the trees. According to a soldier in A Company, 'That was where the young NCOs were fantastic and that is where they really started gripping people. With the best will in the world the company commander and platoon commanders couldn't control it. They just wanted to focus on getting into the right point in the jungle.'

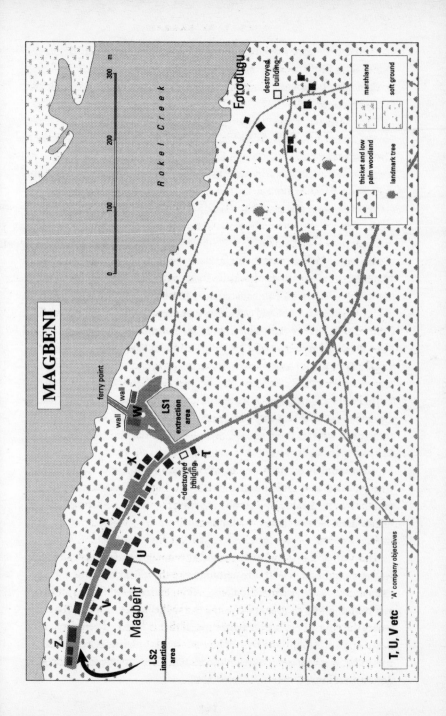

MAGBENI

Rokel Creek

ferry point

wall

wall

W

LS1
extraction
area

X

destroyed
building

T

Fotodugu

destroyed
building

Y

U

V

Z

LS2
insertion
area

Magbeni

T, U, V etc   'A' company objectives

thicket and low
palm woodland

landmark tree

marshland

soft ground

0   100   200   300   m

The Paras pushed forward, feeling the ground becoming firmer under foot as the swamp became shallower. Hooking round to the left until they reached the tree line, the company was quickly in position for the break into the village.

They were wet and muddy; grass and reeds had clogged the linked GPMG ammunition draped around the machine gunners. For Command Sergeant Major (CSM) Chiswell, tasked with securing the LS, there were several lonely minutes as his party waited in the swamp on the side closest to Magbeni for the Chinook to fly back to Hastings to pick up further elements of A Company group and insert them at LS2; the CSM could then move off to join his men.

Twenty-two-year-old Captain Mathews, the Company 2 IC, came in on the second lift. He admitted afterwards that like all the 'Toms' he had been apprehensive: 'We knew the West Side Boys had lots of equipment, mortars, rifles, machine guns and heavy machine guns,' he said. 'There is obviously no set format and obviously that plays on your mind – not being able to predict your enemy's intentions or reactions.'

As the small Special Forces group across the river in Gberi Bana held off the militiamen, the Mk7 Lynx AH helicopters swept in overhead and blasted the West Side Boy positions in Magbeni. Using the SS600 Series 3 thermal imager, the Lynx crews picked the up the cluster of WSB around the heavy machine gun that had opened fire at the 1 Para Chinook and in accordance with the plan raked it with 12.7 mm machine-gun fire until it was silent. The helicopters then moved in to cover the river.

Interviewed afterwards, one of the Para section commanders, twenty-nine-year-old Corporal Simon Dawes from Basingstoke, said simply: 'We came under fire at first and then it was taken out. We had helicopters and we had heavy guns that suppressed the fire.'

The company shook out and began to clear through the village of Magbeni, sweeping from west to east. Now the fetid warmth of the jungle air was permeated with the sharp smell of burned cordite as gunfire and explosions ripped through the village. The thump of exploding grenades and 66 mm LAWs punctuated the fast beat of GPMG fire and the sharper rattle of SA80 rifles firing on automatic. The lead platoon, 3 Platoon, successfully took Zulu, the first of the objectives, which was centred on a crumbling one-storey building, but 2 Platoon came under heavy fire as it approached Yankee, the second objective.

For most of the Paras, this was their first experience of a sustained fire fight. Corporal Dawes said later in an interview: 'This is the first fire fight I have been in where rounds were coming my way.' With the memory of the fighting still fresh, he searched for words to describe the action and added modestly: 'I don't like to talk about that sort of situation but it was scary. But once we got into the fighting the training took over.'

Though the strafing runs by the Lynx attack helicopters had killed or frightened off some of the West Side Boys in Magbeni, a small hard core were standing their ground and fighting back. As the 1 Para Company HQ moved forward to liaise with 2 Platoon, there was an explosion in front of the group that injured seven of the soldiers – who might well have been killed had they not been wearing helmets and body armour.

'There was a loud explosion and we could hear these agonising screams,' said nineteen-year-old Private Julian Sheard. The wounded included Major Lowe, who went down with shrapnel wounds to his legs, the 2 Platoon commander, three of his HQ including his signaller and the OC's signaller.

It was the second critical moment in the operation, but as Prussian General Helmuth von Moltke expressed in the 19th century, 'No plan survives contact with the enemy.' What would see the company through were the clear and concise orders that had been passed down from Major Lowe.

'The OC called me up and told me I was to take over command of the company,' Captain Danny Mathews recalled. It was like a situation on an exercise in which the directing staff remove key players in the command structure and pitch subordinate officers and NCOs into their positions. This time it was for real, but it was a situation that had been anticipated and rehearsed.

Mathews thought fast. Weapons, ammunition and radios were removed from the wounded, who were then dragged to cover. Sergeant Fitzwater took command of 2 Platoon. While an uninjured radio operator transmitted the casualty evacuation (CASEVAC) request giving details of the number and nature of the injuries sustained, the crew of the Chinook lifting off from the Gberi Bana side of the creek with the hostages either picked up the report or was told of the casualties by the JTFHQ. When the plans were being prepared, it had been decided that radio communications would be in clear – although the WSB may have had the PRC352 radio captured along with the Royal Irish hostages, if by chance they were on the same frequency as the raiding party, they would not have time to react to any signals they intercepted. The speed and simplicity of this operation's communications net probably contributed to the quick reactions of the Chinook crew. Demonstrating a piece of superb flying, the helicopter landed under fire on the track running through the village. The wounded were quickly loaded aboard and were on their way to *Sir Percivale*. For the Paras on the ground, the helicopter casualty evacuation was dramatic but also hazardous as the downwash from the rotors peeled the roof off a building close to which they had taken up positions and sent lethal sheets of corrugated iron and timber crashing down.

The casualty evacuation was so fast that Regimental Medical Officer (RMO) Captain Thomas and the company aid post were still running towards the site when the helicopter lifted off. After the initial cries of pain, the wounded Paras were now grimly silent; some were able to walk on to the helicopter but others had to be carried aboard. The wounded reached the operating theatre aboard *Sir Percivale* within twenty minutes of being injured.

The first casualties arrived at around 07.00 hours and a total of thirteen were received on the RFA, where the surgical team fought to save Trooper Tinnion's life. Some wounded were treated for minor injuries, but the medical team also performed emergency surgery. All patients had been treated and stabilised by 18.30 hours and were ready to be flown to the Haslar Royal Naval Hospital in Portsmouth, England. Surgeon Lieutenant Carty said, 'Although we train for this kind of thing, I would be lying if I didn't say that it was very stressful at times.'

Despite the setback at Magbeni, A Company kept up the momentum of the attack with 2 Platoon securing objective Yankee as 3 Platoon moved parallel with them. The GPMG gunners had problems with stoppages because their link was fouled with grass and mud, but they worked quickly to clear their weapons. They then engaged the remaining WSB positions, firing the 11.65 kg machine guns from their shoulders because the thick vegetation made it impossible to see targets when firing from the prone position. They had realised that this would be necessary during rehearsals at the Hastings training area and had practised hard during the work-up for the operation. Under cover of smoke from red phosphorus grenades, 1 Platoon dashed across the open track. By about 07.00 hours, the WSB could be seen withdrawing eastwards towards LS1 and the lead platoon concentrated its fire on the fleeing targets.

1 Platoon assaulted objectives X-Ray and Whiskey, which were close to Rokel Creek. At Whiskey they found the WSB ammunition dump, professionally dug in and with a poncho stretched above it. 3 Platoon then cleared Victor, Uniform and Tango objectives, the buildings south of the track, and moved into a blocking position to cover any West Side Boy counterattacks from units around Laia Junction. The immersion at the swampy LS at the outset of the operation had caused some problems with the radios, but even if electronic communications were less reliable, the human voice worked effectively in the small area of the village. The action had been a classic 'corporal's war', fought by small, well-led groups of soldiers.

Clearance patrols were mounted by 1 Platoon. They pushed out into the secondary jungle to find any WSB who might have concealed themselves nearby, but after 20 m the vegetation became too dense to push through.

It was now 08.00 hours and Magbeni was secure.

The company took up defensive positions, set up Claymore mines to cover their arcs and paid out the brown cable from the mines back to their shell scrapes.

The mortar section was now flown to LS2, but since there was no suitable position for the base plates they were flown to LS1 instead. Here they experienced difficulty adjusting their fire because the dense vegetation concealed the 'splash' of dirt and smoke from the exploding high explosive (HE) mortar bombs and the fall of shot could not be seen even when smoke rounds were fired. The mortar fire controller (MFC) was picked up by a Lynx but unfortunately experienced difficulties with signalling instructions back to the mortar section. The solution was to correct fire by the rather hazardous expedient of aural adjustment. This involves listening for the direction and loudness of the impact and adjusting the elevation and alignment of the barrel accordingly. With minimum charge and barrels elevated almost to the vertical, the bombs fell on the final protective fire (FPF) target close to the forward positions. If there was a West Side Boy counterattack, it was here that the interlocking fire from the GPMGs, the blast of the Claymores and aimed rifle fire would halt them.

A patrol now moved through the village destroying vehicles including the Bedford with the ZPU-2, three 'Technicals' and ammunition including large stocks of mortar ammunition and RPG rounds with PE4 plastic explosives. Petrol and RP grenades were used to burn down buildings.

A Company group had completed its mission and as the main body went firm around LS1, Captain Mathews accompanied two sections on a final sweep through the village.

It was the first year of the 21st century, but the scene was timeless – as the flames crackled and the columns of smoke rose above the jungle, the victors surveyed the scene of their triumph. For many of the young Paras, after the pre-dawn start and a day of combat there was a feeling of relief to be alive, accompanied by creeping fatigue.

Over 130 years earlier, the American writer and historian Oliver Wendell Holmes, a veteran of hard fighting in the American Civil War, had summed up the moment in his book *The Banker's Secret*: 'Life's sovereign moment is a battle won.'

On the ground, the resistance put up by the WSB had actually been much stronger than had been expected. Cornered, some of the gang had fought with little or no thought of surrender. In an interview with Jason Burke of *The Observer*, a veteran of fighting in Sierra Leone commented, 'It is the old problem. We just don't get it. We look at these irregular forces. We look at these kids and young women fighting in trainers and T-shirts. We laugh at the way they wear charms to ward off bullets. We look at their drunken and doped-up leaders and we cannot take them seriously. But these kids have grown up fighting and killing and committing atrocities.

'They also don't understand the rules. No one has ever told them that war is not like a Rambo video, about how soldiers should behave, when to be scared, so they will just stand there and blast away.'

More interesting still was the post-operation analysis by some of the Special Forces. Some reckoned that the full-blooded attack involving the Paras had been unnecessary. The WSB guards could have been killed silently at night and the hostages extracted covertly and exfiltrated from the WSB camp down Rokel Creek by SBS inflatable craft.

Unofficially, even the MoD acknowledged that they were relieved that Operation Barras had suffered only one death and twelve injuries, eleven of them minor. One veteran SAS soldier describing the operation said, 'This was not a clinical, black-balaclava, Princess Gate-type operation. It was a very grubby, green operation with lots of potential for things to go wrong.' However, as Richard Connaughton comments in *Small Wars and Insurgencies*, 'One lesson these unfortunate casualties established was that the UK government was not casualty averse in circumstances where the cause was just.'

Across the river in Gberi Bana, fifteen male and three female prisoners were taken. Their wrists secured with white plasticuffs, they were bundled into the Chinooks along with the bodies of their dead comrades. The prisoners were then passed to the UNAMSIL Jordanian Battalion, which in turn handed them over to the Sierra Leone Police.

Twenty-four WSB died during the raid. Officially, three of the dead were women but the real figure seems likely to have been five. One source close to the operation said that the death toll was probably higher: 'If you followed every blood trail into the jungle you might well be able to quadruple that figure.' D Squadron was so successful at taking prisoners on the north bank because the conditions that had made Gberi Bana an ideal place to keep the hostages – with the creek to the south and jungle and swamp to east and west – now gave the WSB nowhere to run as the SAS swept through the village.

A Company 1 Para had fulfilled its mission of defeating the West Side Boys within their area of responsibility in Magbeni, and there was no call to pursue and destroy the gang. As the helicopters came in before dawn and the darkness filled with the red streaks of tracer fire, the thump of explosions and shouting as 1 Para went into action, the assault on the senses would have been overwhelming. Realising that they were not up against nervous or compliant UNAMSIL troops but rather the overwhelming yet controlled violence of professional soldiers, many of the WSB fled in the darkness through the scrub and jungle and hid.

However, for some, dying in a spectacular fire fight with men of the SAS and the Parachute Regiment was a fate that would have been relished by the youthful members of the West Side Boys, whose short and violent lives had passed in a haze of drugs, guns and girls. Surrender was a concept that did not come easily for militias in Sierra Leone – if you were taken prisoner, your fate would still inevitably be death, but preceded by torture and humiliation.

If you could not escape, it was better to fight to the death.

What went largely unreported in the British media was that the raid would eventually free a total of twenty-two Sierra Leoneans held prisoner by the WSB for weeks or months. Five were women who had been abducted and forced to become 'bush wives' or 'sex combatants'. The men had been used as forced labour.

Emmanuel Fabba, one of the forced labourers, provided *The Daily Telegraph* with the first eyewitness account of the rituals – some terrifying, others humiliating – of life inside Gberi Bana. He said that the militia's commanders regularly pointed their guns at the captured Royal Irish soldiers and threatened to kill them if a rescue bid was mounted.

The camp commandant, the self-styled 'Lieutenant-Colonel' Contobie, was a sadist, Fabba said. He made the captives line up, then bow down in front of him and say, 'Good morning, Commandant.' Fabba commented, 'He used to boast that the British have bowed before only three black men: Idi Amin, Chief Bureh and now him.'

Major Marshall had to ask permission for his men to eat and be given drinking water, and was ordered to clean the wounds of injured militiamen using cheap local gin as an antiseptic. The major and captain were forced to train thirty male hostages in a parade ground drill on the dirt football field, using wooden sticks to imitate rifles. After training, the West Side Boys intended to use the abducted men as fighters. However, the West Side Boys did not realise that these drill sessions also allowed the officers to get to know their fellow captives and enabled them to identify them after the raid was over.

The female Sierra Leonean captives were kept across the river at Magbeni. When Contobie spoke about them, Fabba recounted, he grinned broadly and said they had been stripped and raped.

Kallay lived with his fearsome wife in a house near the captives. He was seen occasionally, surrounded by bodyguards.

One morning, Major Marshall made the mistake of greeting Kallay. Fabba reported that Contobie was furious: 'The commandant went berserk. He asked the major: "Why did you speak to him? Who permitted you?" and then he pushed him away hard.'

The Britons were constantly surrounded by child fighters, some as young as ten, from the gang's Small Boys Unit. 'There were more children than adults,' said Fabba. 'Gangsta rap' music blared from radios and ganja soup – made with marijuana – was part of the daily diet of drugs and drink for the militiamen.

The soldiers spent much of their time locked up in a 13 m by 2.4 m cement-and-mud house, the home of the former village chief. Inside there were mats and blankets for bedding. Armed guards kept watch by the door and window. The only lavatory was a hole in the ground in a metal hut shared by captives and militiamen. Fabba said that during the week he was there, the soldiers were taken to wash once in the nearby Rokel Creek. 'They washed themselves and their uniforms, which they put back on wet.'

According to Fabba, 'Usually, the British kept very quiet. They spoke to each other in low voices and sometimes shared a cigarette. The major did the talking for them if he needed to speak with the West Side Boys.' For meals, the British soldiers mixed tinned composition or 'compo' rations sent in by the hostage negotiators with local bush food such as cassava leaves and coconuts. The militiamen also treated their captives to sachets of cheap local gin called Sasman in Sierra Leone, but known by the WSB as 'morale-boosters'.

Although they were pushed around and threatened, the soldiers were not assaulted, said Fabba. In contrast, the Sierra Leonean LO with them was badly beaten and, it was reported, held in an open pit covered with a wooden grid. Men and women from the WSB had relieved themselves into the pit.

Prior to Operation Barras, Fabba said, the major had assured his fellow captives that there would be a rescue mission.

After the operation had been successfully concluded, there was speculation in the media that Lieutenant-Colonel Fordham had warned Marshall about the imminent rescue attempt by means of veiled speech in a rare radio exchange or on the satellite phone. Another version of events said that a written note had been passed by sleight of hand during one of the negotiation meetings. Whatever the method, the message was said to have been phrased as an innocent expression of affection: 'Sally and Sarah send their regards and so does Dawn.' The SAS were coming at first light.

In reality, to ensure security, it is unlikely that such a warning was given to the hostages and even the negotiating team were not told details of the operation. However, both in Canterbury and Freetown, the presence of the Paras in Sierra Leone was public knowledge and with it the likelihood of an operation to free the hostages. Perhaps a message was passed.

What is more probable is that, being experienced soldiers, the Royal Irish hostages surmised that the time was approaching when direct action would be necessary and Marshall sensibly decided to tell the Sierra Leonean hostages how to behave when the assault went in.

'He came to talk to me in a low voice,' said Fabba. 'He pointed at the wings on his uniform and said the Paras were coming. He did not know exactly when, but he said we should not leave the house when we heard the helicopters. We knew the British were our only hope and had prayed that they would come soon as the West Side Boys had threatened to execute us.'

At dawn on Sunday, the Sierra Leonean hostages survived by lying prone inside their hut when the silence was shattered by gunfire as the SAS patrol attacked and the air filled with the thump of the hovering Chinooks' rotors. Overcome by this terrifying assault on his senses, one captive – Braima Phohba, a student at Bunumbu Teachers College – panicked, ran from the hut and was caught in the crossfire and killed.

'There was so much shouting and shooting, it was terrible,' said Fabba. 'We saw a British soldier outside, so we called out, "Civilian hostages, don't shoot." They brought us out of the back of the building, tied us up and made us lie face down in case we were West Side Boys. The major confirmed our identity later.'

For Binta Sesay, Contobie's heavily pregnant wife, the timing of the attack saved her life and that of her unborn child. Her husband had said that he was going to kill her on Monday because she had urged him to surrender. Sesay had struggled under a bed when the SAS attack hit Gberi Bana. 'I was very afraid, but the soldier spoke to me quietly. He brought me water, lit a cigarette and asked me if I wanted one. He was a friendly man.'

With the two areas secured, at around 10.00 hours the Chinooks began to shuttle WSB prisoners and dead out of the area.

Across the creek in Magbeni, the Paras had located the three Royal Irish Land Rovers and discovered that despite some bullet holes in the bodywork and flat tyres they could still be driven. A helicopter returned from BTC with spare keys for the vehicles. They were then driven to LS1, rigged for underslinging and lifted out by a Chinook. Surprisingly, the Paras found that the Browning HMG on the WMIK had not been fired.

It was now 11.00 hours.

As the heat increased to a sauna-like humidity, the last helicopters carrying the men of D Squadron and 1 Para lifted off in a swirl of dust and leaves and twisting columns of smoke.

In the ensuing silence, the surviving WSB crawled from the jungle around Gberi Bana and surveyed the destruction and carnage.

'There were many corpses and wounded people lying on the ground moaning,' said sixteen-year-old Unisa Sesay, a member of the gang's Small Boys Unit. 'One commander was standing and his friend was trying to remove a fragment from his shoulder. The rest of the people were on the ground.'

Cyrus, aged seventeen, said they had been told that the wounded would be shot and thrown into the river because there were no medical supplies. Both boys said they saw too many corpses and were too shocked to count them. They said that the dead included a Sierra Leonean hostage and a boy of about fourteen from the SBU.

'There were always a lot of them [SBU] around,' said Betty Sams, a Sierra Leonean woman who had been held for ten days at Magbeni by the WSB. 'They were used as servants by the bigger members of the West Side Boys and as bodyguards because none of the older members of the group, especially not the leaders, trusted one another.'

Subsequently, an estimated fifty child soldiers who had fled the fighting went into hiding in the surrounding bush. Fearful travellers along the road from Freetown's peninsula to the interior said that they had spotted armed boys as young as eight roaming the jungle.

Alieu Sissay, who had encountered them on the road, said: 'We wanted to try to coax them out and one or two of us shouted to them, but they just vanished. No one is going to go in there to get them the help they need.'

He said that the smallest in the group, carrying an AK-47 and dressed in underpants and a torn T-shirt, had poked his face out from behind a large leaf and smiled. Another child had pulled him back into the thicket. 'They have no conscience and they have done terrible things,' said Sissay.

Betty Sams said that they were probably led by a fourteen-year-old boy known simply as 'Killer'. 'He was one of the worst. The adults were all scared of him. He was really tiny, he looked like he was eleven or twelve, but when he looked at people, they fell silent. He's likely to be their leader now.'

By a remarkable coincidence, on the morning of Sunday 10 September, CDS General Sir Charles Guthrie was due to give a live interview on the high-profile BBC 1 current affairs programme *Breakfast with Frost*. The interview had been booked back in June and was to have addressed general issues about the British Armed Forces.

At the studio in the BBC Television Centre at Shepherds Bush, there was increasing tension as the general was running late. The veteran broadcaster and journalist Sir David Frost, who presented the programme, was playing for time by reviewing the Sunday papers when Guthrie arrived at the Television Centre. Switching off his secure mobile phone, via which he had been linked to the JTFHQ and DSF in Freetown, Guthrie emerged languidly from his staff car and apologised for the delay.

'I'm sorry I'm late,' he said. 'There's been a bit of trouble in Africa.'

At about 09.20 hours in London, MoD spokesman Major Tom Thornycroft had confirmed to Guthrie that all the hostages were safe. The television production team hurried to check whether the story was being covered by any of the international news agencies – there was nothing.

'There probably won't be anything out for about an hour,' commented Guthrie.

For Frost, the drama of the moment was compelling: 'Now, it's very rare that you get dramatic breaking military news and the key figure of the moment coinciding live while we're on the air. The two together is really rare but that's just what's happening here this morning. In the last few minutes we've learnt that British soldiers in Sierra Leone have this morning undertaken military action aimed at releasing the British hostages who have been held in the jungle for the last fortnight.

'There's nothing on the wires yet, nothing is publicly known, but the man who knows more than anyone else, who has the latest information, is with us. He's the head of the Army and the Navy and the Air Force, General Sir Charles Guthrie. Good morning, Charles, this sounds like amazing breaking news, good news.'

Guthrie was measured in his reply. 'Well, I hope it's good news, we think it's good news. We decided to attack the place where the hostages were being kept at half past six this morning,' he explained, 'so the situation is still very confused. There is fighting going on but the first indications are that the hostages are safe; I don't know what condition they're in but they are safe. I don't know whether we've had any casualties. We didn't want to have to do this, we didn't want to have to assault because it's a very difficult operation, there are big risks in it, but we have done it and the reason we did it is because really our negotiations were getting nowhere. The hostages had been there for three weeks, they [the WSB] were threatening to kill them, or they were threatening to move them to different parts of Sierra Leone and once they'd done that we'd never be able to recover them with ease, which I hope we've done this morning.

'So it's very difficult, but I do want to stress this is a very, very tricky, complicated operation we're doing a long way away in very difficult terrain where, working as a team with the Foreign Office, with the police, our ministers have had some tough decisions to take because if it goes wrong we're in trouble.'

Later, at a press conference at the MoD, Guthrie explained, 'This kind of operation is never without risk. We are not playing some stupid arcade game . . . The West Side Boys were not a pushover. They fought very hard. We did not want to do this, but the clock started turning.'

In fact, when General Guthrie was talking to David Frost, Operation Barras was still in progress with about an hour to run. As a senior officer commented afterwards, 'Until Guthrie spoke, no one in Freetown knew what was going on and the hacks were still in the hotel recovering from their Saturday night hangovers. As it happened, it didn't cause any problems and probably got Guthrie out of a few awkward questions from Frost on the defence budget!'

Soon afterwards, in the security of Freetown, the six newly released Royal Irish hostages had been reunited with their five comrades from the ill-fated patrol. They telephoned their families in Britain and went through a range of medical checks on board *Sir Percivale*.

Lieutenant-Colonel Fordham said that the six were 'mentally and physically exhausted'. He added, 'I saw them on the ship this morning and they looked remarkably well considering the ordeal they had been through. These are soldiers that fell back on training and it demonstrates how good these men were in terms of their strength of character and spirit of endeavour. They are physically and mentally exhausted and need time to recover. They were kept in very poor conditions and they looked after themselves as best they could. They were given little freedom of movement and their basic requirements of food and water were severely limited. When the first five came out they recounted an incident of a mock execution, but it was not repeated. I told representatives of the militia group that I would not tolerate any abuse of the soldiers.'

Pegasus recorded that 'a post-operational amount of alcohol was drunk in celebration' by the men of A Company 1 Para now aboard the RFA *Argus*. In fact, to the surprise of the crew of *Argus*, many of the tired 'Toms', after a few beers, were pleased to be able to clean up and get to sleep. The following day they boarded C-130s at Freetown before changing to a TriStar at Dakar for the final leg back to the UK, arriving home in the early hours of Tuesday morning.

DSF and his HQ along with D Squadron also made their exit on

Monday morning. Within less than twenty-four hours, the word was out in Freetown that the WSB had been defeated and the crews of British military vehicles were greeted by the population with broad smiles, waves and applause.

Democrats, the biggest-selling daily paper in Sierra Leone, came up with a screaming headline that encapsulated the outcome of Operation Barras: BRITS KICK ASS IN WEST SIDE.

British High Commissioner Alan Jones, Peter Penfold's successor in Freetown, was more measured in his assessment of the operation: 'Our policy on terrorism is one of no concessions. Today's result has borne out the correctness of that policy and emphasises our commitment to protect our own men.'

Dr Julius Spencer, who had taken a firm stand on the hostage negotiations, spoke in similar terms: 'It was a very difficult operation. We hope this sends a message to [Sierra Leone rebel groups] to give up their arms.'

In a brief press conference arranged in Freetown, Battalion Operations Officer Captain Cradden, from Sheffield, said that he had been told to start preparing for the operation eleven days earlier. He explained, 'Our part in the operation was to ensure the West Side Boys' heavy guns on the south side could not interfere with operations on the north side and endanger the hostages. We are very proud to have taken part in the battle and to have been of some assistance in securing the hostages.'

Impeccable in regimental beret, stable belt and fresh camouflaged jungle uniforms, Cradden, accompanied by Corporal Dawes, were photographed by the press against a jungle backdrop. Both men knew that the hostages had been rescued by the SAS and looked rather embarrassed as they were paraded in front of the media pack.

To the sceptical Freetown-based international press, it all seemed rather stage-managed and that the Paras were clearly restricted in what they could say. The general feeling was that the press conference had been organised to distract interest from the obvious fact that Special Forces had been used for the hostage rescue.

Two years after the successful operation, on 27 June 2002, Captain Mathews would be presented to the Queen during her Golden Jubilee visit to the armed forces at Portsmouth. He was one of a group of nine servicemen who had recently served with distinction.

At the close of Richard Connaughton's perceptive analysis of the operation, he writes, 'What Operation "Barass" [sic] had again brought into focus was the matter of forces for courses – quantity v. quality. The lesson has consistently been underlined in the post-Cold War period, that half-hearted intervention will not succeed. That is more applicable in Africa than anywhere else . . . The simple quantities approach is unlikely to succeed. It is in the nature of Africans to be impressed by power and by those representative armed forces prepared to demonstrate and use that power.'

The success of Barras, which by the lavish standards of similar operations launched by the United States was fought on a shoestring budget with limited resources, made a lasting impression with US Army officers, particularly those within the Special Forces community. For British soldiers on postings to remote and hostile countries, it sent a reassuring message.

As one experienced observer noted, 'If we had lost this one then there would be repercussions for all our operations worldwide. We would be seen to be fallible, we would be reluctant to risk troops on peacekeeping operations because we would not be sure we could extract them from trouble, we would in turn lose confidence in ourselves and would be less effective. The success of Barras was not with saving the lives of the hostages but with showing that the Brits could pull off something that not even the US could probably have done as well. Settling scores, although satisfying, is a long way down the list.'

Barras and the continued UNAMSIL commitment in Sierra Leone helped to alleviate the gloom of the grim prophecy delivered by American writer and analyst Robert Kaplan's influential *Atlantic Monthly* essay, partially set in Sierra Leone and titled 'The Coming Anarchy'.

He had described the country as engulfed by 'an increasing lawlessness that is far more significant than any coup, rebel incursion, or episodic experiment in democracy', a lawlessness that signalled a world where 'criminal anarchy emerges as the real "strategic" danger'. Africa, and many 'emerging nations', would be marked by 'the withering away of central governments, the rise of tribal and regional domains, the unchecked spread of disease, and the growing pervasiveness of war'.

However, if Operation Barras had not been launched, the African 'sex combatants' and their fellow male prisoners would probably have been murdered when they were no longer useful, or have died of disease at the squalid WSB base. History has shown that harsh decisions sometimes have to be taken, but if the negotiations had succeeded and the British soldiers walked free, or if they had been released by a covert Special Forces operation, the African hostages would certainly have died. The rescue of the British on these terms might have been a tactical success, but would have risked becoming a strategic surrender to the forces of anarchy.

In 1832, Prussian veteran of the Waterloo Campaign von Clausewitz had explained this very concept in his seminal study, *On War*: 'We see, therefore, that War is not only a political act, but also a real political instrument, a continuation of political commerce, a carrying out of the same by other means . . . the political view is the object, War is the means, and the means must always include the object in our conception.'

Operation Barras was a political act. It did more than liberate the Royal Irish or save the lives of the Sierra Leonean captives – or even those of the WSB who subsequently trooped into UN bases to surrender. With its dramatic helicopter assault, gunfire and explosions, it was an exercise in nation-building – a necessarily spectacular endorsement of the rule of law and the elected government in Sierra Leone.

Chapter 9
Aftermath

'If a bin no' na-in de las.
'If I had only known' always comes too late.

Operation Barras had been a triumph and *Soldier*, the British Army's in-house magazine, carried a full report in its October 2000 issue – rather too full for the MoD's liking.

The report, titled 'Tight Security Key to Jungle Rescue Success', said that SAS troops had swooped in by helicopter for a fifteen-minute fire fight on the edge of a swamp. One SAS soldier, trooper Brad Tinnion, was killed in the raid, which left more than twenty-five members of the West Side Boys dead.

Part of the article, under the heading 'Anatomy of a Rescue', read: 'Armed helicopters took off from Freetown, carrying Special Forces and Paras into the jungle. They were flown by pilots from the Special Forces Squadron. Special Air Service troops on the ground, who had been observing the rebels' stronghold for more than a week, warned that the landing would have to be made under fire.' It added: 'The SAS snatch squad in a Lynx [sic] touched down long enough to get the hostages on board. L/Bdr [Lance Bombardier] Brad Tinnion was fatally injured.'

Soldier was in fact reporting information that had already received wide coverage in the national press. However, since the MoD refuses to acknowledge publicly the existence of Special Forces, it ordered that the magazine be destroyed to prevent 'confusion over policy'. Vanloads of the magazine en route to national distributors were called back. Some 90,000 copies were pulped and recycled, at a cost of £70,000. A censored version of the magazine without any reference to Special Forces was then printed and distributed.

An MoD spokesman said, 'The magazine was withdrawn because it was considered to contain information that contravened the MoD's regular policy on disclosure of information. It contained some information on Operation Barras in Sierra Leone. We don't comment on our Special Forces' activities or personnel for fear of compromising their safety. It was an editorial oversight which meant some details were included that we felt contravened that policy. The magazine was reprinted with the offending paragraphs removed.'

Although the magazine is published by the MoD, its editorial team takes pride in *Soldier*'s independence. This was thought to be the first time that the magazine had ever been censored.

One former officer told *The Daily Telegraph*, a newspaper widely seen as supportive of British forces, 'In the main, we don't and will not talk about the SAS and I think the press understand that, but in situations such as Sierra Leone, where it is obvious that Special Forces are deployed, it can look foolish to constantly make no comment after the event. Common sense seems to have gone out of the window.'

He added, 'I see no problem in confirming that Special Forces took part in Operation Barras once the rescue was over and the unit concerned had been pulled out. I also think it is an insult to the SAS and the family of the trooper who died not to give him credit as being a member of the regiment. Surely in death there is no problem in stating he was a member of the SAS.'[1]

The men from D Squadron would have been amused by a conversation that took place some months after Operation Barras that paid tribute to their skills. As the WSB trailed in to surrender in the months following the operation, some volunteered to serve in the new SLA. Following screening, those who were accepted went to Benguema Training Camp (BTC) to begin their training. In conversation with a former WSB, a Light Infantry instructor on the staff – an NCO and veteran of Operation Barras – couldn't resist asking the former WSB a rather obliquely phrased professional question.

'How did you find the SAS?' the instructor asked.

'The SAS found us,' came the slightly puzzled reply.

The Sierra Leone government said that Operation Barras had considerably weakened the militia. Later in September, the Sierra Leone Army launched Operation Salone, a sweep through the villages and territory that had once been the domain of the WSB. The state radio reported, 'The Sierra Leonean Army is now in control of Magbeni, Layah [Laia] – in the jungle – and Masumana, on the highway between Freetown and Masiaka, where the West Side Boys have ambushed hundreds of vehicles.'

A company from A Battalion of the SLA known as 'the Steelbacks' made a sweep through the area and had 'encountered no resistance from the West Side Boys at Magbeni' according to company commander Captain Mohamed Sankoh. He said his troops had prepared 'strong defensive positions' to be ready for a counterattack. The soldiers found that all houses and vehicles in the town of Magbeni had been reduced to gutted shells.

Other witnesses living downstream said that in the days following Operation Barras they saw twenty-one corpses, believed to be those of WSB soldiers, floating down Rokel Creek. Men, women and children in military uniforms were said to be among the dead. Some of these bodies may have been thrown into the river by survivors after the Paras had departed and others may have been killed by the Lynx gunship during the operation and have fallen into the water. What their presence in the river did not indicate was use of excess force during Operation Barras.

Meanwhile, the state radio quoted President Kabbah as saying that the highway between Freetown and Port Loko (a town approximately 48 km north-east of the capital), which had been closed since May when RUF rebels had flouted a 1999 peace deal and taken about 500 UN peacekeepers hostage, had been reopened. He added that the security situation in the country, ravaged by nine years of civil war, was improving.

A formal announcement was then made by the Sierra Leone government: 'Government wishes to congratulate all those who were involved in the operation to free the hostages today, particularly the British forces, for the very professional way in which the operation was planned and executed. Government is very pleased that all the hostages, British and Sierra Leonean, have been successfully freed and that the Sierra Leonean troops that were involved in the operation acquitted themselves well. Although it had been hoped that the situation could have been resolved peacefully, the use of force eventually became unavoidable due to the recalcitrance of those calling themselves "The West Side Boys".'

Johnny Paul Koroma, the chairman of the Commission for the Consolidation of Peace (CCP), said, 'It is now the business of government to enforce its power in that area so that civilians will not be further harassed.'

In the days following Operation Barras, UNAMSIL stepped up patrols along the main highway near the former WSB base. UN spokeswoman Hirut Befecadu said, 'We have increased activity there to make that route once and for all safe. We have indicated that we do not wish to see West Side Boys in that area, we do not wish to see anybody armed in that area.' Befecadu said that Jordanian peacekeepers at Masiaka had prevented an attempt by the West Side Boys, following Operation Barras, to take civilian hostages and use them as human shields to escape.

Now that Barras had been a success, individuals and organisations were keen to say that they had been associated with it, however peripherally. It was a classic example of the military adage 'defeat is an orphan, but victory has many fathers'.

The *Expo Times* of 13-26 September 2000 published comments regarding the operation from two Sierra Leoneans living abroad.

In the newspaper's regular 'Talking Point' section, Wilfred Leeroy Kabs-Kanu – based in New Jersey, USA – wrote:

Nobody will, and should, deny the British the one moment of glory they are basking in now for the immaculate performance of their armed forces at Okra [sic] Hills last Sunday, during which they burst the bubble of the West Side Bullies and snatched to safety the six British servicemen the renegade soldiers have been holding hostage for weeks.

The spectacular and stellar conclusion of Operation Paras [sic] speaks volumes of the traditional invincibility of the Royal Armed Forces. Their marvellous performance in strange and treacherous terrain has won them respect throughout the world and redeemed their ego, which the West Side Bandits almost destroyed with impudent ease.

However, the more we dwell on the British victory, the more we are tempted to ask where the moral responsibility of the former Imperial power starts and ends vis-à-vis her relations with her former colonies. This question comes begging because the weekend's events have shown once again that Britain will only act decisively where her own personal interests are directly threatened. Where the threat to her interests is only peripheral, Britain is not known to act with the urgency and finality of Operation Paras [sic].

However, in a thought-provoking essay contributed to the same newspaper, Kofi Akosah-Sarpong, based in Ottawa, Canada, focused on Sierra Leone and its national psyche:

West Side Boys and the RUF have an evil dynamic. A confused rebel group like the West Side Boys, with their childish demands, childish attitudes, most of whom have not seen peace since they were born and throughout their pathetic lives, at its worst, is a super-mob. A sense of terrible self-pity that is contemptible in an individual is transformed to misguided heroism in the rebel context: a fierce, virtuous assertion of the rebel group, as the West Side Boys displayed against the overwhelming power of the British paratroopers. That is why rebel grievance, whether realistic or not – a rising force in the African scene as the Mano River Union area comes under conflagration – is so dangerous.

The West Side Boys sees itself as victim of the Sierra Leone collapse which has flowered into self-indulgence, coming out frighteningly alive, collective, suddenly legitimized, glorious even. The individual shame – caused by poverty, alienation, self-pity and piety – is transformed into shamelessness. The weak and vicious members of the West Side Boys, whom I was told have been underrated for long in the Sierra Leone scheme of things, transfer their worst defects to the larger misguided 'cause' (who can tell us what they are fighting for after Major Johnny Paul Koroma, their leader of the AFRC fame, has disbanded the group in the greater Sierra Leonean peace and order).

Thus the West Side Boy or RUF brute killer transforming his/her self-pity into selflessness, and by extension, righteousness, portrays himself/herself as a victim of the Sierra Leonean cultural decay and collapse, who is therefore metaphysically justified in all the mayhem they are visiting upon the poor Sierra Leoneans, and which is gradually assuming life in Guinea.

The West Side Boys are mere injured Sierra Leonean virtue catching up. As they say, nothing is more empowering than being a victim. It is the diamond of self-justifications, the humanoid's indulgence. 'Those to whom evil is done/Do evil in return' – W. H. Auden, the great thinker, would have described such attitude of the West Side Boys as if it were one of Newton's laws.

In any case, self-pity congeals to make a stubborn hard shelf. The West Side Boys or the RUF are indifferent to mere world opinion. Before the British paratroopers stormed their Occra Hill base the UN, diplomats and the Sierra Leonean public and their helpless government have talked to them. Their leaders, epitomised by self-styled Gen. Foday Kallay, have manipulated these poor souls to obduracy.

So Sierra Leone becomes, once again, the primary human mystery, the beast potential in everyone, more so in the increasingly alienated African from the fat cats of African cities. Sometimes, the beast can be talked out, as the earlier negotiations saw the freeing of five British soldiers by the West Side Boys for a satellite phone and some food, and calmed and recivilized. Sometimes the beast, once risen among us, needs to be beaten until it is helpless to harm any longer. Sometimes it simply needs to be killed, as twenty-six of the West Side Boys were killed in the British operation.

In Freetown, Lieutenant-Commander Tony Cramp, spokesman for British forces in Sierra Leone, seemed almost understated when he said, 'There is a great deal of relief that the operation was successful. We always planned on such resistance. It is known that the West Side Boys have used deadly force in the past. They have been taken apart by this and hopefully those that remain will see the light and see the futility of what they are doing.'

The British Army had regained its standing in Sierra Leone and in Freetown the *Sierra News* described the donnish Brigadier Gordon Hughes, commander of the British forces in Sierra Leone, in terms that are not normally used for a senior British officer: 'He was like a latter-day Saladin with a relaxed ambience and, like a rock star in a mosh pit, would smile gamely at the gaggle and ululation of greeters.'

Meanwhile, in London, the MoD had issued press releases about the operation giving details of casualties that initially described Bradley 'Brad' Tinnion as a soldier in 1 Para. However, when his rank of lance bombardier and his unit – 29 Commando Regiment Royal Artillery – were listed, it became clear to informed observers that he must have been serving in the SAS. Such soldiers are attached to the Regiment and come to the SAS from a 'parent' regiment or corps. While soldiers may serve for the rest of their career in the SAS, officers normally return to the parent unit after their tour with the Regiment.

Tinnion, a career soldier, had joined the Army at seventeen and as a gunner had passed the tough Commando Course to join 29 Commando Regiment R. A. In 1997 he had taken on and passed the gruelling trial of mental and physical stamina that is the selection course for the SAS. He had been serving with D Squadron for two years. The squadron had been on exercise in Kenya in September 2000 and ten days before Operation Barras, two of Tinnion's friends – Corporal Martin Halls and Trooper Adrian Powell – had been killed in a vehicle accident during the exercise. Brad had attended their funerals at St Martin's Church in Hereford.

Brad Tinnion had requested that his brother, who was also a soldier, be informed if anything happened to him. In September 2000, Tinnion's brother was on exercise in the jungles of Belize in central America, and until he had been told about Brad's death, the outcome of Operation Barras would not be made public.

In Harrogate, Yorkshire, when news of Brad's death reached his mother Phyllis Collins, she summed up the anguish of all mothers whose sons have died in action: 'We are ever so distraught. We had a lovely son and we have lost him for ever.'

For thirty-year-old Anna Homsi, Brad's childhood sweetheart and long-time partner who was pregnant with their first child at the time of his death, the bereavement would be compounded by MoD bureaucracy.

Their relationship had all the character of a marriage and had been tested by the demands of his life in the services. They had known one another for ten years, during seven and half of which they had lived together, albeit disrupted by Brad being sent on courses, exercises and operational deployments. Now that he was in the SAS, they had set up house at Sutton St Nicholas, near Hereford.

She described him as 'the man of my dreams. We are obviously deeply shocked and devastated by Brad's death, but enormously proud he died doing the job he loved'.

Brad was buried in the SAS cemetery at St Martin's Church, Hereford. Around 600 mourners from all over the country attended the full military funeral.

At this point, Anna discovered that although the war widow's pension took long-term partners into account, it did so only if they had been supported by the serviceman for six months before he enlisted. Brad had joined the Army as a teenager, long before he and Anna had set up home together.

Anna would receive a one-time death-in-service payment of £20,000 because Brad had named her as his next of kin, but to support their daughter, born after Brad's death, Anna would receive only £2,750 per year until Georgia was seventeen years old, a total of only £66,750.

Anna felt that she was entitled to a war widow's pension of £18,000 a year and in this she was backed by Mr Paul Keetch, Liberal Democrat defence spokesman and the MP for Hereford, and Mr Tom Reah of the law firm Powell, Eddison, Freeman and Wilks, a stalwart ally, family friend and solicitor.

When Anna announced that she would sue the MoD under the Human Rights Act of 1998 unless she received the same pension as any widow of a soldier killed in action, it was a bold move, but one that attracted wide public sympathy and considerable media interest. Probably because of this, and the MoD's desire to keep the operations of the SAS out of the public eye, Secretary of State for Defence Geoffrey Hoon announced on 2 August 2001 that the case was being examined.

'We have already begun to look afresh at Anna Homsi's case,' he said. 'I have every sympathy for her situation. That work is being taken forward. I am confident we can reach a satisfactory outcome soon.'

At the time, Mr Reah said that Anna was still 'very, very cautious' about Mr Hoon's promise. 'First of all, we haven't seen any details,' he said. 'The other thing is, Anna is not just concerned about herself. What about other people in this situation? An ex gratia payment is not the way to do it.'

MP Paul Keetch said it was an irony that the government had allowed unmarried dependants of MPs to receive benefits but did not extend the same rights to dependants of those who were prepared to risk their lives in the armed forces. 'Mr Tinnion was praised by everybody for giving his life for his country, yet now his country is not prepared to look after his partner and his daughter in a way most people would find acceptable.'

The offer that the MoD finally made to Anna was a single payment of £250,000. When she heard the news, Anna said that it was too early to celebrate. 'Obviously I am delighted they are reconsidering their position. But until we read the small print it is a question of wait and see. They also haven't made clear what they propose to do for long-term partners in the future.'

At the time, off-the-record briefings from the MoD indicated that it was unlikely that there would be any change to their existing policy. However, although the payment Anna received was not a pension, it was a significant shift in attitude which acknowledged the place of partnerships outside of marriage.

Backed by her MP and solicitor, Anna had won a significant victory for the partners of soldiers killed in action or training that would have implications in Operation Telic during the Second Gulf War. Inspired by Anna's stand, there was a cross-party campaign aimed at equalising pension rights in the armed forces, and on Thursday 20 March 2003, the MoD announced that unmarried partners of any British service personnel killed during Operation Telic in Iraq would receive pensions. The decision would apply to both heterosexual couples and same-sex partners and would be offered when a loved one was killed in 'conflict'.

Entitlement to a pension would be awarded to partners where there was deemed to be a 'substantial relationship' and eligibility would be judged according to a range of criteria from financial interdependence, children and shared commitments like mortgages, the prime beneficiary of the will, shared accommodation, length of the relationship and the absence of a legal spouse. The MoD statement said, 'The decision [to award a pension] would be based on a broad assessment of the substance of the relationship and not all of these criteria would need to be met for entitlement to exist.' The MoD also said that the announcement would not affect existing compensation given to all children of military personnel killed in action.

This was all in the future when Geoffrey Hoon visited A Company, now back in Connaught Barracks in Dover, England, on 20 September 2000. He was fulsome in his praise: 'I have no doubt that many years from now, it [Operation Barras] will be seen as an example of how these things ought to be done. You should be proud of your part in it.'

In Freetown, the Sierra Leone government and army held an open-air interdenominational memorial service for Brad Tinnion. Soldiers in uniform and paramount chiefs in traditional robes gathered at the King Tom cemetery. A sign with the Union Flag and the Sierra Leone flag bore the message 'Koya Chiefdom Mourns the Death of Bombardier Brad Tinnion'. Former WSB leader Foday Kallay, who was in the custody of the Sierra Leone Police, recorded a radio broadcast on Tuesday 12 September calling on his followers to give up the fight and go to a demobilisation camp before they were hunted down. After the British attack, more than thirty WSB turned up at a Jordanian checkpoint asking to be taken into the camps rather than go to prison.

In the police headquarters a few days after his capture, Kallay, dressed only in an oversized filthy Calvin Klein T-shirt that almost covered his grubby boxer shorts, told journalist Chris McGreal of *The Guardian* that he had abandoned war for politics: 'No more violence. I want to be a politician.'

Speaking to BBC journalist Lansana Fofana on 11 September, Kallay said that his militia was a spent force. 'He told me he regrets the whole kidnapping saga,' said Fofana, 'and as far as he was concerned the myth about the West Side Boys was now over and that they don't have any more fighting force left there. And in fact he told me that most of his commanders were killed in the operation and others drowned. He was very downcast and very troubled.'

Kallay had grounds for being downcast. The Sierra Leonean government announced in mid-September that it would try Kallay for kidnap and also on counts of murder, rape, extortion and robbery. His fellow commanders, 'Colonel Savage' and 'Colonel Terminator', had disappeared – but their loyalty was in question anyway. Kallay said he had them detained at the time of the attack because they were trying to overthrow him. Perhaps they had realised that his increasingly ludicrous demands during the negotiations would cost them their lives.

With the benefit of hindsight, Kallay said of the airborne assault: 'Their fire power was unmatchable. We could not escape.' Now he realised that he could face the death penalty, along with two other jailed leaders, 'Brigadier Bomb Blast' and 'Brigadier 55'.

The two policemen taking down Kallay's statement used an unorthodox approach to encourage him to talk fully. One threatened to cut off Kallay's arms, just as his followers had hacked the limbs from innocent Sierra Leoneans. The other said that if Kallay did not co-operate in the investigation, they would simply dump him on a street corner and leave him to the mercy of the citizens of Freetown.

Journalist Foday Koroma, writing in the 13 September issue of the *Expo Times*, provided a more detailed and measured account:

Personnel of the Criminal Investigations Department of the Sierra Leone Police Force are this week reported to have been visiting the Pademba Road Maximum-Security Prison to obtain statements from detained members of the West Side Boys.

Sources close to the attorney-general's office say the West Side Boys have already made statements to the CID both at the prison and at the CID headquarters. The sources further state that the Law Officers

Department is considering bringing to trial both the rebels of the Revolutionary United Front and the West Side Boys, as both factions committed the same atrocities such as rape, torture, abduction and arson.

Both parties, the sources continue, also violated the Lomé Peace Agreement signed last year.

The West Side Boys were reportedly taken to the CID headquarters where their previous statements were compared and corroborated . . . Those that may likely face trial include their leader, self-styled Brigadier Foday Kallay, Savage, Bomb Blast and Ibrahim Bazzy.

Binta Sesay, whose capture at Gberi Bana had rescued her from her brutal husband, gave birth to a baby boy in the Pademba Road Jail in Freetown. In the compound outside, her brutish husband's body was among the corpses being offloaded from the back of an SLA truck. The last act of Kallay, their erstwhile commander, would be to identify the bodies for police records.

The Press Association reported that 'twenty-four-year-old Kallay, with his hands tied behind his back, remained impassive as he was made to look at bodies with gaping shot wounds laid out in a mud yard'. The bodies, some of which were barely recognisable, had been zipped into body bags and formally handed over to the Sierra Leone Police. After identification they were placed in a mass grave, quick lime scattered and the hole back filled.

Ibrahim Koroma, the gang member who had provided the first information about the capture of the Royal Irish patrol, had evaded the murderous Kallay, escaped from the gang and surrendered a week before the destruction of the WSB in Operation Barras.

Other members of the WSB had also decided that discretion was better than valour. In the afternoon of 10 September, thirty trooped in to surrender to the men of JordBat 2 at Masiaka. Two days later, eighteen more surrendered to Jordanian peacekeepers at Magbuntoso, 40 km east of Freetown. By 22 September, a total of 371 demoralised West Side Boys including fifty-seven child combatants had been disarmed.

Reports appeared in the Freetown press that the West Side Boys had regrouped and were harassing people in the surrounding villages. Barras had hit only one of eight WSB bases. However, following the operation, Jordanian peacekeepers were quickly deployed to all areas formerly held by the West Side Boys. UNAMSIL military spokesman Lieutenant-Commander Patrick Coker said, 'The acting UN Force Commander, Brigadier-General Mohammed Garba, visited the area yesterday along with the commander of the Jordanian forces who are deployed in that area, Brigadier Ahmed Sehren.'

Coker continued, 'General Garba visited all the villages the West Side Boys used to occupy. The general did not encounter any armed group apart from UN forces during his trip. Various military uniforms and other items left behind by the West Side Boys were discovered in some of the villages visited. Since the raid on the West Side Boys, forty-eight members of the militia had voluntarily disarmed to the Jordanians at Magbuntoso, with eighteen of them disarming on the day of General Garba's visit.'

While this was taking place, Brigadier Peter Pearson, a senior aide to Commander LAND General Sir Mike Jackson, had flown to Freetown to debrief the rescued patrol members. His report described the events that led up to their capture and concluded that 'Major Alan Marshall made an error of professional judgement in diverting from a planned and authorised journey so as to make an unauthorised visit to the village of Magbeni. There his patrol was overwhelmed. Major Marshall made a grave mistake'.

In Freetown, the press reported that senior British defence sources had commented that '[Major Alan Marshall] has repeated at the start and finish of every conversation that he absolutely accepts, as the company commander, full responsibility'.

However, the Sierra Leone Army liaison officer, twenty-eight-year-old Lieutenant Musa Bangura, who was on one week's sick leave following his release, said that the Jordanian colonel at JordBat 2 had asked the British soldiers to take 'a closer look' at the area. Bangura, who was liked and well respected by the staff of the STTT, said that the major and the regimental signals officer (RSO) had been given 'assurances' by the Jordanians before they drove off the highway into the Occra Hills area. Bangura also praised Marshall for trying to protect him during the seventeen-day hostage crisis. After his seven-day leave, the Sierra Leonean officer reported back for duty.

In what amounted to an admonishment, a paragraph in Brigadier Pearson's report addressed to Brigadier Hughes said: 'The Commander of British Forces has been reminded that Sierra Leone remains an unstable and volatile environment and that the deployment of his forces was to be strictly controlled; and that the Commander is to take all necessary measures to ensure that UK forces do not find themselves inadvertently in a position that may lead to their capture.'

This was an overly harsh judgement of Hughes' command. His role in Sierra Leone was not to stifle initiative and restrict the operations of the STTT. During the build-up to Operation Barras, Special Forces were happy to have Brigadier Hughes in place as the senior officer who was the public face of Operation Barras – 'a role he carried out to perfection', according to one informal comment. The snap decision to visit Magbeni had been Marshall's and was taken on the basis of information supplied by the Jordanians.

Back in the United Kingdom, the Sunday broadsheet newspaper *The Observer* wrote that Major Marshall would not face a court martial. Senior defence sources were said to have been impressed by the way he attempted to defend his men from the West Side Boys during their capture, sustaining a savage beating in the process. They were also impressed that he had not sought to avoid blame. 'If Marshall can convince an inquiry that he simply made a mistake by acting on his own initiative, his career will not be damaged,' said a senior source quoted by the newspaper. 'But if he is found negligent in any way a public example will made of him.'

'In his "naming and shaming" by the Army in the past three days,' *The Observer* commented, 'Marshall may feel this has already happened.'

However, many officers and senior NCOs in the British Army, then and now, if they were honest, must have thought of the times when they too had 'gone out on a limb' – in Northern Ireland, Bosnia or the Gulf – and returned safely after taking a calculated risk. These risks sometimes yield unexpected tactical or intelligence benefits and if this happens the officer or NCO is commended for using his initiative.

As one experienced soldier observed:

In war, the front line is pretty well defined and, more importantly, the adversarial relationship between all those on the battlefield is also well defined. Everyone knows where they stand. You expect enemy soldiers, who you recognise by their uniform, to want to try to kill you. You know that success depends on you killing them first, within whatever Rules of Engagement apply. You would not dream of putting yourself openly behind enemy lines in a small isolated group, and advertise your presence to the enemy with little protection other than small arms immediately to hand.

Peacekeeping (PK) is different. The adversarial relationship is completely ambiguous. PK soldiers may be welcomed by one faction one day, resented by others on another. PK forces rely mostly on moral, not physical authority. And the best PK armies are those who have a reputation for professionalism and impartiality, but also packing a hard punch when they do fight conventionally. The British Battalion (BritBat) did well in Bosnia because of this – they were fair and impartial, but when pushed they would fight back and at one stage BritBat became known locally as 'Shoot-Back-Bat'. That gave all British troops in Bosnia considerable moral advantage.

The British approach to PK has relied upon establishing close liaison with the factions, getting out on the ground, patrolling, getting a 'feel' for what is actually going on, what the real issues are at a local level which might ignite local conflict which then might spread. Nip things in the bud and you might be able to prevent things getting out of hand, or at least you can give early warning to everyone else.

This entails risk. European Economic Community Military Mission (EECMM) LOs [liaison officers] and UNMOs [UN military observers] were killed in Bosnia in the early days – they weren't being reckless. They were certainly taking risks, particularly the EECMM who were completely unarmed, but their best protection was their own judgement, about what they could and could not get away with and reading the local situation. You can only develop that feel for things by getting out and about in the first place. Sometimes, luck goes against you. The same is true elsewhere. You cannot win hearts and minds, and truly make a difference, by rumbling around behind armour and hiding in fixed bases.

Marshall could not have predicted that the WSB would react in the way that they did. The same could have happened to numerous other similar patrols elsewhere in Sierra Leone. On a different day they [the WSB] would probably have reacted differently, and nothing more would have been heard of it.

Perhaps his patrol could have deployed differently when they went into the village, with a team covering from way back as he went forward, and therefore they all wouldn't have been so quickly swamped. But even then it would have been difficult for the cover team to extract those who had been taken. Casualties would probably have been high, including members of the patrol.

It is easy for officers safe back in LAND Command and [the] MoD to second-guess what Marshall should or should not have done, and to talk of him making a 'grave mistake' in exercising his initiative. They were not the men on the ground – he was. Even if the route and visit had been planned and registered it would not have prevented his capture.

Another soldier commented, 'We rely on men such as these [Marshall] to stick their necks out in operations across the world. We must therefore be prepared sometimes for things not always to go according to plan. That is why we have contingencies, and why soldiers must have the confidence that we will back them up – come what may. The British Army punches above its weight in many areas. If we lose the courage and "brass neck" of our soldiers we will all join the ranks of mediocrity – and there are plenty of armies already in that vein.'

Looking at how the men in the patrol had been abused and everything they had suffered, all front-line soldiers must have thought, 'There but for fortune . . .'

The months in Sierra Leone had been tough for the Royal Irish even without the events at Rokel Creek. Their STTT had done a 'back-to-back' tour – as one company had departed on completing its training cycle, another had flown in. However, key battalion headquarters and administrative staff including Colonel Fordham had remained in-country and consequently had spent a total of six months at Benguema Training Centre [BTC]. Now, at last, in late November, they were going home and were assembled at Lungi Airport in the equatorial heat, waiting for the RAF C130 Hercules to fly them home.

The RAF had been superb supporting Operations Palliser and Barras but now flights in and out of Lungi via Senegal had become for 'The Crabs', as soldiers know the RAF, perhaps something of a 'milk run'. The soldiers watched as the aircraft landed, taxied and swung its nose around with engines running so that the full heat of the exhausts hit the waiting soldiers. The soldiers muttered unprintable comments about the RAF, but then this *was* a trooping flight and they were patient men – after all, many of them knew the Army aphorism 'Time to spare, fly Crab Air'.

The RAF enjoys a good safety record which it maintains in part by carefully controlling the cargo it carries. Soldiers and even their families can be checked for 'contraband' – corrosive, inflammable, puncturing or explosive items carried in kit or luggage. But what appears to be a sensible precaution can in the eyes of soldiers become an opportunity for the RAF Police to act like petty tyrants, confiscating on a whim items they deem to be contraband.

The Hercules' engines had stopped and as the tail ramp began to descend, the soldiers of the Royal Irish prepared to pick up their Bergans, rifles and webbing and board the aircraft. To their surprise, a section of RAF Police emerged from the interior and moved across the tarmac towards them. The senior RAF NCO explained briskly that before boarding the aircraft, his detachment would conduct a search for contraband.

'What sort of contraband are you looking for?' asked Colonel Fordham, looking steadily at the senior NCO.

'Corrosive, inflammable, explosive or sharp objects, sir,' came the crisp reply.

The colonel paused for a moment and then in the finest parade-ground voice gave the order: 'Company, FIX ... BAYONETS.'

Practised hands moved to scabbards and dull steel glinted as bayonets snapped home on the muzzles of SA80 rifles.

'This, Sergeant Major, is an infantry battalion,' Fordham said. 'We all carry sharp objects.'

The RAF Police senior NCO was a man who could read a situation – there was no search for contraband and the tired Rangers, NCOs and officers of the Royal Irish filed aboard the aircraft.

On the international scene, 2000 was shaping up to be a good year for Sierra Leone. The month of May had marked the beginning of the Kimberley Process in Kimberley, South Africa. What began as a consultation among a number of diamond-producing countries grew into negotiations that culminated in the adoption of the Kimberley Process Certification Scheme (KPCS) by these countries at a ministerial meeting in Interlaken, Switzerland, in November 2002. The KPCS sets an international benchmark for national certification schemes to be implemented by each participant country through national legislation.[2]

By effectively controlling the trade in rough diamonds through national certification schemes, the trade in polished diamonds became more transparent and secure, giving consumers the confidence that the diamonds they were buying were not 'blood' or 'conflict' diamonds, the stones that had funded so much of the fighting in Sierra Leone.[3]

Three years after the rescue operation, UNAMSIL had become a UN success story – it had almost the right number of men and women on the ground.[4]

The UN disarmament programme in Sierra Leone was formally concluded in January 2002 with the symbolic ceremonial closure of the last disarmament centre in the eastern Kailahun District. In March 1991, Kailahun had served as an RUF base from which the rebels had launched their decade-long campaign against successive Sierra Leonean governments.

Following the ceremony at Kailahun, during which eleven senior RUF commanders handed over their weapons to UN officials, the UNAMSIL force commander, Nigerian Army Lieutenant-General Daniel Opande, said that disarmament was complete and that the war in the country was over.

The UN said that despite the formal conclusion of the disarmament programme, the process would continue until 'all parties are completely disarmed'. It would be a 'multi-layered' programme and after the successful collection of small arms, UNAMSIL officials would promote a 'community programme' throughout Sierra Leone to encourage the handover of home-made and tribal weapons. The demobilisation of ex-combatants at centres in Kenema, Tongo Field, Daru and Kailahun would continue until all had been processed according to the terms of the NCDDR (National Committee for Disarmament, Demobilisation and Reintegration).

The success of the UNAMSIL operation, however, came at a human and financial cost. Total UNAMSIL fatalities at 31 May 2003 stood at 109, of whom 104 were military personnel, two were UNMOs and three were support troops. In New York, the UN had approved a budget of £298.24 million for operations between 1 July 2003 and 30 June 2004.

By 2001, the increased stability led to the return of one of the key players in the Sierra Leone economy: the Canadian-listed diamond-mining company DiamondWorks came back to its mineral holdings, including the Koidu Kimberlite Project. The company began construction and redevelopment of facilities damaged during the war. DiamondWorks, through its wholly owned subsidiary Branch Energy Limited, holds a twenty-five-year mining lease ratified by the government of Sierra Leone in 1995.

'The support of the United Nations and the United Kingdom,' the company explained, 'along with the injection of substantial financial and humanitarian resources into Sierra Leone, has facilitated efforts to bring the Koidu Kimberlite Project back into production.'

On 6 April 2001, the MoD announced the decorations that had been awarded for Operation Barras – the operation that had helped to accelerate the UN DDR programme, which in turn led to increased stability and improvements in the local economy.

Two soldiers with the SAS were awarded the Conspicuous Gallantry Cross, a decoration second only to the Victoria Cross. In addition, four Military Crosses were awarded to members of the rescue team, three to the Special Forces and one to Captain Dan Mathews, 2 IC A Company 1 Para. Brad Tinnion, the only named SAS soldier, was 'Mentioned in Despatches'. Five helicopter crewmen from the JSFAW received the Distinguished Flying Cross.

On 1 September 2001, Geoffrey Hoon announced that the final STTT deployed to Sierra Leone, the 2nd Battalion Light Infantry (2LI), would leave the country at the end of that month, having completed its task.

Lieutenant-Colonel Peter Davies, commanding 2LI, said: 'We have set standards of discipline and basic skills that will make the SLA able to defend themselves against rebel activity in this country. It will be a very different army from the one we found. Whether this sets a precedent for involvement in the rest of Africa depends on what happens to the SLA in the next few years.'

As part of the training and restructuring programme, the SLA now had a company-strength Special Forces unit, the Force Reconnaissance Unit (FRU).

Captain Dimor Musa, its commander, said, 'After what we have been through we can feel the difference the British have made in terms of professionalism and command and control. There is hope now that we can look to the future, unlike before when we were living day to day. The British training has bred confidence and things are much more organised.'

Thirty-two-year-old Captain Martin Collin RM, advising the SLA Force Reconnaissance Unit, summed up the mystique of any Special Forces unit: 'The importance of a unit like this in the SLA is that the rest know their army has a specialist unit. If the FRU are about, at the spearhead of operations, that gives them a huge morale boost. It is also something for aspiring soldiers to aim for.'

The withdrawal of the last STTT reduced the UK military presence in Sierra Leone to 360. However, the UK continued to provide military observers and staff officers for UNAMSIL, a training element for the International Military Advisory and Training Team (IMATT) and a force protection element for IMATT consisting of 110 soldiers. The UK would provide around 100 personnel for the 126-strong IMATT, who would join instructors from Australia, Canada and the US.

The withdrawal concluded the successful training of 8,500 Sierra Leonean soldiers by the STTTs. Geoffrey Hoon commented, 'The training assistance provided by the British Army to the Sierra Leonean Army has been a key factor in helping transform the security situation in the country.' A statement by another politician, Gibril Massaquoi, a spokesman for the RUF, confirmed this view. He praised the STTTs' role in rebuilding the country's armed forces.

Sierra Leone is no longer a country ruled by the dictatorship of one party. A plethora of parties emerged for the May 2002 presidential campaign, and although critics may have said that this would not produce good governance, at least the population did not lack for choice. Observers of the political scene recognised some names, notably Koroma, but all countries have their dynastic political families. The names of parties such as Citizens United for Peace and Progress (CUPP) and the Peace and Liberation Party (PLP) reflected the hope and optimism of what is still a young country, with a population whose median age is seventeen.

Although he had denied harbouring such ambitions, Johnny Paul Koroma, erstwhile leader of the AFRC, stood as a candidate representing his own Peace and Liberation Party (PLP). In the interim, he had apparently become a born-again Christian and sought to bring an element of religious evangelism to his ostensibly anti-corruption campaign. Although Koroma won only 3 per cent of the national vote, the PLP managed to exceed the 12.5 per cent threshold in the West-West (Freetown) constituency and gained two seats in the House of Representatives, including one for Koroma. Moreover, Koroma's candidacy won majority support from the security forces, despite rumours that he had sought to engineer a military coup against Kabbah in the run-up to the election. Regardless of his election to the House of Representatives, as a result of his activities in the AFRC–RUF junta, Koroma still faced possible indictment by the international war crimes court.

Ahead are challenges that would daunt a developed country. Eleven years of brutal fighting have left between 75,000 and 200,000 dead (estimates vary) and tens of thousands maimed or psychologically scarred, including upwards of 10,000 child soldiers, forced labourers and sex slaves. In parts of the country, less than 3 per cent of people have access to safe drinking water. For every 1000 babies born, 170 will die immediately and a further 286 before they reach the age of five. The average life expectancy is thirty-seven years.

In spite of these challenges, there have been small but significant indications of a return to normality in the country's recent past.

On 5 September 2001, local youths squared up to UNAMSIL, not toting guns but in a soccer match organised to mark the first anniversary of the liberation of Magbeni. The match was attended by Deputy Force Commander Major-General Martin Luther Agwai. The match between the UNAMSIL Lions Football Club and the local soccer club, the Kompa Yek Stars, before more than 2,000 enthusiastic fans, was part of UNAMSIL's ongoing peace-building and reconciliation activities.

In a brief speech before the kick-off, Major-General Agwai said that the match was an important step on the road to peace and reconciliation in the country. He presented shirts to the village team, which they donned before the match. The strip was purchased with contributions from UNAMSIL personnel. The local paramount chief thanked UNAMSIL for the donation and its efforts to restore peace in Sierra Leone.

And the score? The Kompa Yek Stars won, beating the UNAMSIL Lions by two goals to nil, with both goals being scored during the second half.

Six months later, Magbeni was once again back in the news. A ceremony on 27 March 2002 marked the transfer to community leadership of three primary schools constructed by the UK branch of the US-based Adventist Development and Relief Agency (ADRA).

At the request of community leaders in the villages of Magbeni and Kurankor, ADRA, with funds provided by the UK Department for International Development (DFID), built and equipped three primary schools for hundreds of local children. Each school has six classrooms, furniture, office space, lavatories and a well.

Like the football match, this represented a microcosm of the recovery of the war-battered country.

Also in 2001, a force review of the Sierra Leone Armed Forces was carried out under British Army guidance to restructure them under a unified command. In January 2002, President Kabbah announced that the SLA would be unified with the tiny Sierra Leone Air Force and the moribund Sierra Leone Navy to form a reconstituted force known as the Republic of Sierra Leone Armed Forces (RSLAF). These measures came into effect in April 2002 and led to the expansion of the force to 11,000.

On 12 June 2000, Kabbah had written to UN Secretary General Kofi Annan asking for the international community to try those people who were guilty of crimes committed during the fighting in Sierra Leone's recent past. On 14 August 2000, the UN passed SCR 1315 confirming that a Special Court would be set up. By 16 January 2002, the Court had been established both by the UN and through an act passed in the Sierra Leonean parliament.

The Special Court now sits in the country and applies both international and Sierra Leonean law. Although administered by the UN, it is an independent judicial body. A large team of international prosecutors led by eminent American lawyer David Crane, and including a legal adviser to former US President Bill Clinton, has been assembled. Following the establishment of the Court in 2002, their three-year mandate would focus on a relatively small group of people – perhaps between fifteen and thirty – considered primarily responsible for the worst atrocities and human rights violations.

Among those indicted by the Special Court were former AFRC leader Johnny Paul Koroma, RUF field commander Sam Bockarie, Kamajor leader Sam Hinga Norman, AFRC leader Alex Tamba Brima, RUF commander Morris Kallon, interim RUF leader Issa Hassan Sesay and RUF leader Foday Saybana Sankoh.

The Freetown *Concord Times* reported that former High Commissioner Peter Penfold, a man still deeply committed to Sierra Leone, had asked, following the arrest of Sam Hinga Norman, whether former Vice-President Dr Albert Joe Demby and President Tejan Kabbah would be indicted as well.

In a letter he circulated to British politicians, Penfold pressed for the release of Norman and argued that, 'Although Sam Norman was regarded as the leader of the Kamajors, the southern-based civil militia, this was only one component of the CDF [Civil Defence Force], which was headed by a committee set up by President Kabbah and chaired by the vice-president at the time, Dr Demby.'

He then asked, 'Does this mean that Dr Demby or President Kabbah might be arrested by the Special Court?' He also criticised the US, describing the country's role in the establishment and operation of the Special Court as particularly incongruous – being the main funders of the Court to the tune of £33 million. 'But at the very time when they are pushing the work of the Special Court,' Penfold's letter continued, 'they have signed an agreement with the Sierra Leone government exempting US citizens from being sent to the International Criminal Court for committing atrocities and human rights violations.'

A Truth and Reconciliation Commission was set up alongside the Special Court, but there was confusion over their respective roles. Incorporating a mix of local and international commissioners, the Truth and Reconciliation Commission is chaired by the head of the local Methodist church, Bishop Joseph Humper, and has an energetic Sierra Leonean lawyer, Yasmin Jusu-Sheriff, as its executive secretary. Modelled on the South African Commission headed by Archbishop Desmond Tutu, it provides a platform for victims to relate their painful experiences and for the perpetrators to seek forgiveness. It has no legal powers to prosecute or punish.

In London, foreign correspondent Chris McGreal, who had reported for *The Guardian* from Africa for ten years and covered in depth the events preceding and during Operation Barras, received the James Cameron Memorial Award on Monday 25 November 2002. The judges praised his 'even-handed reporting and analysis of sub-Saharan Africa – without allowing his judgement to be affected by sentimentality or historical guilt'.

The James Cameron Memorial Trust was established after the death in 1985 of veteran investigative and campaigning journalist James Cameron, with money contributed in his memory by his many friends and admirers at the BBC, *The Guardian* and in the public at large. The Trust is administered by the Department of Journalism at City University, London. Each year, a prize is awarded by a panel of judges to a journalist whose work in the British media has been 'in the Cameron tradition'.

On Tuesday 29 July 2003 at 22.40 hours GMT, Sierra Leone moved closer to stability when Foday Sankoh, the man who had brought much of this misery to Sierra Leone, died peacefully from complications resulting from a partial stroke he had suffered in April 2002. Despite this infirmity, he was still listed as the presidential candidate for the RUF Party, but was excluded from the elections on the grounds that he was not a registered voter because he was in jail.

At the time of his death, he was believed to have been in Choithrams Hospital in western Freetown, where he had been moved after the stroke he suffered while being held on the former slave-trading post of Bunce Island. By March 2003, Sankoh's deteriorating health had become clearly visible; after two years of imprisonment he was an increasingly eccentric figure, reportedly refusing to wash or cut his hair, and there were real concerns for his mental health. At one Special Court hearing, he announced, 'I am surprised that I am being tried because I am the leader of the world.' Despite this behaviour, the majority of the now divided RUF continued to recognise Sankoh as the movement's legitimate leader.

A week before he died, the Court had rejected a request to drop murder charges against him on health grounds. In June, Court Registrar Robin Vincent said that the tribunal hoped to send him abroad for medical treatment. However, the Court had then reported that it could not find a country willing to accept the rebel leader even for short-term treatment.

Sankoh's death from natural causes granted him 'a peaceful end that he denied to so many others', Special Court Chief Prosecutor David Crane said in a statement.

Doctors who had been treating Sankoh said that before he died he had lapsed into a 'catatonic state' and was incapable of walking, talking, feeding himself or even recognising his immediate surroundings. For many Sierra Leoneans, Christian, Animist and Muslim alike, this fate was punishment enough for his crimes. They had little confidence in the Special Court and felt that in the end everyone, however high the position they may have held, will receive their just deserts.

One such person was the terrifying Sam 'Mosquito' Bockarie, the instigator of Operation 'No Living Thing'. He had been reported fighting alongside anti-government rebels in Côte d'Ivoire in May 2003. Though Bockarie, now a comparatively old man of forty, was allied with Liberian President Taylor, he was killed by Liberian forces in early May. Liberian officials claimed he was shot dead while resisting arrest. Later, the Liberian government announced that Bockarie had in fact entered Liberia with a large cache of arms in a bid to overthrow the government of Liberia. David Crane commented that he 'seriously doubt[ed] the veracity of the account being offered by the Liberian authorities'.

Bockarie was a wanted man in Sierra Leone, charged with seventeen counts of war crimes, including acts of terrorism, collective punishments, unlawful killings, sexual violence, physical violence, crimes against humanity, use of child soldiers, abductions, employing forced labourers, looting, burning and attacks on UNAMSIL personnel.

On 15 May 2003, Special Court officials reported that Bockarie's mother, wife and two daughters had been murdered outside their home in Liberia.

On 2 June 2003, Liberian authorities transferred a body they said was Bockarie's to Sierra Leone. A forensic investigation established that the cause of death was five bullet wounds in the chest with three exiting from the back and two on the sides, and a stab on the right side of the neck.

Bockarie described his early life as one of acute poverty in the jungles of eastern Sierra Leone. He often went to bed hungry. His father could not afford schoolbooks, and consequently Bockarie was illiterate. What might otherwise have sounded like a plea for understanding is tempered by this grim comment: 'I cannot tell how many people I have killed. When I am firing during an attack, nobody can survive my bullets.'

He was clearly untroubled by his murderous reputation. When interviewed in January 2000 by Steve Coll, the Pulitzer Prize-winning managing editor of the *Washington Post*, he announced during one long account of the war in Sierra Leone, 'I am a good-looking man, a big showman, I like good living . . . You know, I really admire myself.'

Coll noted the general's wardrobe: '[He was] resplendent in quasi-military dress: a felt beret with two pinned stars, combat camouflage, a silver pistol and, around his neck, a medallion in the shape of Africa hooked to a shiny gold chain. He buzzed flamboyantly around town on an off-road motorcycle. He changed clothes frequently – safari suits, European designer wraparound sunglasses, the latest designer jeans and, for a family photo on our final morning, a smart charcoal double-breasted suit.'

Bockarie was a member of the Kissi tribe, born in Kailahun District, and spent part of his early life working as a barber in Kono. Before becoming the field commander of the RUF, he would earn a reputation as a disco-dancing champion, worked as a diamond miner, electrician and waiter and might have been dictating his own epitaph when he said, 'I never wanted myself to be overlooked by my fellow men.'

This wish was unlikely to be fulfilled: the Freetown newspaper *Awoko*

Tok Tok reported that with no living relatives to collect his body, Bockarie would probably be buried by the prison authorities in an unmarked pauper's grave.

In May 2003, Sami, a Liberian businessman whose family has been in the country for four generations, was interviewed by Jon Henley of *The Guardian*. Sami put the terrifying weeks of Operation 'No Living Thing' and the work of the Special Court into a typically Sierra Leonean context: 'It was a time of madness. People want to put it behind them. Raking it all up now could do tremendous harm. These people are history, but this way they'll get another big chance to inflame their followers. This country has other ways, tribal ways, traditional ways, of dealing with them.5

'God or Allah will judge them,' Sami concluded – *Hakeh*, divine justice.

Notes

Chapter One

1 **The Royal Irish Regiment.** The Royal Irish Regiment is the youngest regiment in the British Army, but it has a unique history. Although it was only formed on 1 July 1992 by the amalgamation of the Ulster Defence Regiment (UDR) and the Royal Irish Rangers, it can trace a long pedigree.

The UDR was formed on 1 April 1970. Its area of operations was exclusively Northern Ireland, where it worked alongside the Royal Ulster Constabulary (RUC) against terrorist organisations like the Provisional Irish Republican Army (PIRA). In this role, the UDR became the longest-serving regiment on active service in the British Army – longer than any regiment since the Napoleonic Wars.

In its early days, it had up to 18 per cent Catholic membership. However, Catholics were being targeted by the PIRA, and the UDR suffered an early image problem with nationalists who saw it as absorbing too many former B Specials, a paramilitary-style police reserve drawn from the Protestant community.

During the UDR's twenty-two years of duty in Northern Ireland, a total of 197 serving UDR soldiers were killed in the line of duty and a further sixty former members were killed by paramilitaries after they left the regiment.

In 1988, Queen Elizabeth II granted colours to the nine UDR battalions. However, three years later, in a review of the armed forces, the British government announced that the UDR would be disbanded. The decision was presented as a purely military one, arising from a reduction in forces brought about by the ending of the Cold War. However, by that time only 3 per cent of its members were Catholic and the Irish government regarded the UDR with suspicion.

The Royal Irish Rangers were themselves an amalgamation of the Royal Inniskilling Fusiliers, the Royal Ulster Rifles (originally the Royal Irish Rifles) and the Royal Irish Fusiliers.

The regiment that was proposed – the Royal Irish Regiment – could trace its history back to the Royal Irish Regiment raised as the Earl of Granard's Regiment of Foot and re-titled the Royal Regiment of Ireland in 1695.

A new Royal Irish Regiment had been raised in 1881 and fought with distinction in the Crimean War, in addition to performing the demanding garrison and internal-security duties necessary throughout the British Empire.

In World War I, the Royal Irish Regiment raised a total of ten battalions from its two pre-war regular and two reserve battalions. The additional battalions included two service battalions in Kitchener's 1st and 2nd Armies, a battalion formed in 1917 from the dismounted South Irish Horse, a further service battalion and two garrison battalions. The regiment won forty-two battle honours and one Victoria Cross, but lost 2,780 men as casualties. In total, the Royal Irish Regiment won four VCs before it was disbanded in 1922 on the formation of the Irish Free State.

The youngest recorded Allied soldier to die in World War I was Private John Condon from Waterford, who enlisted in the Royal Irish Regiment aged thirteen and served in the 2nd Battalion. Condon was killed in at Ypres in 1915, but his body was not recovered until 1923, when it was re-interred in Poelkapelle British Cemetery, Flanders. The only personal item returned to his family was a piece of one of his boots stamped with his regimental number – 6322.

The current Royal Irish Regiment was originally made up of eight battalions, later reduced to four. The regiment retained one of the traditional titles by calling its private soldiers 'Rangers'. The 1st Battalion is a general service battalion, an ordinary line infantry unit, which in 2003 was serving with 16 Air Assault Brigade. A company of soldiers from the Royal Irish was among the British Army contingent sent to Bosnia to protect food convoys in 1992. Commanded with distinction by Lieutenant-Colonel Tim Collins, the battalion saw action in Iraq in Operation Telic in 2003, during the Second Gulf War.

The following widely reported speech was given by County Down native Lieutenant-Colonel Tim Collins on 20 March 2003 in Kuwait, near the Iraqi border:

We go to liberate, not to conquer. We will not fly our flags in their country. We are entering Iraq to free a people and the only flag which will be flown in that ancient land is their own. Show respect for them.

There are some who are alive at this moment who will not be alive shortly. Those who do not wish to go on that journey, we will not send. As for the others, I expect you to rock their world. Wipe them out if that is what they choose. But if you are ferocious in battle, remember to be magnanimous in victory.

Iraq is steeped in history. It is the site of the Garden of Eden, of the Great Flood and the birthplace of Abraham. Tread lightly there. You will see things that no man could pay to see and you will have to go a long way to find a more decent, generous and upright people than the Iraqis. You will be embarrassed by their hospitality even though they have nothing. Don't treat them as refugees, for they are in their own country. Their children will be poor; in years to come they will know that the light of liberation in their lives was brought by you.

If there are casualties of war, then remember that when they woke up and got dressed in the morning they did not plan to die this day. Allow them dignity in death. Bury them properly and mark their graves.

It is my foremost intention to bring every single one of you out alive, but there may be people among us who will not see the end of this campaign. We will put them in their sleeping bags and send them back. There will be no time for sorrow.

The enemy should be in no doubt that we are his nemesis and that we are bringing about his rightful destruction. There are many regional commanders who have stains on their souls and they are stoking the fires of hell for Saddam. He and his forces will be destroyed by this coalition for what they have done. As they die, they will know their deeds have brought them to this place. Show them no pity.

It is a big step to take another human life. It is not to be done lightly. I know of men who have taken life needlessly in other conflicts, I can assure you they live with the mark of Cain upon them. If someone surrenders to you, then remember they have that right in international law and ensure that one day they go home to their family.

The ones who wish to fight, well, we aim to please.

If you harm the regiment or its history by over-enthusiasm in killing or in cowardice, know it is your family who will suffer. You will be shunned unless your conduct is of the highest, for your deeds will follow you down through history. We will bring shame on neither our uniform nor our nation.

[Regarding the use by Saddam Hussein of chemical or biological weapons] It is not a question of if, it's a question of when. We know he has already devolved the decision to lower commanders, and that means he has already taken the decision himself. If we survive the first strike, we will survive the attack.

As for ourselves, let's bring everyone home and leave Iraq a better place for us having been there.

Our business now is north.

The other three home service battalions of the Royal Irish supported the Police Service of Northern Ireland, patrolling on foot, by helicopter or by vehicle. They also guarded key points, checked traffic and cleared routes in addition to providing specialist weapons-search teams.

In its first six months of operations, three Rangers were murdered, two locally based and one home on leave from Cyprus. Seven soldiers from the Royal Irish Regiment have been killed by paramilitary organisations

The Royal Irish Regiment recruits on both sides of the border regardless of religion or nationality and, along with the Irish Guards, is all that is left of a host of British Army Irish regiments.

2 **West Side Boys.** The name associated with the gang, like much of their style, was derived from the United States. It had first been used by groups of young New Yorkers with a much older and more honourable tradition.

In the 1920s and 30s when cars were still a luxury, boys and girls from working-class families on Manhattan's West Side played a baseball-derived game called stickball in the streets. They formed themselves into loose teams; some had official names and others were invented or taken from professional baseball teams. Many were sponsored by a neighbourhood café or bar. Three well-known teams were the Rufos from West 66th, the Iona's of West 46th and the Burney Brothers from West 60th. Collectively they were known as 'The West Side Boys'.

However, the name that the gang actually favoured has been reported to have been the tasteless and confrontational 'West Side Niggaz'. It had been popularised in the lyrics of the song 'Fuck Friends' by the New York gangsta rap musician 2Pac or Tupac Amaru Shakur. Shakur became a black youth icon when he was killed in a drive-by shooting on September 13, 1996. In order not to cause offence in press reports and broadcasts, 'Niggaz' became 'Boys' and in some military documents the gang's name was even elevated to 'West Side Soldiers'.

3 **ZPU-2.** Though obsolete, the ZPU-2 is a formidable weapon that fires a 64.4 g projectile that will penetrate 32 mm of vertical armour plate at 500 m.

4　**AFRC.** Despite its grandiloquent name, the Armed Forces Revolutionary Council or Armed Forces Ruling Congress (AFRC) was merely an ad hoc organisation formed from mutinous Sierra Leonean soldiers protesting about status and pay.

The mutiny began early on 25 May 1997 and after eight hours of fighting, the mutineers had seized Freetown and freed Major Johnny Paul Koroma from prison, where he was awaiting trial for an earlier coup attempt. Koroma declared himself Sierra Leone's new leader, forcing President Kabbah to flee to Guinea by helicopter.

Within three days, RUF leader Foday Sankoh had voiced his support for the AFRC and the RUF formed a coalition government with the AFRC. Koroma became deputy leader of the RUF.

The AFRC–RUF regime lacked domestic support and was not internationally recognised; it was characterised by a total disregard for the rule of law and the breakdown of the formal economy. Government offices, schools, banks and commercial services ceased to function. Those who opposed the junta were tortured, murdered or raped, and government buildings, humanitarian relief offices and houses were burned down or looted.

5　**Aminatta Forna** is now a London-based author, broadcaster and journalist. She was ten years old when she saw her father, Mohamed Forna, for the last time in the summer of 1974 in Freetown. He was a mild-mannered British-educated doctor devoted to the fledgling democracy of the newly independent Sierra Leone, where he had held the post of finance minister under Siaka Stevens. But one year after the meeting with his daughter, having resigned from Stevens' government in protest over its repression and corruption, Mohamed Forna was arrested and hanged following a rigged treason trial.

As an adult, Aminatta Forna returned to Sierra Leone to investigate the circumstances surrounding her father's death. Her memoir, *The Devil that Danced on the Water: A Daughter's Quest*, is a passionate and vivid account of an African childhood and the story of an African nation's transition from democracy to dictatorship. In the UK, it was serialised as the 'Book of the Week' on BBC Radio and extracts were published in the *Sunday Times* newspaper. In the US, the book has been chosen by Barnes & Noble booksellers for their 'Discovery' series.

6　**Cocaine.** Long-term cocaine use can lead to loss of concentration, irritability, loss of memory and energy, paranoia, anxiety, and a loss of interest in sex. Excessive cocaine use leading to loss of memory and paranoia would certainly account for the erratic behaviour of the WSB as the hostage crisis developed.

7　**Cannabis.** Since cannabis is an intoxicating and mildly hallucinogenic drug that can impair short-term memory if used to excess, an encounter with an armed man under its influence might well be hazardous.

Chapter Two

1　**Bai Bureh.** Born around 1840, this Sierra Leonean chief was the hero of the 1898 'Hut Tax' rebellion. His father was an important Loko war chief and his mother was probably a Temne from the region of modern Makeni.

As a young man he was sent to Gbendembu, a training school for warriors, where he earned the nickname 'Kebalai', meaning 'one whose basket is never full' or 'one who never tires of war'. Kebalai became a famous war leader in the 1860s and 1870s, serving under a Soso ruler in a long jihad to establish correct Islamic practices. In 1886, Kebalai was crowned ruler of Kasseh, a small kingdom near Port Loko, and given the royal title of Bai Bureh.

The new ruler soon gained a reputation for stubborn independence that annoyed the British administration in Freetown. On one occasion, Bai Bureh refused to recognise a peace treaty the British had negotiated with the Limba without his participation, and on another occasion, he led warriors on a raid across the border into French Guinea. When the British declared Sierra Leone their Protectorate in 1896, they quickly issued a warrant for Bai Bureh's arrest, fearing that he would foment resistance to the new 'Hut Tax'. But they could not capture him, and Bai Bureh organised a large-scale guerrilla revolt that lasted for ten months. He brought warriors from several Temne states under his command, as well as some Loko, Soso and Limba fighters, and held the initiative over a superior British force for the first four months of the rebellion. Bai Bureh acquired a reputation for supernatural powers and was believed to be bulletproof and to have the ability to become invisible or stay underwater for long periods. The British offered a reward of £100 (the equivalent of £5,750 in 2003) for information leading to his capture, but no one would come forward. A Colonial official wrote that Bai Bureh's men 'loved their chief, and remained loyal to him to the very last'.

Bai Bureh was finally captured on 11 November 1898 and taken under guard to Freetown, where crowds gathered to catch a glimpse of the great man. The British exiled him to the Gold Coast (now Ghana), but in a change of heart they brought him back in 1905 and reinstated him as a Chief of Kasseh. Sierra Leone's greatest military hero died in 1908.

Chapter Three

1 **Small Boys Unit.** Currently more than 300,000 children under the age of eighteen are fighting in conflicts around the world. Hundreds of thousands more are members of armed forces who could be sent into combat at any time. Many of these children have been forcibly recruited but some have joined up voluntarily.

According to official estimates, 5,400 children fought in Sierra Leone's civil war, but UNICEF stresses that these are just estimates. A local group, Children Affected by War, believes that the figure is probably closer to 10,000. One rebel group admitted in late 1999 that 30 per cent of its combatants were children.

Musah al Fatau, an expert on mercenaries in West Africa at the Soros Foundation in Dakar, Senegal, said that there are many child soldiers particularly in countries where there has been a breakdown in governance. 'Sierra Leone was a clear example of this, where illiteracy and poverty were quite high and politicians used groups of young people for their political ends,' he noted. Fatau also commented that many children who took up arms there were unable to develop subsequently into responsible adult citizens.

Relief workers have even reported some cases of child soldiers becoming mercenaries and following their elders from one regional conflict to another. Adults were terrified by the SBU combination of youthful brutality and swaggering self-confidence, at odds with their matted locks and tattered clothes. However, appearances belied their tight discipline and fierce loyalty to commanders. Travelling light, they cared little for their personal safety and were at home in the thick forest close to the edge of Freetown.

'Children form part and parcel of mercenary activities in West Africa,' commented Napoleon Abdulai, a disarmament expert working for the UN Programme of Co-ordination and Assistance for Security, noting also that they are often heavily drugged when they are sent into combat. Some former child soldiers say they were forcibly injected with cocaine before being sent into battle. Drugs administered by adults played an important part as a control mechanism.

Abdulai said that many child soldiers in Sierra Leone in the 1990s had been unable to stop their violent way of life and had gone on to become hardcore adult mercenaries in Liberia and Côte d'Ivoire.

They are considered beyond redemption by most Sierra Leoneans. One parent who tried to foster a fourteen-year-old boy as part of a reintegration programme said: 'They live in the jungle like wild animals. They cannot come back into town. They have been made mad and dangerous and no one can control them. I had the boy for six weeks and then I just could not do so any more. He threatened to chop the hands off my children and when I was not looking he tried to rape my eight-year-old daughter.'

Casualty rates among child soldiers are generally high because of their inexperience, lack of training and lower recovery rates from battlefield injuries. Many girl soldiers are expected to provide sexual services as well as to fight. Child soldiers accept an early death because normal life expectancy is low.

Interviewed in May 2003, fifteen-year-old Abass Gbla, who at the age of ten was a sergeant commanding ten boy soldiers in an RUF SBU, is now training as a carpenter. 'Obviously my life is better now,' he said. 'Although with the drugs I have to say I was addicted to the fighting; I felt like a big man. But now I recognise I'm learning a skill, a valuable skill. It will help me to live and to forget.'

2   **Valentine Strasser.** While in power, Strasser was immensely popular with his fellow soldiers. His reputation was enhanced when he was wounded in action while fighting against the RUF.

A flamboyant figure in Ray-Ban sunglasses and designer clothing, he was the youngest head of state in the world. Despite widespread criticism of the Sierra Leone human rights record from organisations such as Amnesty International, the young leader quickly ingratiated himself with world leaders including Bill Clinton, John Major and Nelson Mandela.

However, only eight months into his leadership, Strasser's forces executed twenty-six political opponents on a beach outside Freetown. The international community was appalled, and Britain immediately suspended aid in January 1994.

After he was ousted from power 1996, Strasser led a nomadic life in the UK. He had been given a scholarship on a student visa to study law at Warwick University. He abandoned the course when his identity became known to fellow students and drifted to London where he was reported to have 'worked the doors' as a bouncer at nightclubs.

Strasser showed friends scars above his eye and on his leg and said he had been attacked outside a London Underground station. 'I was going to an off-licence, and then this guy just turned around and came at me with a knife – something like a Swiss Army penknife,' he claimed. 'I was stabbed and I had to be taken to hospital. I couldn't put it down to anything other than racial motivation.'

At age thirty-four he was living in Islington under the assumed name 'Reginald' Strasser and had been unemployed for two years. In October 2000 his identity was revealed. His application for asylum was rejected and he flew to The Gambia.

He was detained there and deported back to Britain, where he was denied entry. He was returned to The Gambia and was detained by military officers in Talinding, 15 km west of the capital Banjul, and questioned in the National Intelligence Bureau headquarters.

In 2003 he was reported to be destitute in Sierra Leone, where one resident commented that he deserved some credit since he was the only former national leader who had ruled Sierra Leone for two years and who was still alive.

3 **Kamajor fighters.** These tribal fighters underwent initiation rights to become part of this secret society. Witch doctors and initiators conducted the ceremonies, which they said gave the Kamajors special powers on the battlefield. A Kamajor child fighter explained, 'Before going out to fight, we would be given special water. The water protects you as long as you don't "spoil" [violate] the laws. It was part of our bloodstream and made us bulletproof.'

These laws were secret but were said to include sexual abstinence. According to Kenneth Kuka, a Kamajor leader, 'Most of our laws have to do with women. The young boys were some of our best fighters because they didn't have girlfriends or women. So the bullets would never penetrate them.'

When the Kamajors prepared to go into action, they would dress in their traditional attire, which included fetishes and talismans. The Kamajors said they must remain clean and pure even to the extent of avoiding contact as conventional as a handshake.

The Kamajors were reluctant to disarm because of their lack of faith in the peace agreement and the intentions of the RUF/AFRC junta. They said they would remain committed to defending democracy 'at any hour, any time'.

According to human rights groups, the Kamajors were also guilty of serious human rights abuses. Some of their attacks had the character of inter-tribal conflicts. As far back as 19 February 1997, the government of Sierra Leone rejected an RUF statement that the ceasefire violations in the northern part of the country were deliberate attacks by Mende Kamajors against the Makeni tribe. The government claimed that the Kamajors were defending themselves against RUF attacks and were doing so with its approval.

Tribal and group rivalry took an unusual turn when fighting broke out overnight on 4–5 October 1997 between government soldiers and the RUF near Congotown, over diamond concessions. According to eye-witness accounts, the RUF taunted the government soldiers with not having the courage to fight the Kamajors.

Other militias within the Civil Defence Force included the Donsos in the diamond-rich Kono region and Tamaboros and Kapras in the north, militias formed to protect their regions from rebel attacks. Hinga Norman, the deputy defence minister chief in the Kabbah government, was made honorary head of the militias and given the title Chief Kamajor.

The militias, in particular the Kamajors, were instrumental in prosecuting the war against the RUF. Initially, they had good relations with the ECOMOG forces, but relations deteriorated due to tensions over the exploitation of the diamond resources. The militias also collaborated with the rebel forces in the exploitation of the war economy.

As in many insurgencies, the war in Sierra Leone was not one in which there were 'good guys' and 'bad guys'. For those working and fighting on the ground, these moral absolutes were relative – everyone was bad, but the 'good guys' were not as bad as the 'bad guys'. Even the West Side Boys, strutting around in their Tupac Shakur T-shirts and mirror sunglasses, were seen as 'good guys' during their time as a pro-government group militia until they went to the 'bad' side and became bandits.

4 **Mammy Yoko.** Somewhat appropriately, the hotel that would be taken over as the UNAMSIL HQ is named after one of Sierra Leone's controversial heroines – Madam, Mami or Mammy Yoko (1849-1906). A latter-day Cleopatra in a world dominated by men, she was a chief who used a mixture of charm and guile to manipulate the British administration in the late 19th century. When the British declared Sierra Leone their Protectorate in 1896, Mammy Yoko commanded her people to pay the new 'Hut Tax', but her sub-chiefs rebelled. They held a secret meeting, blaming Yoko for 'spoiling the country' by supporting the British police, taxes and forced labour. Yoko took refuge in the police barracks, which withstood several attacks by her own subjects, and she was later awarded a silver medal by Queen Victoria for her loyalty.

Mammy Yoko ruled as a paramount chief in the new British Protectorate until 1906, when it appears that she committed suicide at the age of fifty-seven. If true, her reasons have never been altogether clear. A British official wrote that she had obtained all there was to be had in life – love, fame, wealth and power – and felt there was nothing more to look forward to.

The hotel that bears her name was built in 1980 when Sierra Leone hosted a summit of the Organisation of African Unity (OAU). Subsequently it became not only the UNAMSIL HQ (housed on its upper floors) but also a focus for the media.

The 2002 edition of the *Lonely Planet* guide described it thus: 'The hotel still offers twenty comfortable 1st-floor rooms with air-con and cable TV to anyone who doesn't mind the constant hubbub of a UN mission. The hotel has a reasonably comfortable bar that offers a rudimentary breakfast and it plans to reopen its restaurant soon. Thanks to the UN, it also offers the best security of any hotel in Sierra Leone.'

Chapter Five

1 **Text of Major-General Jetley's letter to the UN:**
REPORT ON THE CRISIS IN SIERRA LEONE
Background
  1. The Lomé Peace Accord was signed in July 1999 to end the eight-year-old

bloody civil war in Sierra Leone. The primary reason for the signing of the accord was that a stalemate had been reached in the fighting and the ECOWAS states were finding it extremely difficult to support their Peacekeeping Force – ECOMOG – due to the extreme financial drain on their fragile economies.

2. The accord called for deployment of a peacekeeping force comprising ECOMOG and UNOMSIL to oversee the peace process. This was interpreted by the Nigerians (who formed the major chunk of ECOMOG) that ECOMOG would form a major part of the UN Peacekeeping Force and that this Force would be headed by the ECOMOG Force Commander Maj.-Gen. Kpamber. However, when Maj.-Gen. Kpamber went to UN HQ New York, he was very disappointed to learn that he was not going to be the Force Commander of UNAMSIL and that Nigeria would have three battalions as part of UNAMSIL; out of this they had to concede one battalion to the Guineans. The Nigerians therefore felt that they were not getting a fair deal in the Peace Process in Sierra Leone despite the sacrifices they had made to pave the way for the peace process. This to a very large extent is the genesis of the present crisis. It is my opinion that the ECOMOG Force Commander along with the SRSG [special representative of the secretary-general] and DFC [deputy force commander] have worked hard to sabotage the peace process and show Indians in general and me in particular in a poor light.

Relationship Between ECOMOG and RUF

3. It is well known that public opinion in Nigeria was against the continued deployment of Nigerian troops as part of ECOMOG in Sierra Leone; however the Nigerian Army was interested in staying in Sierra Leone due to the massive benefits they were getting from the illegal diamond mining. Brig.-Gen. Maxwell Khobe was commonly known as the 'Ten Million Man'; it is alleged that he received up to [US] 10 million dollars [£5.5 million] to permit the activities of RUF. The ECOMOG Force Commander Maj.-Gen. Kpamber was also involved in the illegal diamond mining in connivance with RUF leader Foday Sankoh.

4. After the initial fighting between ECOMOG and RUF, the relationship had thawed when a stalemate had been reached militarily. It is understood that a tacit understanding was reached between the RUF and ECOMOG of non-interference in each other's activities; the total absence of ECOMOG deployment in RUF-held areas is indicative of this. I believe that the RUF leader Foday Sankoh was also under the impression that the UN Peacekeeping Force agreed to in Lomé was primarily a rehatted ECOMOG with Maj.-Gen. Kpamber as its boss. The deployment of a neutral peacekeeping force (UNAMSIL) under an Indian General, keen to implement the Peace Accord in letter and spirit, was not what Sankoh had bargained for. He viewed UNAMSIL as a big obstacle in his ambition of becoming the next President of Sierra Leone.

Relationship Between Force Commander, SRSG and DFC

5. The SRSG and DFC had instructions from Nigeria to pursue the agenda for which they had been sent. Keeping the Nigerian interests was paramount even if meant scuttling the Peace Process and this also implied that UNAMSIL was expendable. To this end the SRSG and DFC cultivated the RUF leadership, especially Foday Sankoh, behind my back.

6. I was sandwiched between the two of them which severely hampered my

functioning. Some instances which reflected my predicament:

a. The DFC was sent to Nigeria in Jan 2000, without my approval, on the pretext of resolving the equipment of Nigerian Battalions, clearly a task not forming a part of the charter of duties of the DFC. The DFC returned after 13 days and did not think it fit to meet me for two days thereafter.

b. During the discussions on the rehatting of the Nigerian battalions for 90 days, the DFC spoke openly against the logic given by me. The SRSG conducted the entire conference with a pro-Nigeria bias.

c. Notwithstanding the fact that the SRSG had absolutely nothing to do with military matters, he insisted on knowing the reasons why INDBAT could not deploy on widely separated axes at Koidu and Kailahun as mistakenly planned off the map earlier. Even after my explaining to him in detail, he insisted on arranging a meeting with the DFC, COS [chief of staff] (observer) who had joined UNAMSIL just two days ago and the COS of the force, just to undermine my position and embarrass me in front of my subordinates. In hindsight, it appears that my decision has been vindicated. If I had deployed as SRSG was insisting we would have had the entire INDBAT either disarmed or decimated.

d. With a view to making inroads into the districts of Kailahun and Koidu I sent strong patrols each of KENBAT and GHANBAT to Koidu and INDBAT to Kailahun respectively. While the GHANBAT CO failed to execute my orders, KENBAT could only achieve partial success. It was only INDBAT which successfully reached Kailahun. When I informed the SRSG about the above events, instead of complimenting INDBAT'S spectacular achievement, he, in the presence of my subordinate staff officers like the DFC and CMO [chief military observer], started questioning the rationale of my actions, suggesting that I should have sent joint patrols of all three battalions to Koidu rather than the individual unit identities. At the end I had to categorically ask him to leave the military matters to me since such plans are made and decisions taken after due consultation with my staff.

e. On numerous occasions the DFC has not executed tasks given by me; he has not even bothered to give a feedback weeks after the scheduled date of submission of report of projects entrusted to him.

Events Leading to the Present Crisis and the Conduct of Nigeria during the Crisis

7. The present crisis was precipitated by the incident at Makeni where 10 RUF cadres had voluntarily disarmed and joined the DDR programme. However, this was not acceptable to the RUF leadership which had its own agenda. The complicity of Nigeria in the crisis is evident from the following:

a. The RUF action is timed with the withdrawal of ECOMOG troops from Sierra Leone.

b. The SRSG was on leave at the same time and could not be contacted for at least two days despite the best efforts of New York.

c. RUF intercepts received by DHQ [division headquarters] of Republic of Sierra Leone Army clearly indicate the close relationship between RUF and Nigerians.

d. Initially the RUF effort was directed only against Kenyans and Indians and when this aspect was discussed in the Senior Staff Meeting there was a symbolic gesture at Kambia against the NIBAT-2 company located there.

e. The complete Nigerian company at Kambia was permitted to move to Port Loko, and the two Indian drivers with them were detained. They were later released after I intervened.

f. No fight given by Nigerian troops of NIBAT-2 to RUF at Lunsar and Rogberi, Rokel, Masiaka and Laia Junction.

g. I was given confirmation that the NIBAT-3 company was deployed at Newton, an important location on the Masiaka–Freetown Axis; however when I personally landed there during my recce I found no troops deployed.

h. The DFC has been in constant touch with Foday Sankoh throughout this crisis; he has probably also compromised a lot of my operational plans.

i. It is popularly believed by the locals in Freetown that CO NIBAT-4 took Foday Sankoh in his APC when the demonstrators turned violent at his house. In fact, eye witnesses corroborated this. One of my sources has also confirmed above. He was reportedly kept in custody in the house of CO NIBAT-4 in Freetown, a fact which has been hidden from me so far.

Other Constraints in my Functioning

8. In addition to the above problems, I have also had the following logistics difficulties in the mission to cope with:

a. Transport. The present capability of the mission does not permit movement of one company at a time. Despite this, out of the 20 UN trucks, ten had been given to the private contract organisations called Dyncorp. My staff officers were forced to travel in minibuses and a few gypsies [type of vehicle] on the pretext that the Indian Guard and Admin Company was to provide the transport, whereas the MOU [memorandum of understanding] does not say so.

b. Communications. Even after months since the establishment of the peacekeeping mission, I cannot talk directly to any battalion commander. There are severe shortages of communication equipment in a number of units which have not been made up despite several reminders to the administrative staff. Some battalions have only one radio set in the company available to them. Most battalions have no fax facilities to forward sitreps [situation reports] or reports and returns.

c. Fuel. The fuel contract for the mission has not yet been finalised. On numerous occasions I have had to cancel operational moves because of non availability of POL [petrol, oil and lubricants]. The system of fuel replenishment is based on few POL bowsers held by the UN; fwd dumping facilities or kerb-side petrol pumps have not yet been established.

d. Rations. The troops are still being provided rations on an interim contract. On occasions battalions have got theirs up to seven days late and that, too, with large number of deficiencies. In fact, during the ongoing crisis units like KENBAT at Makeni and Magburaka and INDBAT companies at Kailahun which had been surrounded ran out of food and water and had to be resupplied under fire. If the units had been stocked for 15 days as is normally practiced, the units would not have had to look over their shoulders.

e. Water. As per all MOUs, water supply is a UN responsibility. In the absence of availability of potable drinking water, UN is to provide bottled water to all troops. To date the administrative staff has not been able to dig a single well in the country nor have they provided bottled water. What is most appalling is that troop labour was used for digging these wells. This despite repeated discussions on the issue even in the presence of the CAO.

f. <u>Camp Infrastructure</u>. It was brought to the notice of the administrative staff that due to the heavy rains in the country it was extremely necessary to provide a hard standing in the camp sites of all units. The demand for construction materials was fwd accordingly in Feb 2000. Not a single bag of cement has been received to date and the wet season has already begun.

9. <u>Capability of Units</u>. Most units under my command other than India, Kenya and Guinea have very little or no equipment with them. They have not been properly briefed in their country about the application of Chapter VII [of the UN Charter – Action with Respect to Threats to the Peace, Breaches of the Peace and Acts of Aggression] in this mission for certain contingencies. It is for this precise reason that the troops did not have the mental aptitude or the will to fight the rebels when the situation so demanded, and resorted to handing over their arms on the slightest danger to their life. This aspect enabled the rebels to gain a moral ascendancy and thereby emboldened them to take on the United Nations in the manner in which they have done in the present crisis. Guinea, Kenya and Zambia case in point. Also, units hoped that negotiations would help the rebels see reason. The rebels took advantage of the gullibility of these units and disarmed them.

Conclusion

UN Peacekeeping operations are a combination of diplomacy and tact. Generally in African countries the Peace Accord signed is shaky and fragile. In a mineral-rich country like Sierra Leone, politics has a very major role to play in finding solutions to civil wars. In my case, the Mission Directive given to me, and which I tried to follow implicitly, directly conflicted with the interests of not only the warring factions but also of the major players in the diamond racket like Liberia and Nigeria. As an Indian, and having no hidden agenda to promote, I became a victim of the machinations of these countries. By placing their stooges in the right places they have not only tried to scuttle the peace process but also to try and denigrate me and the country I represent, to promote their own personal ambitions and personal interests.

2 **The Pathfinder Platoon.** This platoon was formed in 1983 at the same time as 5 Airborne Brigade. Since 1996, it has formed part of the establishment of the Parachute Regiment. The Pathfinders are responsible for advance force operations. Chief among these is covert reconnaissance, location and marking of drop zones (DZs), tactical landing zones (TLZs) and helicopter landing zones (HLZs). They may also be employed on target reconnaissance for air and land raids and limited high-value offensive action (OA). Pathfinders may be inserted up to a week before the arrival of the main body of troops. Their role once they have linked up with the main force is that of brigade-level intelligence, surveillance, target acquisition and reconnaissance (ISTAR). This involves operations beyond the range and capacity of the patrol platoons and other reconnaissance elements of the brigade. Reconnaissance could be on foot or in WMIK Land Rovers.

The Pathfinder Platoon has its own selection course and training programme, taking only men from the parachute battalions. Commanded by a captain, Pathfinders operate in four-man patrols, four of which make up a troop under the senior patrol commander, a lieutenant. There are two troops, Air and Mountain, and a small headquarters with a total strength of about forty. Air Troop is trained in both high-altitude low-opening (HALO) and high-altitude high-opening (HAHO) free-fall parachuting, while Mountain Troop utilises only HALO. Unlike the rest of the Paras, the Pathfinders use the M16A2 rifle as their main weapon, often with the M203 grenade launcher attached. They also use GPMGs and the 66 mm LAW is retained. Members of the Pathfinder Platoon often go on to join 22 SAS.

Chapter Six

1 **Toms.** Nickname for soldiers of the Parachute Regiment, derived from 'Thomas Atkins' or 'Tommy', the World War I nickname adopted by journalists from a mythical figure who distinguished himself at Waterloo in 1815. Thomas Atkins may also have been used by army clerks as a signature for illiterate soldiers. It was used by Australian and New Zealand soldiers in World War I as an adjective for British soldiers whom they called a 'Tommy Officer' or 'Tommy Sergeant', but never a 'Tommy Soldier'. The French and Germans picked it up from newspapers and by World War II the Germans knew their adversary as 'Tommy'.

2 **16 Air Assault Brigade.** The Brigade's primary 'war-fighting' role would be strike operations, usually in depth over protracted distances, within a divisional or corps offensive battle. This would require the integration of armed or attack aviation with combined arms in concert with all means of air delivery:
(a) Aviation deep attack with Apache attack helicopters
(b) Cross forward line of own troops or theatre-entry air drop, airland or heli borne operations including seize and hold, area interdiction and large-scale raids
(c) Support to Special Forces.
In operations other than war, three roles were envisaged:
(a) Peace support
(b) Humanitarian relief operations
(c) NEO operations – what 1 Para, with its supporting arms and corps, would be required to do in Sierra Leone.

16 Air Assault Brigade was required to maintain a pool of high-readiness forces for the Joint Rapid Reaction Force (JRRF) from which a range of capabilities could be deployed to meet contingencies:
(a) Deliver the airborne battle group at two to five days' notice to move to conduct early entry operations, whilst in rotation meeting the spearhead commitment at even shorter notice
(b) Deliver the lead aviation battle group at five to ten days' notice to move, also providing in due course a squadron of attack helicopters dual roled for amphibious operations to support 3 Commando Brigade
(c) Deploy remainder of Brigade within thirty days.

3 **The Royal Fleet Auxiliary (RFA).** The RFA is a civilian-manned flotilla, comprising twenty-two ships, which is owned by the MoD. It is managed by the

commodore RFA who is directly responsible to the commander-in-chief Fleet (C in C Fleet) for its day-to-day operation.

The primary role of the RFA is to supply the Royal Navy (RN), at sea, with the food, fuel, ammunition and spares that it requires in order to maintain operations away from its home ports. In addition, the RFA provides the RN with seaborne aviation training facilities as well as secure logistical support and amphibious operations capability for the Royal Marines and the British Army.

The ill-informed might see the RFA as a Cinderella service; however, it has been a key part of RN operations and RFA ships were in the front line during the 1982 Falklands War and both Gulf Wars. RFA vessels also formed part of the British contribution to operations in former Yugoslavia and are often deployed in support of Britain's contribution to NATO and UN peacekeeping operations. At the time of the civil war in Sierra Leone, RFA *Sir Percivale* was over thirty years old and a veteran of the Falklands War, and would play a major part in the operations in West Africa. The ship could carry 340 troops and was fitted with platforms for operating a range of helicopters including Lynx and Chinook.

The RFA employs approximately 2,300 UK-registered officers and ratings who follow career paths and training patterns broadly similar to those of the merchant navy. However, RFA personnel also have a certain amount of specialist training necessary to meet the requirements of operating with the Royal Navy.

Most RFA ships carry, or are capable of carrying, RN helicopters and the personnel required to operate and maintain them. Because RFA ships are often required to operate in war zones in support of the RN, most have a limited weapons-fit for self-defence.

4 **Joint Force Harrier.** The RAF GR7 Harrier has a ground-attack role and can carry up to 4,173 kg of bombs, cluster bombs, 68 mm rocket pods, CRV-7 rockets and AIM-9 air-to-air missiles (AAMs). Although the Fleet Air Arm FA2 Sea Harrier can also carry bombs, its principal armaments are two 30 mm Aden cannon and AIM-120, ALARM and Sea Eagle missiles. Operating as part of Joint Force Harrier, it was reported that the RAF initially found it difficult adapting to the Royal Navy's more robust approach to operations.

Chapter Seven

1 **LAW.** This US-designed one-shot disposable telescopic weapon developed during the Vietnam War weighs only 3.45 kg and is 775 mm long – soldiers can carry up to three tucked into their webbing. It would later emerge that the hut walls at Magbeni were 457 mm thick, but the LAW can penetrate around 300 mm of armour and would prove very effective on the day. If the WSB attempted a vehicle-mounted counter attack, the '66', as the LAW is commonly known in British service, with an effective range of 220 m, could be used to destroy them before they closed with the Paras. The LAW had been used very effectively by Paras and Royal Marines during fighting in Operation Corporate in the Falklands in 1982 – a year before some of the Paras in A Company had been born.

2 **M18A1 Claymore.** This US anti-personnel mine consists of a curved plastic container holding 700 steel balls in a plastic matrix, behind which is a 682 g sheet of composition C4 plastic explosive. The container stands on two sets of folding legs

and has a simple peep sight in the top, as well as two fuse wells for the M4 blasting cap.

As with many items of US military equipment, it comes with a set of illustrated instructions. These are enclosed in the M7 bandoleer, which also contains 30 m of brown cable, an M57 firing device commonly known as a 'Claymore clacker' and an M40 test set.

The mine weighs 1.58 kg and is 216 mm long, 35 mm wide and 83 mm high. When fired, it blasts the steel balls in a fan-shaped sheaf – these are lethal up to a height of 2 m and to a range of 50 m, though the danger area is almost 150 m. There is a back-blast danger area of 16 m.

3   **SAS negotiator.** It is reported that this soldier was later awarded the George Cross (GC) for extraordinary bravery during covert operations in Afghanistan.

He was part of an eight-man team, including SAS and US Delta Force troops, operating in the south-east of the country during mopping-up operations against the Taliban. The sergeant took part in the violent clashes at Kalajangui prison, 10 km from Mazar-i-Sharif, which erupted after a CIA agent was killed by prisoners in late November 2001.

He had warned the CIA man against entering the fortified compound to interrogate prisoners selected from 500 Taliban PoWs, since he was sure the American was risking his life. The SAS soldier very nearly lost his own when he attempted to pull the agent to safety. But the CIA man had already been killed by prisoners with their bare hands, and the SAS soldier had to shoot his way out of the prison. Despite the danger of hundreds of rioting prisoners, the SAS man organised a successful holding operation to keep them pinned down until reinforcements arrived.

In a private ceremony at Buckingham Palace, he became 156th recipient of the GC since it was instituted by King George VI in 1940. The award is of equivalent status to the Victoria Cross (VC).

4   **Joint Special Forces Aviation Wing (JSFAW).** The JSFAW has two Special Forces Flights. The SF Flight in No.7 Squadron at RAF Odiham in north Hampshire near Basingstoke is equipped, like the rest of the squadron, with the Chinook HC.2 helicopter. This flight saw action in Operation Granby in 1991 and Operation Telic in 2003, during the two Gulf Wars respectively. Its pilots are trained in low-level flying and the use of night-vision goggles (NVG), while the loadmasters operate the 7.62 mm miniguns with which the helicopters have recently been mounted.

No. 657 Squadron Army Air Corps operates the Mk7 Lynx AH attack and liaison helicopter and its pilots are also expert in low-level all-weather flying.

5   **The Barras.** For Glaswegian soldiers, the operation name selected from the MoD operational codename list might have raised a smile since it was part of the folk history of that city.

In the late 1800s, Margaret Russell, the twelve-year-old daughter of a policeman, began to look after a fruit barrow belonging to her mother's friend in the street market in Parkhead, Glasgow. A natural businesswoman, she prospered and with the money earned bought a small fruit and vegetable shop in the Bridgeton area of the city. When she married James McIver, they pooled their business acumen and rented out barrows to traders in Moncur Street in the east end of Glasgow for the Saturday market. The market was a success and the area became known to Glaswegians by a corruption of barrows as 'The Barras' – and Margaret McIver inevitably became 'The Barras Queen'. The market survives today, selling a wide range of goods and produce, and now has a towering formal entrance with a metalwork sign reading 'The Barras'.

In Freetown, the popular newspaper *Sierra News* drew attention to the fact that 'Barras' was the last two syllables of 'embarrass' and suggested that the operation was intended to embarrass the WSB. In reality, it was the British Army that had suffered embarrassment. As Richard Connaughton observed in *Small Wars and Insurgencies*, 'There is no doubt that the lives of the remaining seven hostages [including the Sierra Leone Army LO] were at risk, but it also seems likely that Operation 'Barass' [sic] was to some degree about settling scores.'

Connaughton identifies this desire to settle scores as the 'he's taking us on syndrome' that had characterised US Secretary of State Madeleine Albright's obsession with Somali warlord General Mohamed Aideed in 1993. This led to the ill-fated US Special Forces attempt to kill or capture Aideed at Bakara Market in Mogadishu on 3 October 1993.

In 1956, the same syndrome had prompted another unsuccessful military enterprise, Operation Musketeer – the Anglo–French landings at Suez in November of that year. Part of the impetus for the operation was the anger of British Prime Minister Anthony Eden at the nationalisation of the Suez Canal by the flashy Egyptian leader President Gamal Abdul Nasser.

Chapter Eight

1   **Marshland.** Swamps and marshland have always been a hazard for airborne forces. During the D-Day landings in Normandy on 6 June 1944, the 507th Parachute Infantry Regiment of the 82nd Airborne Division landed east of their designated drop zone, codenamed 'T'. This proved to be an area flooded as a result of the Germans damming the River Merderet. Like LS2 in Operation Barras, in aerial photographs the area had appeared to be grassland. Tragically, many of the heavily laden paratroops landing in the dark drowned in these flooded fields. As late as 1989 in Operation Just Cause, the US invasion of Panama on 20 December at 02.10 hours, a wave of 20 C-141 Starlifter transports dropped the men of the 1st Brigade 82nd Airborne Division over Torrijos Airfield. One of the transports was damaged by ground-fire, but the jump was successful, even if some troops landed in the marshes nearby.

Chapter Nine

1   **SAS in Africa.** Operation Barras was not the first recorded intervention by British Special Forces in West Africa. In 1981, in the small former British colony of The Gambia to the north of Sierra Leone, 500 Cuban- and Libyan-backed rebels had mounted a coup while the country's president, Sir Dawda Jawara, was attending the wedding of Prince Charles and Lady Diana. The Gambia had become independent in 1965 and was a peaceful country with less than 1,000 men in its armed forces. During the coup, the plotters not only overran the capital of

Banjul but also took as hostages twenty-eight senior officials, plus the president's wife – Lady Thielal Jawara – and their four children.

The UK government under Prime Minister Margaret Thatcher contacted SAS Group Headquarters to see if the situation could be resolved. At the SAS Regimental HQ in Hereford, the 2 IC Major Ian Crooke decided that he and two SAS soldiers should go to Banjul immediately. Flying in plain clothes via Paris, but carrying small arms, grenades and satellite communication equipment in their baggage, they evaded security checks by using diplomatic contacts.

The French, who had been consulted from the outset of the operation, sent French-trained paratroops from their former colony of Senegal to The Gambia. They had secured the airport by the time the SAS arrived; however, the rebels still held the centre of the capital.

President Jawara had given Crooke permission to use whatever means necessary to release the hostages and defeat the coup. Crooke discovered that Lady Jawara and her children had been moved to the capital's Medical Research Centre (MRC) because one of her children was ill. At the British Embassy, Crooke and his team met Dr John Greenwood, the young British doctor in charge at the MRC. It was explained that the team were prepared to assault the MRC to rescue Lady Jawara and her children. Greenwood would later recall that 'the officer was hard. I got the impression that he was very determined about what he was going to do'. The SAS team entered the MRC disguised as medical staff. However, since the staff at the MRC had developed a working relationship with the rebels, Dr Greenwood persuaded the men guarding the hostages to lay down their arms as they were causing distress to patients. The SAS team then freed Lady Jawara and her children.

Subsequently, Crooke and his men rallied a small group of Senegalese troops who had been repulsed by the rebels and launched a new attack. After four days, the coup collapsed and Jawara returned to lead his country.

2   The following countries have adopted the **Kimberley Process**: Angola, Armenia, Australia, Belarus, Botswana, Canada, the Central African Republic, Côte d'Ivoire, Croatia, Democratic Republic of the Congo, the European Community, Guinea, Guyana, Hungary, India, Israel, Japan, Laos, Lebanon, Lesotho, Mauritius, Namibia, People's Republic of China, Poland, Russia, Separate Customs Territory of Taiwan, Penghu, Kinmen and Matsu, Sierra Leone, Slovenia, South Africa, South Korea, Sri Lanka, Swaziland, Switzerland, Tanzania, Thailand, Ukraine, United Arab Emirates, United States of America, Venezuela, Vietnam and Zimbabwe.

3   **Blood diamonds.** Smuggled diamonds not only funded the wars in Sierra Leone and Liberia but had a wider impact. On 15 November 2002, the UN Security Council Global Policy Forum quoted a report – 'War and Peace in Sierra Leone: Diamonds, Corruption and the Lebanese Connection' – in its AllAfrica series of publications.

It made disturbing reading.

'A new report released by the Diamonds and Human Security Project evaluates probable links between Sierra Leone's large Lebanese merchant community and global terrorist networks in the context of near-collapsed state institutions and the traditional corruption of Sierra Leone's diamond industry. The twenty-eight-page report by Lansana Gberie, Project Research Associate, [was written] after three extended trips to Sierra Leone and other West African countries in 2001 and 2002.'

The report focused on the period since the UN intervention in 2000, but also traced the development of Sierra Leone's diamond industry and the historical role that the Lebanese have played in corrupting it. Various factions in Middle Eastern conflicts, including *Hezbollah* and *Amal*, have in the past raised substantial funding from the Lebanese community in Sierra Leone through the diamond trade. The report argued that although evidence of links between this Lebanese diaspora community and the al-Qaeda terrorist network were 'anecdotal', the allegations were 'supported by generations of dubious activities' by some Lebanese diamond dealers and tangible proofs of contacts between some of them and Middle Eastern terrorists on the US Most Wanted List in recent years.

The report followed up on allegations, made by the *Washington Post*, that al-Qaeda may have gained millions of dollars from the RUF's diamond trade. The author traced the involvement with al-Qaeda of two Lebanese diamond dealers – Aziz Nassour and Samih Ossailly, who were said to be cousins – 'with long-standing business and other interests in West Africa and the Congo'.

The report suggested that the two had proven links to al-Qaeda and stated that Ossailly first appeared in Sierra Leone in 1997, after the AFRC coup, and was introduced to the junta by a Freetown-based Lebanese named Darwish.

'Ossailly, with Nassour, was already the major buyer of RUF diamonds in Liberia,' the report noted. In Freetown, he 'supplied four containers of army uniforms and other military hardware to the (AFRC) junta, apparently in exchange for diamonds, and from the Liberian end, he and Nassour supplied the RUF with weapons, medical supplies and mining equipment'.

In an interview with the Freetown-based *Concord Times*, Gberie played down the al-Qaeda connection. 'The real story – and this is the primary interest of this report – is the corrupting of the diamond industry and the absence of institutional capacity. This is what makes the country so vulnerable. I have stressed the role of the Lebanese, because it is very, very significant. They virtually control the industry in Sierra Leone, and they have resisted all attempts to reform key aspects of the country's economy.'

However, a Lebanese who preferred to be anonymous criticised what he termed the tendency to look for scapegoats for Sierra Leone's economic crisis. He said that it was true that some Lebanese 'like other nationals may have committed crimes. But let us also know that there are very many Lebanese who have contributed to this country in several ways. I have not seen the report. But I think it is unfair to link Lebanese, diamonds and terrorism. And this is inciting the people against the Lebanese'.

4   **UNAMSIL strength.** The authorised maximum strength for military personnel was 17,500, including 260 UNMOs. The strength as of 30 June 2003 was 12,839 troops with 255 UNMOs. The authorised maximum strength for civilian police personnel was 170. The strength as of 30 June 2003 was 125 civilian police personnel. In addition, UNAMSIL had 327 international civilian staff and 584 local civilian staff

The soldiers had come from Bangladesh, Bolivia, Canada, China, Croatia, the

Czech Republic, Denmark, Egypt, The Gambia, Germany, Ghana, Guinea, Indonesia, Jordan, Kenya, Kyrgyzstan, Malaysia, Mali, Nepal, New Zealand, Nigeria, Pakistan, the Russian Federation, the Slovak Republic, Sweden, Tanzania, Thailand, Ukraine, the United Kingdom, Uruguay and Zambia. Working in this demanding theatre had tested some soldiers very hard, but it had also forged friendships across international borders.

The civilian police for UNAMSIL were drawn from Bangladesh, Cameroon, Canada, The Gambia, Ghana, India, Jordan, Kenya, Malawi, Malaysia, Mauritius, Namibia, Nepal, Nigeria, Norway, the Russian Federation, Senegal, Sri Lanka, Sweden, Tanzania, Turkey, the United Kingdom, Zambia and Zimbabwe.

5 **Charles Taylor.** On Wednesday 4 June 2003, the UN Special War Crimes Court for Sierra Leone published an indictment for war crimes against Charles Taylor. As he was relinquishing power in Liberia, the crimes committed in Sierra Leone by fighters sponsored and supported by Taylor were at last beginning to catch up with him.

Taylor, who had been pressed to resign by Washington and West African leaders, adopted a defiant tone when he stepped down from power in Liberia, a country ripped apart by civil war. His exit was marked by a ceremony in the Liberian capital of Monrovia on Tuesday 12 August 2003.

Always a showman (Taylor was also a lay preacher in the Baptist tradition), when accused of war crimes in Sierra Leone Taylor had denied the charges, prostrated himself on the ground and prayed forgiveness before his Lord. When, as president of Liberia in 1999, he was accused by the UN of gun-running and diamond smuggling, he addressed a mass prayer meeting clothed from head to foot in angelic white.

At the ceremony marking his resignation as president he said, 'History will be kind to me. I know I have fulfilled my duties.' He described himself as a 'sacrificial lamb' and implied that he was a victim of US interests.

Charles Taylor was born in 1948 to a family of Americo-Liberians, the elite group that grew out of the freed slaves who founded the country in 19th century. In later years, for what were suspected to be political reasons in order to broaden his appeal to the indigenous African majority, Taylor added an African name, becoming Charles Ghankay Taylor.

Like many Americo-Liberians, he studied in the US and returned home shortly after Master Sergeant Samuel Doe mounted Liberia's first successful *coup d'état* in 1980. Taylor landed a key job in Doe's regime running the General Services Agency, a position that gave him control over much of Liberia's budget.

Taylor later fell out with Doe, who accused him of embezzling almost £548,350, and fled back to the US. Taylor denied the charges, but nevertheless was held in the Plymouth County House of Correction in Massachusetts, detained under a Liberian extradition warrant. Some reports say he managed to escape from the prison by sawing through the bars; others that there was some collusion in his departure by the US who wanted him to overthrow Doe's corrupt, violent and generally disastrous regime.

Taylor's rebellion succeeded partly because of Doe's incompetence, but it was also the fruit of Taylor's cultivation of some surprising alliances. His friends over the years included the once-radical Colonel Gaddafi of Libya, the conservative former ruler of Côte d'Ivoire – Felix Houphouet-Boigny, the current President of Burkina Faso – Blaise Compaore, and a rogues' gallery of businessmen, local and foreign, prepared to flout UN disapproval to make money in Liberia.

It was during this civil war that Taylor sent weapons and fighters into Sierra Leone to destabilise the country.

After winning power militarily, Charles Taylor won elections in 1997. Observers said that although there was some intimidation, it was a reasonably honest election by African standards.

By the summer of 2003, despite vows to return to Liberia, Taylor was still in exile, a lonely figure living in the south-eastern city of Calabar in Cross River State in Nigeria. On 4 December, his isolation increased when the international police body Interpol issued a global notice for Taylor's arrest for the crimes listed by the UN Special War Crimes Court for Sierra Leone. The 'red notice' which appeared on the Interpol web site was not, it explained, an arrest warrant, but national police could use it to make a provisional arrest.

Justice was finally closing in on the man who had helped to fuel the bloody civil war in Sierra Leone.

APPENDIX

Ministry of Defence Press Release: Operation Barras

The MoD was quick to release a censored version of Operation Barras that made no reference to the role of Special Forces.

Serial Number 472
Released at 16.30 hours 10th September 2000
Sierra Leone Press Release:

The objective of this release is to provide further details of the military operation that took place this morning to secure the release of the seven hostages being held by the West Side Boys in Sierra Leone. [From the outset of the planning for Operation Barras, liberating the Sierra Leonean LO was given the same priority as the Royal Irish hostages.]

Introduction

The Secretary of State made clear this afternoon that the decision to launch an operation to release the hostages was only undertaken when it became apparent that the threat to the hostages had escalated to the point that it overcame the risk of conducting the rescue operation. The Chief of the Defence Staff had indicated earlier in the day that there had been a number of British casualties. We regret to confirm that during the action the UK did sustain a number of casualties. One soldier has been killed, one soldier received serious injuries that are not thought to be life threatening and eleven other soldiers were injured. All casualties have been stabilised following treatment by British medical teams who were in support of the operation. Next of kin have been informed. Hostages and casualties will be moved back to the UK as soon as possible.

Background

The risks associated with undertaking any hostage-release operation are very real in any circumstances. As was stated by the Chief of the Defence Staff this morning, the particular circumstances in Sierra Leone made this one of the most complex operations UK forces have conducted for many years. The West Side Boys are a very unpredictable, well-armed and volatile group. They have a hard core of highly experienced jungle fighters. The terrain was also highly challenging. Gberi Bana, the rebel camp, is in a village on the north bank of the Rokel Creek. The camp is surrounded to the north and west by dense secondary jungle and overgrown palm plantations. To the east is a large area of swamp. Across the creek are the villages of Magbeni and Forodugu.

The Operation

The operation was initiated at 06.16 hrs this morning, following detailed planning both in the UK and in-theatre. Members of all three Services were involved in the operation. The assault included elements of the 1st Battalion of the Parachute Regiment, Lynx Attack Helicopters and RAF Chinook helicopters, armed for self-defence. Assistance was also provided by the Sierra Leone Army and the UN mission in Sierra Leone, particularly the Jordanian battalion, which provided security along the Masiaka highway. The assault itself involved a co-ordinated two-prong helicopter assault against the rebel Headquarters in Gberi Bana and the WSB units located in the villages of Magbeni and Forodugu. The northern phase of the assault aimed to release the hostages, thought to be at Gberi Bana. The aim of the southern phase was to neutralise the enemy position on the southern bank of the Rokel Creek that was equipped with heavy machine guns that posed a significant threat to our aircraft.

Outcome of the Operation

The assault on Gberi Bana was highly successful. All seven hostages (including the Sierra Leonian officer) were successfully and rapidly released unharmed and are now safely on board RFA *Sir Percivale*. All British hostages have spoken to their families by telephone. The southern assault was also successful in preventing West Side Boy units south of Rokel Creek from interdicting the hostages as they were airlifted out. This involved the clearance of the rebel camps and involved suppressive fire as the advances took place. Our troops came under sustained fire including from the edge of the jungle. This in turn was countered by our own mortar fire. This action also led to the recovery of the UK vehicles held by the West Side Boys. All UK forces involved in the operation have now left the Gberi Bana region and will return to the UK as soon as possible.

Enemy Forces

The West Side Boys fought fiercely throughout the operation and engaged in sporadic follow-up fighting for some time whilst the UK forces were preparing for their self-extraction having released the hostages. Casualties: details of West Side Boy casualties remain unclear; however, we can confirm over twenty-five dead including three females.

Conclusion

To conclude, this was a very challenging operation conducted out of necessity because of the serious threat to the lives of the hostages. Despite being an operation of great complexity, thousands of miles from the UK, all our mission objectives were achieved. This is a testimony to the skill and professionalism of all those involved. The Prime Minister, Mr Tony Blair, said, 'I cannot pay high enough tribute to the skill, the professionalism and the courage of the armed forces involved.'

Glossary

AFRC – Armed Forces Revolutionary Council/Armed Forces Ruling Congress, Sierra Leone dissident group

AK-47 – Soviet-designed 7.62 mm assault rifle

ANC – African National Congress

AP – anti-personnel

APC – armoured personnel carrier

APP – All Peoples' Party, also known as APC – All Peoples' Congress

BG – battalion or battle group

BTC – Benguema Training Centre, Sierra Leone

Blood/conflict diamonds – rough diamonds obtained by coercion by rebel movements in Africa

BMP-2 – *Boevaya Mashina Pekhota*, Soviet-designed tracked APC. Carries seven troops and three crew, and is equipped with 30 mm cannon and 7.62 mm machine gun

Browning .50 HMG – American-designed 12.7 mm belt-fed heavy machine gun

CCB – Civil Co-operation Bureau

CCP – Commission for the Consolidation of Peace

CDF – Civil Defence Force

CDS – Chief of the Defence Staff

Chinook – CH47 American-designed twin-rotor troop-lift helicopter (capacity of twenty-two to fifty men)

Claymore – M18A1 American-designed directional AP mine, lethal up to 100 m

CO – commanding officer

COBR – Cabinet Office briefing room

CSM – company sergeant major

CSS – combat service support

DACOS – Deputy Assistant Chief of Staff

Deconflict – directing military air operations to ensure that there is no risk of collision

DDR – disarmament, demobilisation and reintegration centres

DSF – Director Special Forces

EAA – evacuee assembly area

ECOMOG – ECOWAS Military Observer Group

ECOWAS – Economic Community of West African States

EO – Executive Outcomes, a South African private military company

FAA – Fleet Air Arm

FOB – forward operational base

FPF – final protective fire

FRU – Force Reconnaissance Unit, Sierra Leone Army Special Forces

G2 – intelligence

G3 – operations

G4 – logistics

GPMG – general-purpose machine gun, Belgian-designed 7.62 mm belt-fed machine gun

Harrier – F/A2, British-designed Fleet Air Arm vertical-takeoff jet fighter

Harrier – GR7, British-designed RAF vertical-takeoff fighter ground attack aircraft

HE – high explosive

Hercules – C130, American-designed transport aircraft (sixty-four or ninety-two paratroops capacity)

HMG – heavy machine gun

2 IC – second in command

II – image-intensifying night-vision equipment that amplifies ambient light

IMATT – International Military Advisory and Training Team

IO – intelligence officer

JHC – Joint Helicopter Command

JRRF – Joint Rapid Reaction Force

JSFAW – Joint Special Forces Aviation Wing

JTFHQ – Joint Task Force Headquarters

KPCS – Kimberley Process Certification Scheme, diamond certification scheme

L2 – British-designed HE grenade

LAF – Libyan Air Force

LAND Command – the British Army HQ in Wilton, Wiltshire, responsible for UK land forces

LAW – US-designed 66 mm shoulder-fired one-shot light anti-tank weapon

LMA – leading medical assistant

LO – liaison officer

LRR – long-range rifle

LS – landing site

Lynx – AH7, British-designed helicopter armed with rockets, machine guns or anti-tank missiles

Lynx – HAS.3, British-designed naval attack and reconnaissance helicopter armed with homing torpedoes, sea-skimming anti-ship missiles and machine guns

M203 – US-designed 40 mm grenade launcher fitted to a 5.56 mm M16 assault rifle

MA – medical assistant

MAMS – Mobile Air Movements Squadron

MC – Military Cross

MFC – mortar fire controller

MFO – Military Freight Organisation

Mil Mi-8/17 'Hip' – Soviet-designed troop-lift (twenty-eight men) and attack helicopter

Mil Mi-24D 'Hind' – Soviet-designed attack helicopter armed with rockets, missiles and cannon

Mi Mil-26 'Halo' – Soviet-designed troop-lift helicopter (eighty men)

MoD – the UK Ministry of Defence, sometimes referred to as 'the Mod'

MRU – Mano River Union
NCDDR – National Committee for Disarmament, Demobilisation and Reintegration
NCO – non-commissioned officer
NGO – non-government agency
NoK – next of kin
NRC – National Reformation Council
NVG – night-vision goggles
OAU – Organisation of African Unity
OC – officer commanding
O Group – Orders Group, formal issue of orders by a CO to subordinate commanders
OMC – operational mounting centre
OP – observation post
OpSec – operational security
OrBat – order of battle
Para Reg – the Parachute Regiment
PJHQ – Permanent Joint Headquarters, also known as Northwood
PK – peacekeeping
Plasticuffs – self-locking nylon loops normally used as electric cable ties
PLP – Peace and Liberation Party
PMC – private military company
QM – quartermaster
QM (T) – technical quartermaster
Regiment, the – colloquial name for the SAS
REME – Royal Electrical and Mechanical Engineers
REMF – Rear Echelon Motherfucker, US Army slang from the Vietnam War
RFA – Royal Fleet Auxiliary
RM – Royal Marines
RMO – regimental medical officer
RN – Royal Navy
Royal – informal name for a Royal Marine
RP – red phosphorus – smoke grenade
RPD – Soviet-designed belt-fed light 7.62 mm machine gun
RPG7 – *Reaktivniy Proivotankovyi Granatomet* 7, Soviet-designed shoulder-fired
    rocket-propelled grenade
RRC – rigid raiding craft
RSLAF – Republic of Sierra Leone Armed Forces
RSLMF – Republic of Sierra Leone Military Forces
RSQM (T) – regimental quartermaster sergeant (tech)
RSO – regimental signals officer
RUF – Revolutionary United Front
SA80 – British-designed 5.56 mm assault rifle
SADF – South African Defence Force
SAS – Special Air Service, British Army Special Forces
SBS – Special Boat Service, Royal Marine Special Forces
SBU – Small Boys Unit
SF – special forces
Sikorsky S-61 – American-designed troop-lift helicopter (thirty men)
SLA – Sierra Leone Army

SLE – spearhead lead element
SLPP – Sierra Leone Peoples' Party
SO1 – Staff Officer 1, lieutenant-colonel
SO 2 – Staff Officer 2, major
SO 3 – Staff Officer 3, captain
Squaddies – British soldiers
SSD – State Security Division
STTT – short-term training team
Tac – tactical
TI – thermal-imaging night-and-day vision equipment that detects different heat patterns
'Tom' – informal name for a private in the Parachute Regiment
TRAP – tactical recovery of aircraft and personnel
Triage – prioritising the urgency of treatment for battle casualties at a field hospital
ULIMO – United Liberian Organisation
UN – United Nations
UNAMSIL – United Nations Mission in Sierra Leone
UNOMSIL – United Nations Observer Mission in Sierra Leone
UNMO – United Nations military observer
UN SCR – United Nations Security Council Resolution
WMIK – weapons-mount installation kit, machine gun mounting on a Land Rover, known to British soldiers as a 'Wimik'
WO2 – warrant officer class 2
WSB – West Side Boys, West Side Soldiers, West Side Niggaz, West Siders or The Boys – Sierra Leone militia
ZPU-2 – Soviet-designed twin-barrelled 14.5 mm anti-aircraft gun

A Note on Conversions

At time of writing, the conversion rate for £ Sterling, the US $ and the Euro was as follows:

£1 = $1.8 = Euro 1.43

Other useful conversions:
1 km = 0.62 miles
1 metre = 1.09 yards
1 kg = 0.157 stone or 2.205 pounds

Bibliography and Websites

BBC – http://www.bbc.co.uk

Britain's Small Wars – http://www.britains-smallwars.com

Center for Media, Education and Technology – http://www.cmetfreetown.org

CIA – The World Factbook – http://www.odci.gov/cia/publications/factbook

Connaughton, Richard, 'Operation "Barras"', *Small Wars and Insurgencies*, Vol. 12, No 2, Summer 2001, Frank Cass Publishers.

Cry Freetown – http://www.cryfreetown.org/participants.html

Expo Times – http://www.expotimes.net

Forna, Aminatta, *The Devil That Danced On the Water*, London, HarperCollins, 2002

Fox, Robert, *Eyewitness Falklands*, London, Methuen, 1982

Geraghty, Tony, *Who Dares Wins*, London, Little Brown, 1992

Globe & Laurel, July /August, September/October, 2000, c/o *Navy News*, HMS *Nelson*, Portsmouth, UK

Government Guide – http://www.governmentguide.com

Greene, Graham, *The Heart of the Matter*, London, Heinemann, 1948

International Institute for Strategic Studies, *UNAMSIL's Troubled Debut* – http://www.iiss.org

International Travel Maps: Sierra Leone: Scale 1:560,000, Vancouver, International Travel Maps

Jane's Defence Glossary, Coulsdon, Jane's Information Group, 1993

Jane's Geopolitical Library, Coulsdon, Jane's Information Group, 2000

Jang Group of Newspapers – http://www.jang-group.com

Kaplan, Robert, *The Coming Anarchy*, *Atlantic Monthly* February 1994, Boston

Lonely Planet: West Africa, Victoria, Australia, Lonely Planet Publications, 2002

Navy News – http://www.navynews.co.uk

Pegasus, The Yearbook 2000, Winter 2000, RHQ The Parachute Regiment, Colchester, UK

Royle, Trevor, *A Dictionary of Military Quotations*, London, Routledge, 1990

RTE Interactive News – http://www.rte.ie/news

Scully, Will, *Once a Pilgrim*, London, Headline, 1998

Sierra Leone Web – http://www.sierra-leone.org

Sierra Leone Government – http://www.sierra-leone.org/govt.html

Sierra Leone Culture – http://www.sierra-leone.org/culture.html

Soldier Magazine, September 2000, Aldershot, UK

Spicer, Lieutenant-Colonel Tim, OBE, *An Unorthodox Soldier*, Edinburgh, Mainstream, 1999

Stewart, Ian, *Freetown Ambush*, Canada, Penguin/Viking, 2002

The Daily Telegraph – http://www.telegraph.co.uk/news

The Guardian Unlimited – http:/www.guardian.co.uk

Washington Post Magazine – http://www.washingtonpost.com

Windfall Films, *SAS – the Real Story*, Channel 4

Wintle, Justin (ed.), *The Dictionary of War Quotations*, London, Hodder and Stoughton, 1989

All Orion/Phoenix titles are available at your local bookshop or from the following address:

> Mail Order Department
> Littlehampton Book Services
> FREEPOST BR535
> Worthing, West Sussex, BN13 3BR
> *telephone* 01903 828503, *facsimile* 01903 828802
> *e-mail* MailOrders@lbsltd.co.uk
> (Please ensure that you include full postal address details)

Payment can be made either by credit/debit card (Visa, Mastercard, Access and Switch accepted) or by sending a £ Sterling cheque or postal order made payable to *Littlehampton Book Services*.
DO NOT SEND CASH OR CURRENCY

Please add the following to cover postage and packing

UK and BFPO:
£1.50 for the first book, and 50p for each additional book to a maximum of £3.50

Overseas and Eire:
£2.50 for the first book plus £1.00 for the second book and 50p for each additional book ordered

---

BLOCK CAPITALS PLEASE

name of cardholder ....   *delivery address*
                                                (if different from cardholder)

address of cardholder ....

....

....

     postcode ....   *postcode* ....

☐ I enclose my remittance for £ ....

☐ please debit my Mastercard/Visa/Access/Switch (delete as appropriate)

card number ☐☐☐☐☐☐☐☐☐☐☐☐☐☐☐☐

expiry date ☐☐☐☐   Switch issue no. ☐☐

signature ....

prices and availability are subject to change without notice